"Having heard that Sir John Houghton was to publish his autobiography I was very much looking forward to reading it – and I was not disappointed. I enjoyed In the Eye of the Storm *immensely. It is a wonderful account of a life of science and faith, much of it lived in the public eye (not always a comfortable position). This autobiography gives us a lovely picture of John Houghton as a man of real integrity, who despite his very distinguished career in meteorological science, has retained his essential humanity, his graciousness and modesty. He deals with successes and difficulties, with happiness and sadness with equal honesty. His care for God's creation shines throughout these pages, from his deep love of mountains (which I share) to his practical and very informed concern about climate change. Highly recommended."*

John Bryant, Professor Emeritus of Biological Sciences,
University of Exeter

"John Houghton is a seminal figure in modern British science. His contribution to the understanding of climate change was crucial. He did more than anyone else to alert Margaret Thatcher to the issue and it was very much as a result of his scientific insights that led her to go to Rio and to be so strong an advocate for action against climate change. John is animated by a search for truth and by his deep belief in the stewardship we owe to a Creator God."

The Rt Hon. John Gummer, Lord Deben

"Writing in the eye of the storm, Sir John presents a model of integrity that inspires all of us to persist in the pursuit of truth in all things; we see greatness rising from humility, truth contrasted with vested misrepresentation, and devotion emerging from despair."

Dr Calvin B. DeWitt,
Professor of Environmental Studies Emeritus, University of Wisconsin-Madison and President Emeritus, Au Sable Institute.

"With captivating narrative, this book brings to life the full sweep of the inspiring accomplishments of Sir John Houghton, a legend in our field. The passionate scientist, and his integrity and commitment to God's truth and his creation, shines throughout this illuminating, intimate, and eminently well-written picture of the birth of modern climate science. A must read!"

Katharine Hayhoe, director of the Climate Science Center
at Texas Tech University

IN THE EYE
OF THE STORM
THE AUTOBIOGRAPHY OF
SIR JOHN
HOUGHTON

SIR JOHN HOUGHTON
WITH GILL TAVNER

LION

Published by Lion Books
an imprint of
Lion Hudson plc
Wilkinson House, Jordan Hill Road,
Oxford OX2 8DR, England
www.lionhudson.com/lion

ISBN 978 0 7459 5584 1
e-ISBN 978 0 7459 5782 1

First edition 2013

Text Acknowledgments
Scripture quotations taken from the Holy Bible, New International Version,
copyright © 1973, 1978, 1984 International Bible Society. Used by permission
of Hodder & Stoughton, a member of the Hodder Headline Group. All rights
reserved. "NIV" is a trademark of International Bible Society. UK trademark
number 1448790.
p. 189: Extract from *Bulletin of the American Meteorological Society*, Volume 77
Issue 6 (1996) © American Meteorological Society. Reprinted by permission.

Picture Acknowldgments
Every effort has been made to trace the original copyright holders where required.
In some cases this has proved impossible. We shall be happy to correct any such
omissions in future editions.
Cover images: Photo of Sir John Houghton © Sylvain Guenot. GOES-13 satellite
image of Hurricane Irene just 28 minutes before the storm made landfall in New
York City. NASA/NOAA GOES Project
pp. 65, 79 Diagram of Nimbus 4 used by kind permission of NASA.
p. 270 Map of Bangladesh from Broadus, J.M. 1993. Possible impacts of, and
adjustments to, sea-level rise: the case of Bangladesh and Egypt. In Warrick,
R.A., Barrow, E.M., Wigley, T.M.L. (eds.) 1993. *Climate and Sea-Level Change:
Observations, Projections and Implications*. Cambridge: Cambridge University Press,
pp. 263–75; adapted from Milliman, J.D. 1989. Environmental and economic
implications of rising sea level and subsiding deltas: the Nile and Bangladeshi
examples. *Ambio*, 18, 340–45.
Plate section: Cartoon depicting the IPCC Science Working Group, published in
Nature magazine, used by kind permission of David Perkins.

A catalogue record for this book is available from the British Library

Printed and bound in the UK, August 2013, LH26

CONTENTS

LIST OF BOXES

LIST OF FIGURES

PREFACE

I have been privileged to live during a time when the science with which I have been involved – that of the atmosphere, weather, and climate – has progressed enormously: progress made possible by the exciting combination of developments in observations from space, and rapid advances in the power and potential of computers.

For a long time I have intended to write my scientific story, always imagining that I would find the time when I retired – but then I never seemed to retire! When a letter came out of the blue from Gill Tavner asking if she could help me to write my autobiography, I was surprised at her temerity, but felt prepared to pursue her suggestion of being my ghost writer. Gill already shared my faith and had a great heart for the environment, including the problem of climate change. She soon picked up the basic science and painstakingly worked out how to present my work and thought with accuracy and sensitivity. She was a pleasure to work with and ended up doing something for me that I could never have done for myself, for which I am extremely grateful.

I am also very grateful to those during my life who have been my mentors, students, and colleagues in scientific and other projects and in organizations that I have been privileged to lead. Both those of you named in the book and the many others who aren't – I want to thank you all. Working in teams towards common goals has not only resulted in real achievements, it has also been great fun. I wish also to thank all those who have helped with material for the book.

To my wife Sheila I feel great gratitude, not only for her support and patience during the many hours of the book's preparation, but for her companionship during many of the story's events. I am also grateful for the support of my first wife Margaret during the earlier years.

Gill and I would both like to thank the team at Lion. Particular thanks must go to Ali Hull for commissioning the book, for her encouragement, and for helping to form the story's eventual shape.

I trust and pray that this book may not only describe a particular piece of interesting scientific history but that it may stimulate individuals, communities, and the world's nations to take action to combat the threat of severe damage to our world from human-induced climate change.

John Houghton

"IT HAS TO BE ABSOLUTELY TRUE"

I approached Sir John about the possibility of working together on his autobiography in 2009. I thought it might be a story with themes of epic proportions: scientific advances, faith, and the planet earth.

Since our first meeting in his Welsh hillside home, knowing and working alongside Sir John has been a pleasure and a privilege. Unerringly tolerant of my slow grasp of his science and always respectful of my opinion, he has allowed the development of a relaxed working friendship. I will always value this. Both he and Lady Sheila have welcomed me into their cosy home and busy lives with warmth. Hard work though these visits might have been, they have also been great fun. Hours spent with the audio-recorder, the computer, and stacks of books and papers have been interspersed with windswept lunchtime walks together in the Welsh hills.

Our work has involved many hours of face-to-face interviews and further hours on the telephone. Boxes of literature have travelled between our homes, as have numerous redrafts of chapters. I spent two days locked away in the British Library, listening to another interview.[1] In 2010 I joined Sir John and Lady Sheila in Oxford to celebrate 40 years of involvement with Nimbus, which afforded me the invaluable opportunity of meeting some of the key participants in Sir John's story: Des Smith and Jim Williamson among others.

In the later stages of our work, Sir John passed chapters around friends and former colleagues to verify facts and events, thus increasing our confidence in the account contained in these pages.

One phrase, frequently repeated by Sir John, sums up his approach to the challenge of memory and autobiography: "it has to be absolutely true". Such attention to detail and insistence on the truth has resulted in a thoroughly honest book; highly appropriate to Sir John's personality.

This is an important story which we both hope and pray will have a positive impact. While I have been honoured to play a part in telling it, the story is all his.

Gill Tavner

1

WHY WEREN'T WE WARNED?

At 4 a.m. on Friday 16 October 1987, the south-east of England experienced its most intense and destructive storm since 1703. Fifteen million trees were blown down, including many ancient and historically significant specimens in places such as Kew Gardens. Everyday life, particularly in and around London, was plunged into chaos. Hundreds of thousands of people in the south-east of England were left without power, many for over two weeks. Damage in the London area was immense, with buildings battered both by wind and falling trees. The city's transport systems were unable to operate, while the BBC and other TV stations had to broadcast from emergency facilities. Eighteen people lost their lives.

According to the newspapers over the following days, I was to blame.

As director general of the UK Meteorological Office, I held overall responsibility for weather forecasting, and the papers felt that we hadn't given an adequate warning about the storm. Like most people in Britain, I was asleep in my bed when the storm struck, having just returned to my home near Oxford from a meeting in Geneva, a day earlier than scheduled. I remember that my flight home was very bumpy: the weather seemed to be getting wild, but I must admit that I didn't give it a great deal of thought at the time. I knew we'd forecasted rough weather, and that we expected a windy night.

Even on the Friday morning, only hours after the storm had struck, I knew little about its devastating power. Having decided to complete an important and urgent paper before going into work, I was busy at my desk from an early hour. My colleagues at the Met Office, thinking I was still on my way back from Geneva, didn't try to contact me for several hours. At that time, there didn't appear to be any need to do so.

Learning about it from my radio when I went to make a coffee mid-morning, I immediately called my Met Office colleagues, who updated me. Even then, although troubled by what I heard about the storm, and saddened particularly by the loss of lives, the full force didn't really hit me. As my colleagues assured me that they were coping fine without me, and as there didn't seem to be a great deal I'd be able to do if I went in, I returned to my desk.

By rather insensitive coincidence, it was the Met Office Annual Dinner Dance in Windsor that evening. I would see my colleagues then, and they would fill me in on anything more I needed to know. They did. By the end of the evening, appreciating more fully the storm's severity, and understanding that our forecasts might not have given an entirely accurate picture of the course it would eventually take, I realized that we would have some important issues to address. I was therefore better prepared for what followed.

On Saturday morning I found myself in the eye of a media storm. The *Daily Mail*'s headline shouted: "WHY WEREN'T WE WARNED?" I read in that article that I bore the weight of responsibility for our failure to forecast the storm accurately. Outraged journalists and the angry public needed someone to blame, and the line of responsibility led directly to me. I fielded numerous telephone calls from newspaper, radio, and television reporters. In the spaces between, I spoke to several colleagues about what our response should be.

By Sunday, my home was surrounded by reporters and photographers. On a private basis, this was embarrassing as we were holding a small family party to celebrate my recent engagement to Sheila. On a more public basis, it was alarming. Although the reporters were all very pleasant, listening politely as I tried to explain the whole situation to them, some of them were excited by the possibility that my job might be on the line. According to them, this suggestion had already been made by a junior minister in the Department of the Environment. "What do you think of that?" they demanded.

"That is the first I've heard of it," I replied. I told them that I would be meeting senior people at the Ministry of Defence, the Ministry responsible for the Met Office, on Monday morning to brief them about the storm. As soon as I had managed to close my front door, I picked up my phone and arranged a press conference.

The next morning, the papers really went for me. After a blistering article about my alleged incompetence, *The Sun*[1] invited readers to take part in a telephone poll as to whether or not I should be sacked. In our defence, we hadn't failed entirely to predict the storm. However, even though our forecasts from as early as the previous Sunday had been giving notice of likely stormy weather for Thursday or Friday; even though shipping forecasts had warned of unusually strong winds ranging from "severe gale force 9 imminent" (issued on Thursday at 18.10) to "storm force 10 increasing violent storm 11 imminent" (Friday at 02.35); and even though we had warned emergency and transport services to take appropriate preparatory action, the newspapers considered our warnings inadequate. The emergency services, however, were satisfied with the advance warning we had given them.

It seemed that there were two main problems. The first was that our 9.30 p.m. TV forecast had concentrated more on heavy rain than on wind, as we thought at that time that the exceptionally strong winds would be confined to the Channel and northern France. The second problem was our TV forecast on Thursday lunchtime, which has since gone down in forecasting history, an excerpt from it even featuring in the 2012 Olympics Opening Ceremony.

Wisely, the presenter Michael Fish advised viewers to "batten down the hatches". Unfortunately, he then offered reassurance: "Earlier on today, apparently, a woman phoned the BBC and said she'd heard there was a hurricane on the way. Well, if you're watching, don't worry, there isn't." He went on to add that the weather would become "very windy", but that most of the strong wind would be "down over Spain and across into France".

It is not in my nature to panic or react angrily to events; instead, at times of crisis, I usually find myself considering what my responsibility might be at that moment. And so, early on Monday morning, shrugging off *The Sun*'s attack, I went into the Met Office headquarters. My future at the Met Office wasn't my primary concern: I felt it was important to get the press conference underway.

Not long after I arrived, I heard that the Ministry of Defence had given strict instructions that no representative of the Meteorological Office, including me, should talk to the press. I thought this was a ridiculous stance to take, and as far as I was concerned, absolutely impossible. The Met Office on the whole had a very good relationship with the press; if we refused to talk to them now we'd be in bigger trouble than ever. The public wanted to know why they hadn't been warned earlier, and it was our responsibility, as far as was possible, to respond to their questions and concerns.

I continued making arrangements for the press conference to take place that afternoon at the London Weather Centre. Just before lunch, I went to the Ministry, where I met the Permanent Secretary and told him that I had set up a press conference for that afternoon. Although far from pleased that I was going against instructions, he listened to my account of what had happened. He then accompanied me as I went to meet Sir George Younger, the Secretary of State for Defence, who agreed readily that our press conference should go ahead and allowed me to continue with the necessary arrangements.

Little did we know that something apparently even less predictable than the weather was about to rescue us. This day, 19 October 1987, was to become known as Black Monday: the day the stock market crashed. By midday, media interest was drawn away from the weather and focused upon the financial world. Our press conference went by without a hitch, perhaps because so few reporters were there. I'd been bailed out by the world's great financiers in a way I could never have anticipated.

In response to *The Sun's* poll about my future, I later learned that about 2,500 readers had voted that I should go, beating the 2,000 who phoned to say I should stay. Not a bad result, I thought. In spite of the vote being narrowly in favour of sacking me, Michael Fish and I both kept our jobs. In fact, it's fair to say that the incident earned Michael a degree of celebrity, giving his public profile quite a boost. This humorous fellow and good forecaster was soon and still is in high demand as an after-dinner speaker.

There were far more serious matters to consider than the storm's impact on our careers. Had the storm been forecastable? If so, why had we underestimated its strength and incorrectly forecasted its track? What could we learn from what had happened? How could we ensure that our forecast would be more accurate next time there was an exceptional storm?

Back at the Meteorological Office, away from the glare of public scrutiny, we studied in the finest detail all of our data relating to the storm. It gradually became evident to us that we had actually had access to enough information to have predicted accurately the strength and the path of the storm. With better science, better computing capacity, better operations, better technology, and better assimilation techniques, we could indeed have forecast it.

All of us at the Met Office realized that we could learn a great deal from this unusual storm. We needed to grasp with both hands the opportunity it provided for us to move forward.

Forecasting the weather involves two main elements. The first is the collection of information describing the current weather. Measurements of atmospheric temperature and pressure are made from land surface stations, ships, and aircraft around the world and from satellites in space. The data is collected and transmitted to meteorological centres around the globe. The second element is the forecasting part. With the help of computers these millions of data elements are put together and checked to form as complete a description as possible of the current weather. This provides the initial conditions from which we run a computer model that works out how that pattern is likely to develop.

There are inherent problems with this whole process of data collection and interpretation. Met Office computers receive enormous quantities of data, which sometimes do not arrive on time. Indeed, some data which would have helped us predict the storm arrived after the forecast and therefore did not contribute to that day's model. Sometimes, incorrect data reaches us, which can throw the computer badly off course. You have to try to weed out these data errors before they reach the computer, a process heavily reliant upon experience and scientific judgment. One way to weed out strange results is by comparing them with the last computer model, or with what we might usually expect. Therefore, there is a danger of ignoring any extreme or unwanted readings on the assumption that they are wrong. But, of course, if these extreme readings happen to be correct, they are the most important readings of all. Professor Gordon Dobson, my Oxford professor of atmospheric physics, had once asked me, "How can you be sure your corrections are correct?" drawing my young attention to the importance of questioning results, of checking and checking again.

I remember one occasion when the Met Office received a call from a ship being tossed around in the mid-Atlantic, saying,

"We've got a force 10 gale here which isn't on any of your charts." This had happened because the data describing this storm, being so far from what the model was suggesting was correct, had been disregarded. Conversely, on another occasion, thanks to the inclusion of false data, which actually should have been weeded out, we invented an entirely fictitious storm in the Pacific.

Our detailed analysis of the events leading up to the Great Storm of 1987 led to many significant improvements in the forecasting ability of the Meteorological Office. It was instrumental in moving us forward. With extra investment from the government, we improved the quality of the data collection process and the way in which data was assimilated into the computer models. More importantly, the government agreed to invest in improving the Met Office's computing capacity, and we were able to refine the computer models used in our forecasting. The Met Office became better equipped for the future. As a result of our internal inquiry and the subsequent improvements, similar storms elsewhere in the UK in early 1990, and many storms since then, have been very well forecast. But that was not considered to be newsworthy, and the press showed little interest.

A scientist's job, and passion, is the observation and continuous questioning of the unknown in a determined quest for the truth. In fact, investigation of the unexplained and the sometimes apparently inexplicable is one of the major methods of scientific advance: scientists have to pay attention to apparent anomalies in case they are telling us a story of huge importance. Sometimes, however, the anomalies are wrong and, if accepted as fact, can be very misleading. In much of science, as in weather forecasting, there is a range of uncertainty.

Climate science is no different. One of the difficulties with which climate scientists have often struggled is how best to present our varying degree of uncertainties to the public. How can we, like TV weather forecasters, be confident enough to convey what we think will happen, while also explaining that there is some uncertainty? How can we show, with sufficient clarity, enough of the big picture, enough of the truth, to prevent future generations asking the haunting question of 17 October 1987, "Why weren't we warned?"

2

THE INCUBATION OF
A SCIENTIST

From as early as I can remember, I wanted to be a scientist. I was always very keen to find out how things worked and I was forever making things. One of my earliest memories is of being taken behind the clock face of Big Ben while the bell struck 12, by a friend of my dad's who was in charge of building maintenance at Westminster. It must have made as much of an impression on my five-year-old mind as it did on my ears, because upon returning home I hurried to make a cardboard model of Big Ben.

Although cardboard was adequate for some jobs, what I particularly loved making were little electrical gadgets. A major inspiration to my young mind was a book I was given as a prize when I was about eight years old. Alfred Powell Morgan's *The Boy Electrician*,[1] as I have since discovered, influenced many boys of my generation. I enjoyed enormously using material I found around the house to make the devices described in that book.

As well as the mechanical side of things, I was equally fascinated by the mysteries and the beauty of the natural world around me, which seemed to pose so many questions: questions to which I wanted to know the answers. How did things work? Where did they come from? What? How? Why? I never had any doubt at all that I wanted to search for these answers; that I wanted to be a scientist.

At the unusually young age of nine years old, having been identified during my primary years as a promising pupil, I was accepted into Rhyl Grammar School in North Wales. Here, I was very fortunate in having an exceptional physics teacher, Cledwyn Williams, who encouraged and further inspired my early interest in that subject. By the time I reached sixth form, there were only two of us in my year studying physics: myself and Ivor Jones. Cledwyn Williams allowed us free access to the new physics laboratory, where we worked together from textbooks, made up our own experiments, and tried to solve problems ourselves. Only when we were really stuck did we approach our teacher. It was a marvellous, exciting start for me: an early opportunity to develop the valuable skills of independent learning, and of trial and error.

My elder brother David was particularly fascinated by the weather and knew from an early age that he wanted to be a meteorologist. He mounted thermometers and a rain gauge in the garden at home, and for a long time he recorded all his measurements meticulously. He went on to study physics at Manchester University, followed by a Master's in meteorology at Imperial College, London, and eventually joined the Meteorological Office. Little could we have imagined as boys how closely we eventually would work together. In contrast to David's sense of vocation, I was never sure what sort of scientist I wanted to be. I simply knew that I wanted to search for answers. I wanted to search, just as I'm still searching now, for the truth about God, the universe, and everything. Focusing on small, intricate details, I hoped to build a better understanding of the big picture, whatever that might mean.

I was born on 30 December 1931 in a village called Dyserth in the countryside of North Wales. When I was two years old, we moved to Rhyl where my father was a history teacher at the grammar school. Dad loved books and knowledge, particularly religious history. Over his lifetime he built up a personal library of well over 30,000 volumes, all bought from second-hand bookshops. He also contributed to what became an exceptional library at Rhyl Grammar, where I spent hours reading books that were to prove formative to my future interests: books about exploration, adventure, and science.

Adventure and exploration provided me with further ways of finding out about the world. I loved exploring the Welsh countryside, with its coast, rivers, streams, hills, and mountains. With school friends or my brothers, I would cycle, scramble, and climb with great enjoyment. My other brother Paul is 11 years younger than me, so in my late teens I was able to accompany him on his own journeys of discovery. He too went on to study physics at Oxford before becoming a physics teacher. It's interesting to trace back the ties and interests that define you throughout your life. My early love of mountain walking and the sea has never left me, nor has my passion for science and exploration. And I still have very close relationships with both David and Paul.

Our parents came from the Manchester area. My mum, born Miriam Yarwood, was brought up in Eccles as a Strict Baptist.[2] She became a mathematics teacher for a while, which was when she met my father. She gave that up after marriage to become a housewife, like most mothers of her generation. She was a lovely, loving lady, unfortunately troubled by painful osteoarthritis for most of her adult life. When Dad first met her, he was a Methodist with quite liberal views, but he was soon influenced by discussions with his future father-in-law, and by the time he married my mother he had become a Strict Baptist himself. A Victorian by birth and also by style, this combined with what developed into increasingly strong religious views to make my father rather an unbending man.

On Sundays we all used to attend the Plymouth Brethren Assembly in Rhyl, where Dad took a leading role.[3] During the war years (1939–45) we had open house on Sunday afternoons for soldiers from a nearby army training camp. My brothers and I enjoyed their company and made friends among them. The music, conversations, and walks for a while became part of our normal family life.

We were aware, during these years, of sounds that must have troubled the soldiers back in their camp at night. Living less than 20 miles from Liverpool as the crow flies, we could hear German bombers flying overhead on their way to bomb the city. The eastern sky still burns bright red in my memory as fires devastated the city, killing so many innocent people.

My parents held very strong beliefs, which I respected and still do, although I didn't always agree with them. Evolution, in particular, caused quite a few problems between my father and me. Believing strongly in the authority of the Bible, Dad was opposed to the theory of evolution as proposed by Darwin (see Appendix 1). It was not that he read the Genesis story of creation in six days literally; he accepted the scientific evidence that creation had taken a very long period of time rather than just six days. However, he could not accept that God's creative process might have been an evolutionary one, involving chance events. That scientists would often use evolution as an argument against the existence of a creator God confirmed him in this view.

From an early age, science having increasingly captivated my interest, I became aware of the scientific evidence for evolution. Unlike my father, I didn't see any problems with this. It was increasingly clear to me that the universe is God's creation. As science was the means by which I would be able to explore and describe God's creative work, I could not see how there could possibly be conflict between science and faith. Still, it was a sensitive subject and as then I didn't know enough about either science or faith to engage sensibly in deep discussion, it was better avoided.

I went to see my father on the day before he died. By this time, I was in my fifties. "You know, John," Dad said, "there are some things on which we've never agreed." I said I was very aware of that but of greater importance were the many things on which we did agree. Nevertheless, my rebelliousness on that particular issue, and on others, obviously troubled him to his dying day.

Having joined Rhyl Grammar two years early, I was only 16 when I completed my Higher School Certificate examinations, the predecessors of "A" levels. It was time to leave home for university. I was all geared up to follow in David's footsteps and go to Manchester University when we received news that, on the basis of what were apparently excellent results, I had been awarded a scholarship to Jesus College, Oxford University. This Meyricke Scholarship saw me, as a frightened but excited 16-year-old, leaving my family and home in North Wales to travel alone to Oxford.

I arrived in Oxford in 1948 to find that there was no room for me in the college, so I had to find some digs in the town. Not only was I 16, but I was a rather young 16 from a strict Christian background, with very little experience of anything other than home, and still with a child's ration book. Because of the war, men who should have gone to university over the past few years had gone instead to the battlefield, so I found myself in a college full of older, far more experienced men, many of whom were just back from the war.

Strange though this situation was, I didn't mind it too much. Some of the men were kind enough to take me under their wings. The tutors were understanding; but the man who particularly stands out was the tutor for admissions, John Griffith, whom we all came to know fondly as Johnny G. He became a friend right from the start. Although Johnny was a classics tutor, his father had been a physicist and he therefore had a tremendous interest in the subject, which would prove important to me in later years.

Early on I forged some strong friendships within the university Christian Union. Like many churchgoing youngsters who leave home for the first time, I was wondering what sort of Christian I was; whether or not I really believed. If I didn't believe all that my father believed, could I still call myself a Christian? Among the student Christian community were people whose thinking was far more liberal than anything I'd encountered before, allowing a much freer interpretation of the Bible. I became involved in discussions about the Bible and the nature of God that Dad would have considered heretical.

Of great interest to me was how to relate my fledgling faith to the real world, and in particular to science. Through discussions within the Christian Union I gradually began to find my feet. My science had always seemed to demand an intelligence behind the universe, otherwise, I wondered, where could the laws of nature have come from? As far as I could see, science is the exploration and discovery of the world; science did not create the world, and therefore does not negate a creator. I was baffled that science and faith should be so often seen as contradictory, if not in direct opposition with one another. It didn't make sense to me. Once in Oxford, my thinking on this gradually became more coherent.

In later years, while a research student at Oxford, I joined the Research Scientists Christian Fellowship (RSCF), which encouraged me to consider further the relationship between science and faith. I was greatly influenced by the thinking of prominent scientists such as Sir Robert Boyd, one of the pioneers of space astronomy, and Donald Mackay, who was an exceptionally clear thinker and writer on the workings of the brain. Through free discussion of the Bible and through their searching, often challenging, questions, these men and others helped to mentor and support us young students as we tried to find our way. Through the RSCF we organized meetings and conferences to introduce topics relating science with faith to sixth formers. Presenting at such events helped me to think about these issues.

It wasn't just exploration of my faith that kept me occupied outside academic study. As I was in Oxford, I felt I ought to give the rowing club a try. Being rather slight of build, and younger than everybody else, I was an easy choice for cox, which I enjoyed for a while. When the novelty wore off, however, I reflected that it wasn't much good being in a sports team if I wasn't getting any exercise. Besides, all that shouting in damp weather had given me laryngitis. Turning my back on the river, I took up tennis and squash instead.

During the first year of my degree I read mathematics under the guidance of a brilliant young mathematician called Edward Thompson. Each week I took to him the problems over which I had often toiled for hours, sometimes with little success. With great elegance and economy of technique, Edward would indicate in a few lines how to demolish both the problem and my attempt at solving it, a process that rarely took more than 10 or 15 minutes of the one-hour tutorial time.

An awkward silence invariably ensued: awkward for me at least. While he sat back in his chair, puffing away at his pipe, I would sit and stare at my work. Then, after a suitable interval, I would excuse myself. "Well, if that's all, Sir, perhaps I should go." "Yes, good idea, yes," he would reply. So we had rather silent tutorials. Deflating though it might have been, I learned a lot of mathematics in those first 15 minutes of every hour.

As a child I had developed quite a taste for adventure, which continued into my student days. After that first year at Oxford, a friend and I took on the midges and mixed weather of Scotland in a cycling and camping trip. I raised the money for that trip by picking bilberries in Wales. Another summer, five of us joined in purchasing a 20-year-old London taxi with a folding hood. With a maximum speed of about 30 mph we drove through France, Belgium, Germany, Switzerland, and Italy as far as Venice, camping out each night. A particular highlight was finding ourselves mixed up with the Tour de France, so we drove along with our hood down, waving to the crowds. I spent a later summer hitch-hiking with a friend through Denmark and Norway where we climbed some of Norway's highest peaks.

Back in Oxford for my second year, I moved on to study physics under Claude Hurst. He was probably the best physics tutor in the university, a claim evidenced by the statistic that over a period of 14 years during his time at Jesus College, from the mid 1940s to around 1960, seven of the top firsts in Oxford physics came from Jesus College. For my first tutorial with Claude at the beginning of my second year, he had asked me to write an essay on some physics topic. His dry comment was, "We'll get you writing better essays than that." And he did, for which I'm grateful.

During my degree course, I particularly enjoyed lectures on atmospheric physics and meteorology given by Gordon Dobson and Alan Brewer. When I gained my degree in 1951, I followed in the footsteps of so many of Claude Hurst's students, gaining the top first in Oxford in my year. I therefore had a free choice over my doctorate course. I decided to join Gordon Dobson and Alan Brewer's small team of researchers, some of whom were involved in developing new ways of observing the distribution of ozone (O_3) (see Box 2.1 below) in the atmosphere, where it acts as a trace constituent, providing information on the circulation in that part of the atmosphere. Others were interested in the principles of cloud formation. All crammed into two small rooms at the back of the physics laboratory, we got on very well together, learned a lot from each other and had a lot of fun.

The earth's atmosphere was a fascinating area of study, about which there was still a great deal to learn. The atmosphere is divided into several distinct regions, each with its own characteristics. As they all follow the earth's spherical shape, their names carry the suffix "-sphere". Working outwards from the earth, the sphere within which we live is the troposphere, where the temperature falls with increasing height. Above that is the stratosphere, which stretches from about 10 km above us to a distance of about 50 km. Still travelling away from the earth, the next is the mesosphere (approximately 50–100 km), then the thermosphere. The region above these is often known collectively as the ionosphere, because it contains particles that have been ionized by collision with particles from the sun.

Gordon Dobson was a great experimental scientist whose remarkable pioneering work measuring ozone in the atmosphere had begun as early as the 1920s. In 1924, he devised an instrument to measure ozone in the stratosphere. In developing what became known as the Dobson Ozone Spectrometer, he pioneered the principles of remote sensing: measuring atmospheric quantities from a distance.[4] His legacy is still evident today, as even now the principles of remote sensing are still very much in use, and the density of ozone is measured in Dobson units.

Box 2.1 Ozone (O_3)

The gas ozone is a molecule made up of three atoms of oxygen (denoted by O_3). Ozone is created when normal oxygen molecules (O_2) are split into separate atoms by ultraviolet sunlight and one of the lone oxygen atoms joins another oxygen molecule. It is present in the stratosphere in about 10 parts per million.

Ozone's presence in the atmosphere is vital as it absorbs ultraviolet sunlight that would be destructive to many life forms if it were not absorbed before it reached the earth's surface. Ozone is also important because by absorbing sunlight it warms the atmosphere. Temperature therefore rises with height in the stratosphere, preventing vertical motion upwards, making it a particularly stable region.

I still remember Gordon Dobson's advice, which I recalled in the aftermath of the Great Storm. I was making instruments to measure how much infrared radiation was emitted by the atmosphere, both upwards and downwards at different levels. I'd created a little device for doing this, but I had to make all sorts of corrections to the instrument to ensure accurate readings. I showed Dobson my corrections. "Ah," he said, "but how do you know your corrections are correct? Why don't you make two radiometers, make them physically as different as you can, and see whether they both give you the same answer?"

I went away and did precisely as he had suggested and got the same answer for both. This thoroughness gave me great confidence that what I was doing was right. It was another invaluable lesson for my future.

Similarly impressive and influential was Dr Alan Brewer. He had made the first measurements from aircraft of the very dry stratosphere and had worked with Dobson to propose what became known as the Dobson–Brewer circulation of the stratosphere, which explained the dynamic relationship between ozone and water vapour. He was a highly skilled instrument maker and experimental physicist, who also had a remarkable understanding of dynamic as well as physical meteorology.

I was Alan's first research student and his only one at the time, so he had a lot of time and enthusiasm to support me. We developed a great friendship, which lasted throughout his life. When Alan died in 2007, I was invited to write his obituary and to speak at his funeral. I had come to him as a very green experimental researcher, and his influence on me was enormous. He taught me how to conduct experimental research and how to build instruments, about the atmosphere and how it behaves. I'm still immensely grateful to him.

My DPhil project was concerned with the lower stratosphere, which contains most of the atmosphere's ozone. Dobson's measurement of ozone had shown that there was more ozone over the poles during the long winter nights than over the equator, where ozone is created through the action of sunlight. This seemed to imply a flow in the lower stratosphere, tending to move air from the equator to the poles. If this were the case, it would also involve a downward movement of air at mid latitudes that might be detectable from accurate radiation measurements. Such measurements were the subject of my project.

For three years I designed and built radiation-measuring instruments and learned a great deal about the transfer of radiation in the atmosphere. It was fun working with Alan. We took the instruments we had built up to the Royal Aircraft Establishment at Farnborough, where we mounted them onto small, recently decommissioned military Mosquito aircraft, which could fly to an altitude of 40,000 feet, well into the stratosphere. The body of the Mosquito was made entirely from plywood.

My device was about 10 cm square, and we needed to fit two of them to the craft; one on the top and one on the bottom. On our first visit, we discovered that my device didn't quite fit onto the aircraft as we had hoped. I can remember Alan Brewer sitting astride the plane with a brace and bit, drilling holes into it. You couldn't conceivably behave in that way now; but it was great fun. Unfortunately, I had failed the compression chamber test, so I wasn't allowed to do the test flights to the highest levels. A friend called Phil Goldsmith, who was working for the Met Office at Farnborough, undertook those flights on my behalf. Nevertheless, the lower flights were thrilling, sitting on my seat constructed of a selection of bungee cords, with only a thick sheet of perspex between me and the whirring propeller. I'd sit there writing down measurements as we flew. Many of our flights were at night because that gave us optimal conditions for our measuring. It was also more exciting.

Although I thoroughly enjoyed working toward my doctorate and learned a tremendous amount about building, testing, and using instruments, Alan and I didn't really succeed in our aim. Because of the variability of the atmosphere, I was not able to achieve the accuracy required to draw useful inferences about stratospheric circulation. This I explained in my DPhil thesis. I felt therefore somewhat frustrated that, when I completed it in 1955, I was still far from seeing the big picture of the atmosphere's behaviour. I had merely taken a few interesting snapshots.

3

GLIMPSES OF THE BIG PICTURE

I completed my doctorate when I was 23. Aware that I was likely to be called up for National Service, I was keen to stay in science rather than go into the armed forces. When a National Service opportunity arose at the Royal Aircraft Establishment (RAE) in Farnborough, I leapt at the chance. Having flown in the Mosquito with Alan Brewer from there, I was quite familiar with the set-up and some of the personnel. It was therefore with a mixture of relief and excitement that I accepted an appointment as research fellow in atmospheric physics at Farnborough.

My appointment came about largely as a result of Alan's connections at Farnborough, where my task would be to lead a team investigating the transparency of the atmosphere to infrared radiation at different wavelengths. The detection of radiation in the atmosphere allows the identification of heat sources, such as aircraft or missiles. Much infrared is blocked out through absorption by different gases present in the atmosphere, so it is important to identify regions in the infrared spectrum where the atmosphere is largely transparent. Our results could therefore be of considerable military importance.

We succeeded in making some of the first measurements of the distribution of minor atmospheric constituents at different altitudes. Besides their military use, such measurements would tell us a lot about the atmosphere's composition, and be of great scientific interest.

Aware that the results of our work could be used in military applications, I was quite pleased to be able to contribute in this way. The army had been of great value in the world I'd been brought up in, and of course science had played an important role in the war effort. I even found myself pulled into projects other than my main one. The British dropped their test hydrogen bomb in the Pacific at that time, and I helped with predictions of how the transparency of the atmosphere would affect the safety of the aircraft, and how the bomb-flash might be seen in different parts of the atmosphere. However, whatever the project, it was always the science itself that fascinated me. And this was particularly so in the case of the science of the stratosphere.

Because of possible attacks from the air during the war, the RAE had established outstations in the countryside, one of which was Ambarrow Court, a lovely old country house near Sandhurst. This was where our infrared team was based. It was a glorious piece of National Trust land. We were a team of enthusiastic young scientists, and, of course, working closely together for what was to be four years, we developed firm and long-lasting friendships. When we weren't working, we enjoyed walking through the woods. Among the members of the team was Des Smith, an excellent scientist and innovative thinker. Like me, Des's expertise was in the development of devices relevant to the detection and measurement of infrared radiation.

Des and I were quite competitive characters. Sometimes, on long walks together, we would lock antlers in physical challenges. Once we dared each other to climb a not-yet-connected electricity pylon. I was relieved when Des decided to climb down at the same point as I had. Des was also a great mountaineer and sportsman, which led to hikes together in later years when we were fortunate enough to attend international conferences in beautiful places. My life has been punctuated by exciting and happy days with Des. When my first wife died, he decided to cheer me up with a ski-climbing trip to Austria. It was brilliant and extremely cathartic. I've never been so exhausted in all my life. Working with Des at Farnborough was just the beginning of a long-lasting and important friendship.

Des was more bullish than I was back then, and the same is probably still true. Some friends and colleagues have commented that we have the same determination, but Des's approach is more upfront. I'm one of those quieter, more subtle operators who go behind the scenes. These differences probably made us effective. Just as our expertise was complementary, so were our personalities. Of course, we had plenty of disagreements, some fiercer than others; we were young, eager, and ambitious to move our science forward. The inevitable friendly rivalry between us proved a great catalyst to our work; after all, the origin of the verb "to compete" is "to strive together", and that's exactly what we have always done.

Those four years at Farnborough were great fun. Carrying our apparatus from place to place, we would race around the lanes in an old 1.5 tonne Bedford truck. The back roads from that part of Hampshire to the Farnborough airfield were quite something. The others in the team seemed to find my driving frightening: they said I drove too quickly, using the fact that I once drove into a wall as evidence. I also had a car with a freewheel knob by which I could disengage the engine and freewheel to conserve petrol. Passengers tended to dislike that. The aircraft we were now using were more exciting than my car: the craft on which my device was to be mounted was a Canberra two-engine jet aircraft, the predecessor of the Nimrod. As we flew around up in the stratosphere, I had to lie on my front in the nose of the plane, taking and recording my measurements.

The instrument we were devising, building, and using was an infrared spectrometer, which used a "diffraction grating" to separate infrared wavelengths, in a similar way to a prism's separation of visible light. We were working to develop the best spectrometer possible within the limitations imposed by the size of the aircraft available to us. The spectrometer was pointed at the sun so that the absorption of the sun's radiation by the atmosphere above the aircraft could be measured at different infrared wavelengths. Knowing how the different gases in the atmosphere absorbed infrared radiation provided us with information about atmospheric composition, in particular the concentration of carbon dioxide, water vapour, and minor gases such as nitrogen oxide and methane.

It was the first time anybody had really got a comprehensive set of spectra of that kind, and the results helped increase understanding of how the physics and chemistry of the atmosphere relate to its circulation. This work at Farnborough was a good introduction to the more complex devices we would later develop, which would one day play a significant role in monitoring our changing climate.

On 4 October 1957, just before I was due to leave Farnborough, the Russians launched Sputnik 1 (Figure 3.1), the first ever space satellite to be launched successfully into an orbit of the earth. This was to prove a key event in my life. Up went Sputnik, and round it travelled, many orbits a day. It was amazing. For the first time ever, most of the earth was visible to a satellite twice within each day. Des and I were captivated. This is it! we thought. Here is this eye in the sky. If only we could put an instrument on board something like Sputnik and get measurements of infrared radiation emitted from the earth and its atmosphere, that would be a wonderful way forward to understanding the global atmosphere and the global climate more fully.

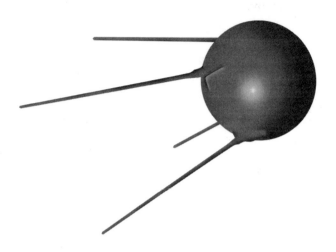

Figure 2.1: Sputnik 1. The first ever satellite to be launched successfully into an orbit of the earth

From then on, Des and I were to spend a great deal of time pondering the possibilities of more accurate atmospheric measurements by combining our sciences. No longer content with local measurements only, we wanted to see how the atmosphere behaved as a whole, because that is precisely what it does. For instance, the weather pattern of the UK is influenced by the entire global weather system: it is not an independent, self-contained system. To forecast the weather more than a few days ahead in the UK requires knowledge of the whole atmospheric circulation, including that in the southern hemisphere. To be able to understand more about the whole earth's atmosphere by viewing it from space would be an enormous advance on the situation of discontinuous observations at a few earth-based locations, which was all that was possible at that time.

Box 3.1 Weather and Climate: How They Differ

Weather describes what we experience at different locations and in the relatively short term – days to a week or two at the most. In addition to regular variations from season to season, weather in general shows a lot of natural variability. Over periods of up to about a week ahead, weather shows some predictability, making forecasting possible.

Climate is simply described as average weather – averaged over periods of months to years to show variations from place to place, season to season, and year to year. Over the past million years, the global climate has varied with a series of ice ages triggered by regular variations in the earth's orbit around the sun. We are currently in a warm period in between ice ages.

The possibility of looking down continuously from above with instruments orbiting the earth raises the question of how predictable climate is in the shorter term, for instance over the next century, and whether observations from space of the atmosphere, oceans, land, and ice would make it possible to predict in advance climate changes, especially those that might be triggered by human activities. Later chapters will enter into the excitement of how some of this is being realized.

The technology of remote sensing of the atmosphere, pioneered by people like Gordon Dobson, had so far involved looking up into the atmosphere from the earth, or at the most from balloons and aircraft. Instead of our remote position being on the ground, or relatively close to the ground, on an aircraft, Des and I hoped our measurements might one day be taken from above. There would be two main advantages to this. First, information about the higher atmosphere would be available, uninfluenced by interference from the lower atmosphere, but more importantly, we would gain data on a global scale: a bigger, more complete picture.

The lightning bolt of Sputnik's launch seemed to jolt our brains with a new electric impulse. We started thinking furiously and innovatively, toying with all sorts of ideas of what we could do from a satellite. What kind of instrument could we use? What measurements might we take? What secrets might the atmosphere hold? Our big vision, if we could find a way to achieve it, was to devise an instrument to investigate global atmospheric circulation. We knew that circulation is driven by differences of density, which itself depends on temperature. The radiation emitted by molecules within the atmosphere contains information about atmospheric temperature structure: the higher the temperature, the more the molecules vibrate and the higher the radiation they emit. If we could isolate the radiation coming from different atmospheric levels, we would know the temperature at those levels. Our target gas was carbon dioxide (CO_2) because, second only to water vapour, it provides the strongest infrared radiation emitted by earth to space. Furthermore, as CO_2 is uniformly distributed throughout the atmosphere, it would give us a global picture of atmospheric temperature structure.

Box 3.2 Measurement of Atmospheric Temperature Structure from Space

In the molecule CO_2, the three atoms involved are in a straight line: $O - C - O$.

The oxygen atoms vibrate relative to the carbon atom and in the process emit infrared radiation in an amount that depends on the temperature of the CO_2. The higher the temperature, the more radiation is emitted. The radiation leaving the atmosphere at different wavelengths will have come from different depths in the atmosphere, enabling the temperature at different atmospheric levels to be monitored. Our target gas was CO_2 because, second only to water vapour, it provides the strongest infra-radiation emitted by earth to space. Furthermore, as CO_2 is uniformly distributed throughout the atmosphere, it would give us a global picture of atmospheric temperature structure.

Less than a year after Sputnik went into space, I returned to Oxford, inspired and brimming with new ideas. I couldn't begin work soon enough.

4

RETURN TO THE SPIRES

I arrived back in Oxford on 1 January 1958, just two days after my twenty-sixth birthday. While the city's famous dreaming spires still held their attraction, my focus was now fixed far beyond them and into space, my mind racing with all sorts of exciting possibilities. Things would never be the same again.

Our eyes had been opened to a measurement future we could never have imagined. It wasn't just us: the whole scientific world, particularly in the area of meteorology, was awakening to the wonder of new opportunities. Two years after Sputnik, America responded by launching its first weather satellite, which sent back fascinating photographs of the cloud structure of entire weather systems; images we had never seen before and the first near-global view of the earth's atmosphere. Further significant advances were surely imminent.

I was already aware that other scientists, particularly in the United States, were working in the area of infrared spectroscopy. Undoubtedly, they too would be thinking about taking future measurements from satellites. Exciting though it would certainly have been to find out what they were doing and to exchange ideas, I have never been one to sit back and look forward to other people's results: I'm too restless for that. I need to be actively seeking the truth for myself. I desperately wanted to learn more, and to be involved in the development of an instrument that would take measurements in space.

After a long and influential career, Gordon Dobson had retired from his personal chair as professor of meteorology, leaving a vacancy which was filled by my friend and former supervisor Dr Alan Brewer. I slotted happily and comfortably into Alan's vacated role as university lecturer in atmospheric physics, in which capacity I soon took on my first research student, Jim Williamson. An extremely capable young man, Jim was and still is very tall, with a sharp intellect and enquiring mind. Although eight years apart in age and experience, a difference more significant in youth than in maturity, we worked excellently together. Jim was as fascinated as I was by the challenges of measuring atmospheric temperature and radiation. His doctoral research project involved measuring infrared radiation from water vapour, using instruments he designed and built specifically for use on a small balloon. Jim's arrival at Oxford was the beginning of what was to become a wonderful partnership. In fact, Jim's scientific skills have greatly contributed to the success of my own career well beyond those early days.

While I returned to Oxford, Des Smith and another friend from Farnborough, John Seeley, went to Reading University to develop their work on optical devices and instruments, which would necessarily be an important part of any measuring device we might build. The fact that launching ourselves into the space age would necessitate continued partnership with Des and John was in itself exciting. Des and John in Reading, Jim and I in Oxford: our two fields of scientific expertise would need to work closely together, each exploring the boundaries of its own discipline.

Thanks to my early flights in the Mosquito with Alan, and then my four years' work at Farnborough, I had accumulated considerable experience in taking measurements of the atmosphere from aircraft. I had also accumulated a lot of data. Immediately upon my return to Oxford, I was involved primarily with analysis of the data I had brought back from Farnborough. Nevertheless, the equally demanding challenges presented by building a satellite-based instrument continued to occupy my mind. When I wasn't analysing data, I was thinking about how we might establish a space science programme at Oxford.

In 1958, the British government had decided to invest a substantial sum of about £6 million into space science. This money was allocated through the British National Committee for Space Research (BNCSR) under the chairmanship of Sir Harrie Massey, a professor at University College London. I was quite optimistic that Alan Brewer might accept an invitation to join Sir Harrie's committee, which would have been a help in keeping us informed about the committee's work. However, Alan declined. Although disappointed, I wasn't completely surprised by his decision, knowing that his interest in space science was limited, and that he tended to prefer working closely on the science rather than involving himself in troublesome committees.

Besides, Alan's mind was otherwise occupied. Shortly after my return to Oxford, I had been asked to fill his place temporarily while he spent a year at the Massachusetts Institute for Technology (MIT) in Boston, USA. He only returned to Oxford for a relatively short time, before leaving again in 1962 to take up a permanent position at the University of Toronto, where he would study measurements of atmospheric ozone, his main area of academic interest. I admire his strength in having maintained his focus.

Following Alan's departure, I found myself progressing through the ranks of academia. I had already joined my former tutor Claude Hurst as a fellow and tutor in physics at Jesus College. Now I was invited once again to step upwards to fill Alan's place and I was elected to the position of reader[1] and head of the atmospheric physics group. My vacated lecturer position was filled by a Cambridge scientist, Desmond Walshaw, who had already been involved in work with Gordon Dobson, so, accordingly, his main area of interest was ozone. Also from Cambridge we soon welcomed Clive Rodgers, who came to work on the theory of remote sensing from space.

Throughout the 1960s, a remarkable group of highly talented young scientists were attracted to my department as research students. Alongside Jim Williamson, some notable names were Peter Abel, who came in 1962; David Pick, who arrived a year later; Fred Taylor, who came in 1966; and John Barnett, John Pyle, and Howard Roscoe, who arrived later in the decade. And so, shortly after my return to Oxford, I was in the privileged position of leading a growing team of excellent, committed scientists and research students, all thinking how we might be able to obtain meaningful measurements from space.

Our primary motivation was, as ever, curiosity: we were curious to know more about the behaviour of the stratosphere in particular. This departmental fascination with the stratosphere's circulation, which had given rise to Dobson and Brewer's pioneering work and had continued through my own DPhil work, had attracted our present research students and was therefore shared by all of us. Scientists still understood fairly little about this circulation, which was not yet adequately measured by existing meteorological methods. Observing it from space was almost our holy grail.

We received some valuable advice from an eminent American meteorologist called Vern Suomi. He said that instead of concentrating solely on the stratosphere, we really must take measurements lower down in the troposphere too. This was difficult to do because we had to deal with complications associated with the variability of clouds. Nevertheless, we followed his advice and, providing the sky was clear, found that we made useful measurements right down to the earth's surface. It had been sensible advice.

It is probably worthwhile explaining here very simply how our work at the time relates to the science of climate change today.

We were using carbon dioxide (CO_2) to measure temperature at different levels in the atmosphere. Understanding temperature at different levels helps us to understand the atmosphere's circulation and therefore its behaviour. Carbon dioxide is also a major contributor to the greenhouse effect, which influences climate change. So, CO_2 helps us to measure temperature, and it also influences the earth's climate.

Scientists had known for over a century about the greenhouse effect, a natural phenomenon first recognized in 1827 by the French scientist Jean-Baptiste Fourier. Fourier identified that radiation from the sun enters the atmosphere, much of it reaching the earth's surface and warming it. To balance this incoming radiation, infrared radiation is emitted upwards by the earth's surface. Some of it is blocked on the way out, as it is absorbed by gases in the atmosphere such as water vapour and CO_2, which act like blankets, keeping the earth's surface about 20 °C warmer than it would otherwise be. These are called "greenhouse gases" because they act like the glass in a greenhouse, which lets the sunlight through but prevents the infrared radiation from inside the greenhouse from getting out, so keeping the greenhouse warm. Without greenhouse gases in the atmosphere, the earth's surface would be much colder; in fact it would be covered with ice. Naturally occurring greenhouse gases therefore help to maintain the delicate equilibrium supporting life on earth.

However, the greater the greenhouse effect, the warmer the planet will be. An enhanced greenhouse effect is caused by higher levels of greenhouse gases in the atmosphere than would naturally occur. The concentration of these gases is increased by human activities such as the burning of fossil fuels and deforestation. By this effect, more radiation is trapped and the earth's average surface temperature increases.

Box 4.1 The Greenhouse Effect: How Does the Earth Keep Warm?

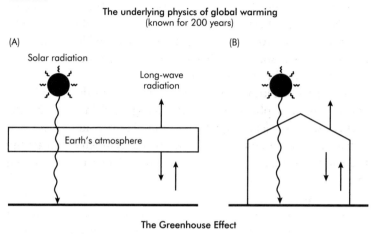

The underlying physics of global warming
(known for 200 years)

The Greenhouse Effect

The earth's atmosphere (A) works in the same way as the glass of a greenhouse (B)

However, our work wasn't driven by concern about rising global average temperature, nor even about CO_2 concentration. That concern would develop in the future as we and other scientists noticed unexpected patterns in data we received and models we created. All we wanted to do then was to take measurements and learn more about the earth's atmosphere. How could we have foreseen, in the early 1960s, where the world would be post-2010, half a century later?

Parallel to thinking about a future measuring device, I was considering more efficient methods of analysing data. This was the late 1950s/early 1960s: the dawn not only of satellite technology, but of the age of computers. In 1958, Oxford University had invested in its first computer: a Ferranti Mercury. With its complexity of thousands and thousands of valves and circuits, this magnificent machine occupied an entire house at 19 South Parks Road. The director of the computing laboratory,

Professor Leslie Fox, was an excellent man who was keen to introduce this computer within the sciences as well as in his own discipline of mathematics. As soon as the computer arrived, I was interested in the possibility of using it for radiation calculations, which were too difficult to do by hand.

With remarkable serendipity, not only was my department attracting talented British scientists, but the attractions of Oxford itself were drawing visitors from further afield. Oxford is a beautiful city and the university has a historic and international reputation for excellence; factors which have always made it a very popular destination for academics from overseas, most specifically, in this case, from America and Canada. In 1960, Walter Hitschfield, a professor of meteorology at McGill University, Montreal, came to spend a year working in Oxford. Keen to learn about radiation transfer [2] in the atmosphere, Walter decided to join me in trying to find a way of computing infrared radiative transfer calculations. He quickly proved to be adept in this new computing technology.

Walter and I stumbled along together very well until, eventually, having worked out exactly how many calculations the computer would have to perform to analyse the data involved, I went to visit Leslie Fox to discuss how his Ferranti Mercury might help. I explained to Leslie just what we wanted to do. He listened patiently.

"How long do you think that would take?" I asked. I imagined this thing was all-powerful. I was wrong. My question was followed by a long silence during which I shifted anxiously from foot to foot. Would it be weeks? Months?

Finally, Leslie sucked in a breath between his teeth and smiled. "That would take you around one million years."

This wasn't what I had hoped to hear. I went away to think. We might have hit a significant obstacle to our progress, but this just meant that we would need to find a way around it. We would have to break down the task into smaller and more efficient processes. We wrestled with this problem until eventually, in 1961, Walter and I successfully carried out the first computer line-by-line calculations of radiative transfer in the atmosphere and applied them to atmospheric ozone. We had forged a way forward. I learned at once the immense future potential and the present limitations of the computer. This, my first experience of complex computing, had been great fun because it was all so new.

Although absorbed by the challenges we had posed ourselves, I had always known by instinct and experience that we cannot neglect other parts of our lives: we need personal, physical, and spiritual health to maintain our intellectual health.

Outside my work, I became aware that visiting students and academics from overseas, particularly from Africa and Asia, often found it difficult to find accommodation in Oxford. In an effort to address this problem, some colleagues and I set up a small committee, which I chaired. A few years later, having acquired funding from a generous individual grant and the British Council, we bought a large house in north Oxford. This house became the North Oxford Overseas Centre (NOOC) and was soon home to a vibrant community of people from many different parts of the world. Before long, with demand for rooms within the centre exceeding the rooms available, it became necessary to buy a second house. The purchase of this second property came so close to failure that our eventual success really felt like an answer to prayer. The NOOC, now with around fifty single rooms, six doubles, and four self-contained family flats, continues to provide a wonderful home to lots of people year upon year.

I was also busy with my church connections in Oxford, and I enjoyed several hiking holidays in the Alps. One of my most memorable Alpine adventures was with a group of friends, all far more experienced and skilled Alpine climbers than I was. We traversed Switzerland's Bernina Ridge at over 4,000 metres high before heading to the Jungfrau region. Nearing the end of our descent from the Gross Fiescherhorn a heavy snowstorm meant that we had to continue roped together, often up to our waists in drifts. Being the lightest in the party, I had to take the lead, the argument being that I would be the easiest to pull out of trouble if necessary. It was an exhilarating experience.

Much more importantly, while attending my brother David's wedding, I was introduced to Margaret, a medical doctor with a great interest in and talent for working with physically handicapped children. Margaret and I married on 7 April 1962. That summer we flew out to Boulder, Colorado, where I had accepted a temporary position in the Bureau of Standards. In my short time there, I gained valuable knowledge and experience, of which more in Chapter 5. This was almost a zenith for me: a few months in which my love of hiking, my new wife, and my work all came together in one glorious place on the edge of America's Rocky Mountains.

Upon our return to Oxford, Margaret and I moved into a family home we had built in Begbroke, near Woodstock. I felt myself blessed with so many wonderful things: exciting, stimulating work, youth and energy, a wonderful wife, great friends, and in 1964 a happy, healthy, beautiful daughter, Janet.

At work, I now had the honour of being a member of the small Senior Common Room at Jesus College, which provided a very friendly community. I remember with great fondness some of those colourful characters. John Griffith in particular was proving to be a great friend and extremely supportive of my team's space work. Happy and secure in my personal life and confident of the support of my academic colleagues, I worked hard to lead my team forward.

Not only was I continuing to develop as a more complete scientist, but I was learning many of the skills of cooperation, teamwork, and leadership upon which I would rely so heavily in my later career. The stereotype of a scientist as a lonely, secretive figure shut away in his dark laboratory like Victor Frankenstein couldn't be further from the truth. Scientists have to get together. Just as it had been for Walter and me, and as the culture within my space team evidenced, cooperation really is crucial for progress and has proven to be an important part of the ongoing work on climate science. A scientist's work depends very much upon interaction with other scientists. Scientific teamwork can know no boundaries, so even international boundaries have to be crossed. In all areas of science, great work is being carried out simultaneously all around the world and scientists must get together if we are to come at all close to seeing the big picture.

There were already many international bodies through which scientists from around the world could share their work. Sometimes, keen to keep up to date with my side of the work since Farnborough, Des Smith would attend. For young, ambitious scientists like us, these meetings were invaluable ways to inform ourselves about the world's most up-to-date science, and meet some of the most eminent and fascinating scientists.

In 1959 I attended one such meeting in Oxford. It was a joint meeting between the International Radiation Commission (IRC) and the Ozone Commission. Des was there again, this time having volunteered to run the bar, which he did in his usual gregarious manner. During this meeting I met Mikhail Budyko for the first time, an influential Russian scientist, who was probably the most respected climatologist in the world at that time. He was accompanied by Kirill Kondratiev, a radiation expert who was rector of the University of Leningrad, and politically a powerful man in Soviet Russia.

Towards the end of the week, Alan Brewer and I invited Budyko and Kondratiev to take a drive with us along the Thames Valley to London. Although Budyko was a keen Anglophile, and in spite of Kondratiev's political influence in Russia, they were rather sheepish about accepting because they had a Soviet-employed minder to control their movements when abroad. However, they managed eventually to slip away from him and join us. We were able to stop off in such wonderful places as Henley, where Kondratiev was keen to row on the Thames. His wife was a rower and had competed there in the past. It was a glorious English summer day, and as we drifted along the river, Budyko asked me, "Is all of England this beautiful?"

Late that evening, we dropped them back at the Russian Embassy Hotel, and that was the last we saw of them for several days. Although they had numerous appointments the following week, they failed to turn up: they were being punished for having stepped out of line. Despite such controls on their movements, keeping in touch with both of these fascinating men for many years was made easy by the numerous scientific meetings we attended.

Another significant meeting of the IRC took place in Leningrad in 1964. Seven of us flew out to Helsinki, to cross the border into Russia by train. Not only was the meeting of great interest to us, but it was an interesting time to visit Leningrad, still in the grip of Communism. It would be almost another 30 years before this would change. In spite of the magnificence of some of its architecture, it was an austere place. From the moment of our arrival, we found it difficult to relax in the oppressive atmosphere. At about 2 a.m. one morning during that week, I was woken by my hotel telephone. I picked it up, to be greeted by Kondratiev, who told me that he intended to nominate me as Chairman of the IRC. He pressed me very hard to accept and it took all of my bleary-eyed wit and will power to say no. I just couldn't do it because I didn't have the time. In spite of the flattery of being offered an international role, this particular one would not have been at the top of my wish list. Later, when more alert, I reflected on his tactic of getting me at my most vulnerable.

Some years later, just after the 1968 Russian invasion of Czechoslovakia, I attended a conference in Bergen, Norway, with Kirill Kondratiev. On the first day, there was a degree of tension because we didn't know how these events in international relations might affect relations in the scientific community. We didn't know whether or not we should mention such things. Kondratiev stood up to open the proceedings. He said how pleased he was to be at the conference and that he felt it should be a free and open meeting, in which he would be fighting for freedom and democracy. I thought this was very clever because without any dangerous reference to the political situation, he had let us know his own position. Although a party man, he was not on the side of his masters on this issue. I feel privileged to have known Kondratiev. He has been, without a doubt, one of the colourful characters in my life. We remained in touch as friends until his death in 2006.

Mikhail Budyko has also been of importance throughout my career. We were, for many years, good friends. He even invited some of us to his home one evening during that IRC meeting in Leningrad. Furnished and decorated in a heavy Victorian style, with several locked cupboards full of English novels, his home bore witness to his love of English culture. Although we got along together very well, our relationship was to suffer decades later when difficult discussions within the Intergovernmental Panel on Climate Change (IPCC), to which I will refer in Chapter 14, caused tension between us.

That, however, was years in the future. Back in 1971, I attended another meeting in Russia, this time a meeting of the International Union of Geodesy and Geophysics (IUGG) in Moscow. Alan Brewer flew over from Toronto, providing a wonderful opportunity to catch up with a dear and much-missed friend. One night, several of the UK delegates, along with Alan, went out for dinner together. Service being very slow indeed, we found ourselves at the dinner table for five and a half hours, so, of course, we talked about many different things: science, family life, mutual friends, and our experiences in Russia. I remember Alan half-joking that there would probably be a hidden microphone in the flowers on the table.

Towards the end of the evening, a waitress approached us and handed one of us a piece of paper, upon which was written the word POWAPAK. "Tell me about powapak," she demanded. Rather perplexed, we explained briefly what jobs a power pack might do, and she went away, leaving us rather puzzled. Reviewing our topics of conversation during the course of the long evening, we realized that we had laughed about an unusual power pack, which Alan had devised for a particular piece of equipment. We stared at the vase of flowers.

As we left the restaurant, we were quiet. We remembered briefly having also discussed a young Russian scientist who, during the course of the conference, had opened up to Jim and me about the problems of living within such an oppressive regime. We desperately hoped that we hadn't mentioned her name or any other means of identifying her. We would never know whether anything happened to her as a result of talking with us. When our plane took off at the end of the week, we breathed a collective sigh of relief. We had gained some scientific knowledge from the conference, and we had all deepened our understanding of the world.

Visits to science conferences, both international and domestic, continued to play an important role in the partnership between Des's team in Reading and mine in Oxford, and whenever we got together, we continued to share ideas for an instrument which might measure temperature remotely at different atmospheric levels from space. Between us, we had acquired such a wealth of knowledge of infrared spectroscopic techniques; surely we could come up with something. But there were so many other problems to overcome, assuming of course that we met that first challenge. Once the instrument was devised, how would we build it? How and where would we test it? How would we persuade NASA to allow it onto a satellite? If they did, how would we gather and analyse the data? Where would the money come from? It seemed impossible. Perhaps that's what made it so compelling. When we were all together, ideas flew around like balls on a pinball table.

The early part of the path to our position and dreams at that time had been forged by some brave and admirable people. In 1784, a Frenchman, David Bourgeois, wrote exuberantly about the potential of the newly invented hydrogen and hot air balloons. Enthusing about their numerous uses, with great foresight he included weather prediction.[3] A century and a half later, in 1935, Captains Stevens and Anderson of the United States made a record-breaking balloon ascent into the stratosphere.[4] Further advances in aircraft had gradually made it easier and safer for other scientists to follow. Now, the development of satellite technology offered still further potential. How much further could this science go? Or more to the point, how much further could our teams take it?

5

BREAKTHROUGH

The year in which I married Margaret, 1962, was significant in many ways. While in Colorado, I worked in a group led by David Gates, one of the few scientists at the time to have begun to realize the possibly damaging effects of increasing CO_2 in the atmosphere. I also had the privilege of learning a great deal about computing from Bill Benedict, a scientific leader in the field of computer calculations concerning radiative transfer. This period also saw my first visit to NASA's Jet Propulsion Lab in California. Through all of this, I was accumulating invaluable experience and knowledge. It didn't take a great mind to see how important an understanding of computers was going to be to our future work. Although I'd made a good start in all of these areas, I was very aware of how much I still had to learn.

It was also in 1962 that Des and I made an important breakthrough in our quest for the instrument that had been our holy grail. Flying home from a conference in Stockholm, we were, as usual, racking our brains to think how we could possibly measure the atmospheric temperature structure at different levels from above. Suddenly, Des said, "I wonder if we could use the CO_2 itself as a filter?" I stared at him. I knew immediately that this was the breakthrough we had been seeking. Des's idea unlocked the gate to a vast new area of thinking, and the rest of that flight from Stockholm was spent in animated, excited discussion. This was definitely it. Returning to Oxford I very quickly made a simple device exploring Des's suggestion. Crude though my prototype might have been, it did everything we wanted. The Selective Chopper Radiometer (SCR) was born.

Des had come up with the principle that was to form the basis not only of our first instrument, but of our future ones too. We would finally be able to satisfy the technical challenge that so far had stumped us: that of collecting enough infrared radiation from different levels for temperature to be measured accurately. In theory, the SCR, if we could make it work, would give us the information we needed about the radiation emitted by CO_2 molecules at different levels all around the earth, and from those measurements we would be able to derive temperature at those levels.

Des's idea was to have two cells, one containing CO_2, the other without CO_2. A mirror would oscillate between the two cells about 15 times per second (Figure 5.1). Its purpose would be to arrange for the radiation from the atmosphere to pass through the cells alternately on its way to the radiation detector. Some of the radiation emitted by atmospheric CO_2 would be absorbed by the CO_2 in one of the cells. We could then compare the energy coming out of the cells reaching the detector. This process

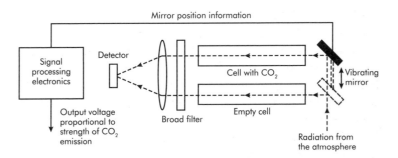

Figure 5.1: Diagram of Selective Chopper Radiometer

is called "chopping". The chopped signal would be a measure of the radiation emitted by the atmosphere at a particular level. For results with the necessary accuracy, absolute precision and calibration of every part of the instrument would be necessary. We had identified and defined our challenge.

Anybody who has ever tried to push their knowledge, their experience or anything else beyond its normal limit will recognize the first problem we faced: scepticism. "It's not possible," we were told on numerous occasions by serious-faced people shaking their heads. "You can't do what you're proposing from a satellite."

We were all young and eager, some might say stubborn. Any doubts or discouragement we encountered served to make us more determined. I think perhaps the timing was optimum for Des and me to push this forward. We were probably just the right age: younger than the establishment but experienced enough to have some decent scientific credentials. Nevertheless, our ideas were still nascent at this time, and a lot more would have to happen to allow any of our plans to reach fruition. If we were going to succeed in our mission to send our science hundreds of kilometres further than ever before, we would need all the determination and self-belief we could muster, as well as all of our experience, knowledge, and scientific skill to develop our thinking. Our teams would need to work together seamlessly, and we would need funding.

Devising the system by which radiation from CO_2 would be identified, collected, and measured, although absolutely key to the development of the SCR, was a small first step. For the entire instrument to succeed, not only would our measuring technology have to advance considerably, but we would have to consider the immense physical demands that would be placed upon an instrument being launched into space. A satellite would carry an instrument an awfully long way, much higher than we had ever had to consider in previous instrument designs. Our new instrument would therefore have to be sufficiently robust to withstand the extremes of vibration caused by the rocket launch itself, and the extremes of temperature it would experience in space, as well as the effects of space's vacuum.

In addition, a satellite-borne instrument would have to be very small indeed; dinky, in fact, with a typical maximum dimension of less than 50 cm. The instruments we had been building at Farnborough were considerably bigger than that. Furthermore, it would have to operate on only very few watts of power from solar cells, whereas we had until now been able to rely on up to 1 kW. It would also have to have longevity built into its design: it would probably be expected to transmit reliable data to the earth for about 10 years without any maintenance from us. We would never be able to service it at heights of over 1,000 km above our heads.

Finally, it would need an excellent mechanism through which to feed back the vast quantities of data we expected it to collect, and we would need a mechanism to receive and analyse that data. Exciting challenges lay ahead. There was certainly room for a little help along the way. But from whom?

Continuing the remarkable accumulation of key people in Oxford at that time, an American scientist, Lewis Kaplan, arrived just a short time after Des's breakthrough, to spend his sabbatical year with my team. I was thrilled. I already knew about Lewis because, in 1958, he had written a definitive paper on how to measure temperature by measuring radiation from CO_2 from space. His excellent ideas about dividing the infrared spectrum had formed the background to our early thoughts for our SCR. While Lewis knew the physics involved, and the principles of taking the measurements, he was not an instrument man. That, we could provide. We could potentially work together very well. Not only that, but as Lewis worked for NASA in the Jet Propulsion Laboratory in California, his connections were likely to prove invaluable.

At about the same time, we were also privileged to welcome John Shaw from Ohio State University, an infrared spectroscopist with great interest in the atmosphere. John had a strong interest in the use of computers in spectroscopy. The arrival of these men, along with all of those mentioned previously, was an enormous boost to my small department, especially as I was still trying to find my feet. Our skills and expertise in different but related areas would complement each other. Thanks to this great blessing of the separate decisions of so many key people to come to Oxford, we were all in exactly the right place at the right time to be at the forefront of meteorological science as it rocketed into the future. Our hopes and plans were now realistic. These men were instrumental in setting me up in space science, for which I have always been extremely grateful.

Throughout the 1960s, our growing team worked hard to develop and test our Selective Chopper Radiometer. From the original concept, it gradually evolved to become a six-channel radiometer, allowing us to take measurements from different levels of the atmosphere. Based upon Des's idea of using CO_2 as its own filter, the theory behind the SCR was actually quite simple. Although we had to be completely accurate about its sensitivity, it wasn't, in the end, too difficult to build, compared with other pieces of spectroscopic equipment.[1]

Securing funding provided us with an early challenge. Most of the money directed towards Sir Harrie Massey's committee, mentioned in Chapter 4, was being granted to scientists looking up into space; astronomers studying the stars, or physicists studying the interactions of the outer layers of the earth's atmosphere with incoming particles from the sun, much higher than the stratosphere. As I've said before, we were unusual in that we proposed to look downwards, *from* space. Ours wasn't fashionable physics at all. Underestimating the challenging scientific problems involved, people tended to look at our science as the equivalent of stamp collecting. Eventually, however, Sir Harrie Massey's BNCSR granted us the money we needed to move forward, at least as far as being ready to submit a proposal to NASA.

At around this time, Lewis Kaplan, Des and I attended a space science conference in Miami, where Lewis took the opportunity to arrange an informal meeting between the three of us and Morris Tepper, NASA's head of Earth Observation Programmes. He showed great interest in our ideas. We talked as we walked around the bars of the different Miami hotels. Into one hotel after another we walked, looked around, and walked out again, paying little attention to our surroundings, or indeed to anything else, so absorbed were we in our conversation. I sometimes wonder whether this might have been the only ever Miami pub crawl in which no one had a single drink. It would appear that the meeting went remarkably well, as from that point on our connections with NASA strengthened. We were to find them very generous with the help we needed, both in time and resources.

By 1963 we had developed the technology for the Selective Chopper Radiometer sufficiently to be able to submit a substantial proposal to NASA. Once again, Lewis Kaplan helped us enormously. Once the proposal was submitted, we waited anxiously for NASA's reply. When it eventually came, although very encouraging, it also made it clear to us that we still had a lot more work to do. "We are interested in your ideas," they affirmed, "but you still have no experience at all of instruments in space. The best thing you can now do is to build a balloon-borne or aircraft-borne SCR and use it to make real measurements in the field. When you have achieved that, update and resubmit your proposal."

We understood that they wanted more concrete proof not only of the SCR's potential, but of our own, before they would be able to commit any resources to helping to develop our work further for use on a satellite. Fair enough, we thought. It was time to put our science, our ideas, and eventually our instrument and our nerves to the test. The Atomic Weapons Research establishment at Aldermaston had spare capacity, which, thanks to some negotiating by Sir Harrie Massey, they were prepared to devote to us. This meant use of both their facilities and their manpower. They became, in simple terms, our factory.

Over the following three years we continued working to perfect the design of the Selective Chopper Radiometer. It was a busy time. Des and I were occupied not only by our day jobs, but we were working together on a textbook, *Infra-Red Physics*.[2] As we were giving so many lectures in our fields, we felt that we should gather our knowledge into a book. Oxford University Press (OUP) agreed to publish it. It was largely thanks to our wives that we ever completed that book. Margaret and Gill set up a monthly dinner, claiming that they would only cook for us if we had made significant progress since our last dinner. It was fun, and the book was eventually published in April 1966.

6

WE HAVE LIFT-OFF

By 1 June 1966 we were almost ready to launch and test our balloon-borne SCR and gain some meaningful readings, which would enable us to resubmit our proposal to NASA. We knew that we were cutting things rather fine. NASA's deadline for receipt of completed proposals was 10 June 1966. This gave us a window of just under two weeks to test our instrument in the air and post the results to NASA. Not only that, but Margaret and I were expecting the imminent birth of our second child. Still, 10 days would surely be enough. After all, we only needed one successful flight. We would launch the balloon in week one and submit the completed proposal. Margaret would give birth in week two. No problem.

Des and I worked together on the written proposal. When it was finally completed and we had triple-checked it, I left the document with Des in Reading. He ran off the required 40 copies of it, putting them in envelopes, leaving them unsealed so he could include in each a short note about our successful balloon flight before sending them. The note, we hoped, would be able to state that the SCR had been successful and that results would soon follow. The plan was simple. As soon as we had a successful launch, Des would take the envelopes to Heathrow and put them on a Pan Am flight to NASA. The rest of the team simply had to launch a balloon.

We reached an agreement with the Ministry of Defence for them to allow us to use their airfield at nearby Larkhill on the Salisbury Plain for the launch of our balloon. We drove our prototype SCR to the airfield. The balloon, and two spares in case of need, would already be there, waiting for us. Wrapped in foam and polystyrene to protect it from the elements, our precious instrument, on which our research student Peter Abel had done a lot of the work, was now about the size of a dustbin, so "the Dustbin" became its name. It weighed about 5 kg. To carry this weight, we needed a 40-foot-diameter balloon, and launching this would demand a degree of specific expertise; more than we realized. Although we had done plenty of balloon work, we had never launched one this big before.

Having put everything in place for the launch, we drove home to Oxford and waited for the Meteorological Office to forecast a particularly still, clear night. We waited and waited. I remember it clearly as a period of waiting. Margaret could have our baby at any time, while my career might very much depend upon me driving to Larkhill at any time. I hoped and prayed that the two would not coincide.

Fairly early within the 10 days we were told that we had the right weather conditions – twice. On both occasions we drove expectantly from Oxford to Larkhill. On both occasions we drove home again in the early hours of the morning, the weather not having been quite still enough to launch our balloon. As the deadline drew nearer, and the early days of June flew by, our opportunities for a still night were reducing. Finally, on the evening of Wednesday 9 June, the evening before NASA's deadline, the Met Office told us that conditions were perfect for launching a 40 ft balloon. The sky was clear and there was virtually no wind. We had three balloons; three chances to get it right. One of those balloons *had* to carry our SCR into the sky. We drove once again to Larkhill.

It was one of those wonderful June evenings when the warm air carries the promise of the summer ahead and daylight holds darkness at bay. Comfortable in our shirtsleeves we carried the balloons, their canopies, and the Dustbin into position. The plan was that I would keep hold of a bucket containing weights, tied to the base of the balloon, while the others would inflate the balloon. Only when the balloon had lifted the weights, which simulated the weight of the Dustbin, would we be able to attach the Dustbin itself. The results would come back to us by radio. The SCR would come back to us if someone found it after it landed, read the addressed label on it, and was good enough to send it back.

Kneeling on the damp grass, I watched as the balloon inflated. The gas rose to the top of the balloon's 40-foot interior, leaving the rest floppy. The lower part would only inflate when the balloon reached thinner air. I looked up in some awe and then looked down at the bucket containing the weights. Soon, I felt the upward pull of the helium beginning to try to lift the bucket skywards, but I held on. Everything seemed ready. The balloon was ready to go. Jim was approaching me, carrying the Dustbin.

Suddenly, the upward force that had gradually been lifting the weights disappeared. I heard a noise – *Pffsscchhttt*. The balloon tore itself loose from the ring that formed its neck and shot upwards. We stared in awed silence and disbelief as it grew smaller and smaller. When it became nothing more than a tiny speck in the evening sky, we turned to one another. What had gone wrong? Solemnly, we prepared the second balloon. This time, we took extra care attaching the balloon's neck to the bucket. Once again I felt it pulling against gravity and lifting the weights; once again, Jim and the Dustbin drew near. So far, so good.

Pffsscchhttt!

Once again, I found myself staring upwards, this time in greater dismay, as our second balloon followed our first, leaving the poor Dustbin abandoned, earthbound, still within Jim's grasp. To this day, I can still see those two balloons sailing into the distance.

We had only one more balloon and only a few more hours. We really had to sit down and think now. What was going wrong, and what could we do about it? As we examined the two necks, which had been left tethered to the bucket when the balloons escaped, a possible cause of the problem dawned upon us. The bucket had two handles, one at each side. We had attached these to either side of the balloon's neck. This was obviously the area of weakness; the arrangement was putting too much strain on the fabric near the neck. Could it simply be that we needed a single point of suspension, in order to allow the balloon to sway more freely above the bucket? Was that the answer?

We were all silent as we filled our modified, last-remaining balloon with gas. If the Dustbin was left behind again, no version of our Selective Chopper Radiometer would ever make it onto a satellite. I watched the point at which the bucket was now attached to the fabric. I felt the familiar pull on the bucket. I held on. Finally, when the weights were being lifted off the ground, Jim and I replaced the bucket with our precious Dustbin. I held my breath, and released the balloon. Off it went – up, up, and away – carrying with it all our hopes and expectations. It was an exhilarating moment. Grateful that America is several hours behind the UK, I rushed into the airbase to call Des and tell him to put the slips into the proposals and the proposals onto the plane.

Five days later, Margaret gave birth to our son Peter.

We couldn't at any point have contemplated giving up on our balloon. Just like life, science is rarely plain sailing. There are always surprises in store. There are frequent disappointments and failures but a scientist has to learn from these and move on, there being often a great deal more to learn from failure than from success. In exploring the wonders of this world in all its complexity, we can hardly expect to get things right easily. What would be the fun in that anyway? A good scientist should never give up because, with a great deal of thought, persistence, and hard work, discoveries are made and effective instruments built.

Again, as in life, many of those who give up are only a whisker away from success – they just don't know it.

The SCR, in due course, was returned to us by somebody who came across it lying in a field.

After the late nights at Larkhill, and with a two-year-old daughter and a newborn son in my life, I didn't have much energy to celebrate the balloon's launch. Besides which, we were still awaiting NASA's response. I felt much more like celebrating a few months later when we received the news that NASA had accepted our proposal and had reserved space for our SCR on the platform of Nimbus 4 (Figure 6.1), due for launch in 1970. NASA told us that they were very impressed by the timing of our proposal and our thorough, professional document. It wasn't until very much later that we were confident enough to tell them the full story.

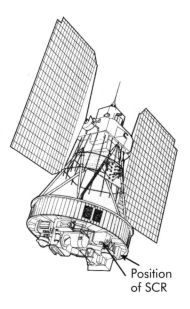

Position
of SCR

Figure 6.1: The scientific instruments are mounted on the base of Nimbus 4.

We now had to set to work improving and testing the SCR. Not only did we have to manage the science, we had to manage our budget. Further development of the SCR would cost about £200,000, which, in the late 1960s, was a huge amount of money. We would have to pay for manpower, components, computers, liaison with industry, building, and testing. We had estimated all our costs with great care. Now we had to work within them. We had to build our instrument, put it through rigorous testing, and deliver it in perfect working order, within our budget and within an immovable deadline of about six months before the launch. To miss the deadline or deliver an imperfect instrument would mean the satellite would go without our SCR. Nimbus would not, could not, wait.

Nimbus 4 was to be a very sophisticated satellite for its time. It would be stabilized so that its base was always facing the earth, no matter where in its orbit it might be. It would be only 3.5 metres high, and the platform for instruments only about 2 metres in diameter. The satellite weighed 500 kg and had 450 watts of available power, which was much greater than most earlier satellites. NASA didn't grant platform space easily, but once they had awarded it, they offered a great deal of support to teams developing the instruments; teams like ours.

The plan was to launch Nimbus 4 in four years, and the people at NASA were ready to help us. This period of preparing and modifying the SCR and working with NASA engineers for the first time was extremely exciting. Even now, after 40 subsequent years in science, most of us still consider those years to have been the most fascinating scientific project we have ever been involved in. It was both exciting and exhilaratingly challenging.

NASA personnel were generally pleased to be assigned to an Oxford-based project, thoroughly enjoying their frequent visits to the city. The Senior Common Room at Jesus College, led by the ever-enthusiastic Johnny G, made them all feel very welcome, but they claimed to be particularly drawn by the formality of college dinners at high table, and the almost ritualistic drinking of port that followed. I suppose I took such traditions for granted, sometimes even finding them irksome. Nevertheless, I always appreciated the stimulation of university life and the daily thrill of living in a city like Oxford, which breathes history onto everybody passing through. The city inspires you with the ideas of great thinkers from the past, so you look up at the spires rather than down at your feet. Like me, NASA engineers enjoy looking up.

The NASA team gave us a great deal in return for Oxford's hospitality. Besides being generous with their expertise, they were stimulating and great fun to work with. Through the knowledge and advice they made available to us from their team of top space engineers, we were privileged to learn a great deal about putting instruments on satellites. Sometimes their help was less esoteric. I remember on one occasion flying back from a visit to NASA with my pockets full of thousands of pounds worth of space-qualified integrated circuits not available in the UK. I wouldn't get those through customs now. I certainly wouldn't get them for free.

Parallel to developing the SCR, we devoted a great deal of time and energy to developing our computing capacity, in terms of both hardware and our own expertise. Space experiments generate a huge amount of data, much of which remains unanalysed at the time, or even well into the future. However, we realized that all of the data received by the SCR must be analysed in its entirety if it was going to help us in our intention of understanding the global atmosphere and its circulation. It seemed essential to me that, even though we were only a small university group, we should look after receiving and analysing the data from our instrument ourselves. I didn't want to pass that responsibility on to anywhere else; after all, the information it would reveal was our main interest.

Although computing technology was advancing rapidly, the Physics Department at Oxford University still didn't have a computer of its own, and we could hardly monopolize Leslie

Fox's Ferranti. Now, 40 years on, it seems remarkable that we were building an instrument for a satellite but still didn't have a computer, particularly as the purposeful use of the former depended entirely upon the latter. This was largely because, before our work was accepted by NASA, I had difficulty convincing the Space Research Council of our need to analyse all of our data when other space experiments were only analysing small proportions of theirs. Once we had been accepted by NASA, it was easier to convince them of our need for an effective data management facility to calibrate and analyse all the data.

From 1967 to 1968, Jim Williamson spent a year at the Goddard Space Flight Center in the States, looking at the computing potential of receiving data from a satellite. While there, he succeeded in negotiating with NASA the use of their satellite-tracking facility in London to receive the data from our SCR. Meanwhile, back in Oxford, Clive Rodgers developed a way of turning radiation measurements into temperature information by a process called retrieval. Clive was rapidly becoming a world-leading expert in the mathematics of this. He was particularly excited when Jim managed to acquire a fairly advanced computer: a PDP 8.

Things had moved on in computing: unlike the Mercury, the PDP 8 used transistors rather than valves, and is now recognized as the world's first successful commercial mini-computer. "Mini", however, is a relative term. The PDP 8 was too big to be housed in the old lab we were using, so we needed to find somewhere else. I found an empty attic room in the science area of Oxford, where we set up our equipment and established the data link with NASA. The plan was for the data to be transmitted from the satellite down to the NASA tracking station in London, which would then transmit it to us in our Oxford attic room.

Testing our device was as important as building it. You cannot send an instrument into space without testing it thoroughly at every stage of its development. This painstaking, demanding process takes many months. You have to start early, because if anything goes wrong you have to return to the drawing board. Building the equipment we would need for testing was our immediate priority. To test thoroughly we would have to do all that we could to simulate the conditions our instrument would encounter at various stages of its journey on board the satellite, not only in space, but during the launch itself. This would mean subjecting our device to extremes of vibration and temperature at a wide range of air pressures. We had to build a high-vacuum chamber within which we could adjust and monitor the temperature very precisely over a wide range. In the chamber there must be no stray radiation to compromise the measurements. We also had to ensure that we had a system in place to receive and analyse data and other feedback constantly.

As many forward-looking companies were keen to get involved with space instruments, both to develop their expertise and build for the future, we found good partners with relative ease. Elliott Brothers, later to become Marconi's, built most of our space hardware. They also carried out tests on a vibration table, onto which they could secure our instrument and subject it to prolonged, brutal shaking. Many of the tests would last for hours. We worked out a shift rota to allow consistent testing through extended periods, lasting days and nights. Although a demanding time for our team, it was exciting.

The worst thing about the whole process was witnessing our intricate instrument, the fruit of many months of painstakingly detailed work, being put through these rigorous tests. We would watch data emerge as our instrument was heated and cooled to extremes in a vacuum and shaken so much that if anything in there wasn't quite right, or was keen to break, it would do so. At times, our hearts were in our mouths, but we knew that it had to be done. Sometimes, things did go wrong and weaknesses were revealed.

Some components didn't survive the long hours of relentless testing; they yielded, broke, and had to be replaced by improved versions and tested again until right. Eventually, when we had tested the SCR as thoroughly as possible and it had survived all of our attempts to destroy it, it was ready to go to America for further testing by NASA.

The dubious honour and responsibility of accompanying the SCR on its flight to the States fell to me. As the instrument was fairly small, I had hoped to take it with me into the cabin, but upon departure from Oxford I was presented with a series of very well padded, very large boxes, which I couldn't get through the cabin door. Instead, I had to watch them being loaded into the hold. I couldn't take care of them as I had planned. Once on American soil, I was held up at immigration.

Finally emerging on the other side, I found the boxes abandoned in a pile in the corner. I gathered them together and took them to a town in Pennsylvania called King of Prussia, where General Electric was assembling Nimbus 4 for NASA. Now safe and secure in capable hands, our SCR would be well cared for. We were still involved in the testing programme, sending students and technical staff over there on a rota as our representatives, to look after the instrument and to take the necessary measurements. The SCR stood up very well to the rigours of NASA's tests.

While the SCR was with NASA, I too was in the States on a three-month visiting professorship at the University of California, Los Angeles (UCLA). We went over the Atlantic on the fairly new liner, the QE2. Margaret, Janet, Peter, and I had a marvellous time, living in an apartment near the sea in Santa Monica. Working in a large department in a prestigious American university was fascinating. In contrast to what I had so recently experienced, many people seemed to work alone; some didn't even know their colleagues' names.

I gave a series of lectures to research students, and I was fascinated by their subsequent comments. They said that they had enjoyed the lectures more than any they had received before, because they liked the conversational style of delivery, which was new to them. They liked the fact that I admitted when I made mistakes. Their professors, they claimed, had to be right all the time. I found this interesting at the time, and still do upon later reflection. Science is full of uncertainty; that, after all, is what drives us to find out more. As scientists, we must always acknowledge the degree of our uncertainty/certainty. Far from being a weakness to be concealed, uncertainty is a scientific strength, if we accept that science must always be honest. This point about acknowledging uncertainty was to become of immense importance in my later work with the IPCC.

That three-month stay in California was a welcome break after the intense work on the first SCR, as well as a valuable learning time for me. UCLA had a lot going on in parts of meteorology I knew little about. Looking back, it was another important part of my quest for the big picture, both in international academia and in a new area of specialization.

By the time Nimbus 4 was ready for launch, my family and I were back home in Oxford. On Wednesday 8 April 1970, our team's first instrument designed for use on a satellite was launched into space. None of us attended the launch in California. Instead, we chose to huddle in our attic room, listening to events on our private data and voice link to NASA and awaiting the first data signals. Johnny G was there too, as interested and enthusiastic as ever.

Cramped though it might have been, it was extremely exciting. Our links to NASA enabled close communication with flight control. We listened to the launch and then waited a few nail-biting hours before any data arrived. The first signals served to confirm that the technology both in space and on earth was working. Jim was at the Goddard Space Center for the launch, and it was he who sent down the line those first data signals, allowing Clive Rodgers to do a quick calculation, which provided the very first profile of atmospheric temperature in the stratosphere from space. And then the data began to pour through in a series of numbers needing our close attention. It was thrilling to be at the cutting edge of space technology and climate science.

The SCR provided the first detailed global observations of the stratospheric temperature structure from a satellite about 700 or 800 km above the earth's surface. It observed for the first time the detail of very large planetary-scale waves in the stratosphere known as stratospheric warmings, the effect of which can be differences of up to 50 °C at the same stratospheric level.

In the short term, the data we received from the SCR needed a great deal of interpretation, and we had to keep checking the SCR's calibration, both of which occupied much of our time in the following months. John Pyle, a research student, and Bob Harwood, an expert in atmospheric dynamics who had recently joined the department, were developing a two-dimensional computer model to help explore the behaviour of the stratosphere (Box 6.1), to which our data was highly relevant. In the longer term, our faithful, robust little SCR continued to return reliable data to earth for ten years before Nimbus 4 was finally decommissioned in 1980.

Box 6.1 Computer Modelling of the Atmosphere

In the study of the atmosphere, computers are essential, first to make it possible to analyse the large amounts of data that are collected by satellite-borne instruments and secondly to develop and run mathematical models that simulate and predict the atmosphere's future circulation. To make predictions, observations of the state of the atmosphere at different levels in terms of the parameters of temperature, wind strength and direction, and water vapour content have to be inserted into the computer model. Then using the equations of motion first described by Isaac Newton in the seventeenth century, the model parameters are integrated to determine the atmosphere's behaviour at any future time.

Weather forecasting using such computer models was first attempted in the 1950s. However, it was not until the 1970s, when computers at least 100,000 times faster than those of the 1950s became available, that practical weather forecasting using such models became possible. Computers used for weather forecasting today are faster by about one trillion (million million) times than those of the 1950s.

The two-dimensional models of the stratosphere set up by Harwood and Pyle in Oxford were simplified in that they studied changes with latitude and height only, and averaged motions and parameters around circles of latitude – hence reducing substantially the computing requirement at that time.

Further information about more recent computer modelling can be found in Chapter 26.

As I hope I have shown, the opportunity for rapid advances in atmospheric science was largely created by the development of satellites, but another flame was needed to truly ignite the touchpaper. Instruments in space would amass so much data that it would take centuries for a human brain to analyse all of the information. The simultaneous development of satellite technology and computing technology was essential. It was like an explosion, blasting apart all of the previous boundaries.

If you'll forgive a second metaphor, these two enormous waves of progress carried us forward at a tremendous pace. Without such waves, no matter how skilful a surfer might be, they can't advance. Looking back now, I feel like a fortunate surfer who was privileged enough to be in the water just as the big waves came, with just enough skill and experience to stay on my board.

In so many ways, both personal and professional, those years in Oxford were of immeasurable value to me. Both of my children had now started school; Margaret had found fulfilling work; and my own work was exciting and challenging. I still feel a sense of wonder and gratitude that, just as the technology advanced, I should have found myself surrounded by so many talented and committed people whose accumulation in Oxford during that brief period was absolutely crucial.

7

FURTHER WORK WITH NASA

The ongoing process of applying for funding was always both complex and time-consuming. We had to put forward a detailed proposal and design for our device before building it, and we had to estimate our costs with great attention to detail. In the period between delivery of our SCR to NASA and the launch of Nimbus 4, with our SCR still on the earth, we were already working on a proposal for a new, modified, and improved version to travel on Nimbus 5.

It is perfectly understandable that the Space Research Funding Committee to whom we now had to apply should find this situation rather odd. We had yet to prove the effectiveness of our first instrument, and we already wanted to improve it. This must have caused the raising of a few eyebrows. They must have thought to themselves, "These guys haven't put anything up yet and now they want another half a million pounds. That's ridiculous." Just before Christmas they said, "Sorry, not this time."

This was potentially disastrous for us. Des and I wrote a long and strong letter to Sir Bernard Lovell, who was the Chairman of the appropriate board of the Science Research Council, asking for the decision to be reversed. We pointed out that it would be the end of the show for the Oxford space programme if they didn't fund us. NASA was already inviting us to put an instrument on their next satellite, and once again they were offering their support. If we had to pull out it would be the end of that invaluable relationship.

Sir Bernard Lovell was an excellent man, and to our great relief, he succeeded in getting the SRC's decision reversed. And so, in 1972, two years after Nimbus 4, Nimbus 5 was launched, carrying with it an improved version of our Selective Chopper Radiometer. Of course, by then our team was working on a device for Nimbus 6.

We succeeded in securing places for our instruments on all four of the Nimbus satellites in the 1970s. While the first had cost about £300,000, the device for Nimbus 7 cost over £1 million. It was a very demanding period. It often seemed to me that there was a nadir period about 12 months before launch, when things wouldn't work as we hoped and we had to work out why and make the necessary adjustments. In 1972, recognizing the demands of running this Space Research Group, I resigned my position as tutor in Jesus College. In 1976, in recognition of my space work, I was elected to a personal professorship at Oxford University.

Other changes lay ahead. The second half of the 1970s saw difficult times for my family. In 1976, Margaret was diagnosed with breast cancer. She was only 44 years old; Peter was 10 and Janet 12. The doctor told us that Margaret probably had five years to live, but was unlikely to live for ten. With Janet and Peter still so young, we were faced with the prospect of a devastating family loss. But Margaret was positive from the start. Throughout her battle with cancer, we both did our best to support and guide our children, maintain our faith, and retain our responsibilities within our professional lives.

Margaret and I were also worried about Peter. While Janet was very happy and making excellent progress in school, Peter definitely wasn't. For some reason, primary school just wasn't working out for him. He was very artistic and brilliant at drawing, but reading was causing him problems. When Peter was diagnosed with dyslexia, we were relieved to have discovered the source of his troubles and keen to help him address them.

After considerable soul-searching and school-searching, not to mention some long discussions with our 10-year-old son, we made the decision that Peter would go to St David's College in Llandudno, North Wales. A school specializing in children with dyslexia, St David's has a strong outdoor, active ethos. Margaret and I weren't keen for Peter to go away to boarding school, but he himself had few such qualms, so anxious was he to escape his Oxford school.

St David's did a marvellous job. One of the first things they did with Peter was to put him in a boat and teach him to sail. Before long he was sailing for the Welsh schoolboys' team: Peter had found his vocation. That change of school changed the direction of Peter's life for ever. Via work in Bermuda, France, and Florida, he now lives in Annapolis on America's east coast, with his wife Kendra and their two children Max and Sam, earning his living sailing, maintaining, and racing large yachts.

Meanwhile, Margaret's battle with cancer continued. Sustained by the knowledge that many friends were praying for us, we prayed regularly ourselves. The Bible tells us that God will answer prayer, and there were indeed times during Margaret's illness when we felt that our prayers were being answered. At other times, I felt less certain. Inevitably, I found myself exploring in new ways my own personal relationship with God. This became a formative time in my faith.

Margaret and I shared the belief that God works through medicine as much as through apparently inexplicable miracles. Accordingly, many of our prayers were for rapid advances in cancer treatment during the next few years, and indeed we did come across some treatments that worked. A mastectomy cleared the cancer for two or three years, but it returned and the struggle continued. One of Margaret's friends from her medical student days was working on cancer treatment at the Royal Marsden Hospital in London. She strongly recommended to Margaret that she try Tamoxifen, a new drug only recently available for use. With some reluctance, our Oxford GP agreed to give it a go.

It was like magic! The effects of the Tamoxifen were almost immediately visible. What had been a steadily increasing number of lumps on Margaret's chest began to disappear. Every few nights we would count their diminishing numbers. Our GP's initial reluctance to use the drug was perfectly understandable, as he had previously tried it with two patients on whom it had not worked at all. For Margaret though, the Tamoxifen held the cancer at bay for a further three or four years. We felt our prayers were being answered.

It was terrible to know that Margaret was ill, and to see her suffer, but she was invariably brave and cheerful. Of course, her ongoing battle affected us all greatly, but as she insisted throughout, life had to go on.

Soon after the Nimbus 4 launch, our team had some new ideas for the instrument we planned for Nimbus 6. We were working on a device that would extend the range for measurements to about 90 km. This would enable us to measure the atmospheric temperature structure in the mesosphere as well as the stratosphere, allowing the investigation of the circulations of both regions, including how they are coupled together and how they interact with the tropospheric circulation. We called it the Pressure Modulator Radiometer, or PMR. Instead of the SCR's multiple cells and oscillating mirror, the PMR had in its optical path only one cell, into and out of which air was pumped by an oscillating piston. A balloon-borne PMR was successfully flown by Fred Taylor while he was a research student, and another research student Peter Curtis very effectively led the team designing and building the PMR for Nimbus 6.

While developing the PMR, we realized with delight that it had remarkable further potential. In the early 1970s Fred had taken a position at NASA's Jet Propulsion Laboratories in California, where he became involved in missions to other planets. Being particularly interested in measuring the structure of Venus's atmosphere, Fred suggested that we should build a PMR for NASA's Pioneer Venus Orbiter. We did, and when it reached Venus in 1978 that particular PMR became the most distant piece of British hardware in space, providing detailed information about the temperature structure in the Venus atmosphere.

As usual, our supportive friend Johnny G was fascinated. By this time he held the honourable position of Oxford University's Public Orator. On 27 June 1979, he referred to our Venus PMR in a public oration.[1] Observing, correctly, that the national press had "completely ignored this exciting achievement", this classics expert decided to set the record straight with a verse in the style of a Latin elegiac couplet:

Kindly Venus, thou that linkest
Lovers all in time and space,
Art thyself henceforth encircled
In a satellite's embrace.

The PMRs on Nimbus 6 extended observations of the atmosphere's temperature structure up to an altitude of about 90 km, where the information they obtained confirmed features of the circulation of warmer air between the two polar regions.[2]

In the 1980s and 1990s, PMRs were used by the UK Meteorological Office for mounting on Tiros satellites. Tiros was the operational series launched by the United States Meteorological Service for making routine operational meteorological measurements from space. Measurements from the Tiros PMR clearly show steady cooling of the stratosphere over this period because of the increase in concentration of atmospheric CO_2: the blanketing effect of CO_2 results in warming at the earth's surface but in cooling above the "blanket" in the stratosphere, confirming clearly the operation of the greenhouse effect in the atmosphere as a whole. More than 10 years after the launch of our first PMR, our team was awarded the Rank Prize for Opto-electronics for its design and development.

For the last of the Nimbus satellite series, Nimbus 7, launched in 1978, we devised an ambitious new instrument, the Stratospheric and Mesospheric Sounder, or SAMS. Although based on some of the same principles and devices as its predecessors, instead of looking downwards at the earth's surface, SAMS scanned the limb of the atmosphere (see Box 7.1) to enable measurements to be made of radiation emerging from different heights in the stratosphere and mesosphere, providing a longer path along the atmosphere and enabling more sensitive measurements. It included a number of PMRs, allowing us to observe radiation

Box 7.1 Scanning the Limb of the Atmosphere

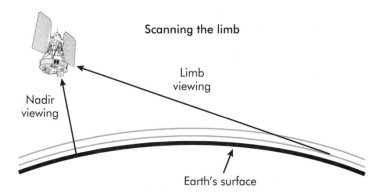

(Above) Limb and nadir viewing.

Scanning the limb of the atmosphere enables measurements at different heights but requires a telescope on the satellite to collect enough radiation and a narrow field of view.

from a number of minor atmospheric constituent gases in addition to carbon dioxide, such as methane, water vapour, and nitrous oxide, so providing measurements of the distribution of atmospheric composition as well as temperature.

However, all good things must come to an end, and by 1979 NASA's attention and resources were turning away from the Nimbus project and towards America's high-profile Space Shuttle programme. Nevertheless, the Nimbus series had been a great success. Observations from instruments mounted on four of the seven satellites sent back data for over a decade, leading to enormous progress in scientists' understanding of the structure and dynamics of the earth's atmosphere. The observations also provided early identification of the changes that were beginning to occur in temperature and other climate parameters as a result of increasing "greenhouse gases", especially carbon dioxide, because of human activities such as the burning of fossil fuels.[3]

Many other technologies were developing during the 1970s, including aviation. This was when Concorde was built. As a result of my involvement with work on ozone, I was invited to fly on one of the Concorde prototypes before it went into service. It was quite a bizarre day. We left Heathrow at 8 a.m., flew to Newfoundland for a coffee and I was back in my office by lunchtime, having crossed the Atlantic twice. This led me to reflect on technology's progress since those Mosquito flights with Alan Brewer – from Mosquitoes to Concorde; from balloons to satellites. Progress, however, comes with dangers of its own.

Concern was mounting that supersonic aircraft, flying higher than other aircraft, well into the stratosphere, could potentially, through chemical interactions, destroy ozone in the stratosphere. In short, we thought they might be destroying the ozone layer, which plays a crucial role in protecting the earth from the strength of the sun's radiation. Dr Paul Crutzen, who was working on a research fellowship in my Oxford department in the early 1970s, was one of the first to study the chemistry of the ozone region and how it might be affected by human activities, such as emissions from aircraft. He was a very bright, interesting fellow whose work was to have great influence upon the development of knowledge at the time. Years later, he shared a Nobel Prize for work he had done in Oxford proving that nitrogen oxides from aircraft could indeed damage ozone in the stratosphere. Later in the 1970s it was discovered that chlorine compounds, specifically chlorofluorocarbons (CFCs) released in very small quantities from aerosol cans, were also damaging ozone, particularly in the colder, polar regions.

However, in spite of high levels of concern, it was several years before the threat to the earth's ozone layer was taken seriously. NASA had initially disregarded some satellite data and, to a degree, the work of Paul and other scientists, on the basis that it seemed inconsistent with what they expected. In 1982, when scientist Joe Farman, working with the British Antarctic Survey ,discovered astonishing dips in levels of ozone above Antarctica, even he doubted his own results. He replaced his trusty 25-year-old ground-based Dobson instrument with a new one, but the dip in readings continued. By 1984, Farman's readings forced NASA to review their earlier data from space. All the evidence for the hole was there, but it had been overlooked.

This is yet another good example of scientists' dependence upon teamwork, and of how easily we can make mistakes by overlooking things. This recognition of the earth's peril led to what Mark Lynas calls "humanity's finest hour",[4] when scientists were able to guide world governments and industry to introduce swift measures to reduce the danger, resisting some powerful corporate vested interests at the time, which is clearly detailed by Lynas. The same degree of action and resolve is now necessary if the world is to avoid the most dangerous levels of climate change. The success of the action taken to sort out this particular ozone problem is encouraging proof that we can do it.

Alongside the space programme, I was giving lectures on meteorology. Largely self-taught on this topic, I felt the lack of a comprehensive textbook to help me. At that time, most meteorology textbooks looked rather like geography books, but meteorology relies heavily upon physics. As I was sharing my knowledge in lectures while also assimilating a great deal of new knowledge, I decided to gather my lectures together in the form of a meteorology textbook that would resemble more closely a physics book. The only way I could manage to write the book was to go early into my office each day immediately after dropping Janet at school. I'd work from 8.30 to 10 a.m. every day, with my door closed. *The Physics of Atmospheres* was first published in 1976 and I'm quite proud that, now in its third edition, it is still used as an informative textbook in a rapidly growing field.

8

NULLIUS IN VERBA: TAKE NOTHING FOR GRANTED

During the 1970s, while working on *The Physics of Atmospheres*, I was bitten by the writing bug and began to think about sharing my thoughts on faith and science in a small book. I have always felt wonder at the beauty and complexity of the universe, and my life, right from childhood, has involved a continuous quest for truths about it in both science and faith. I felt a compulsion to gather together my thoughts and ideas. Having already spoken on the compatibility of science and faith to a large number of different audiences, I didn't think it would be too difficult to turn such presentations into a book.

With these thoughts in my mind, I received a timely letter from John Stott, an influential Christian leader and founder of the London Institute for Contemporary Christianity (LICC), the purpose of which was to stimulate thinking about faith and Christian action in the world. John wondered whether I might consider helping with a week-long summer school on science and faith at LICC. Enthusiastically, I accepted his invitation. Not only did I thoroughly enjoy the lively discussions, but they proved to be a valuable testing ground for my ideas for the book. John Stott wrote to thank me afterwards, saying that those on the summer school had reported having particularly enjoyed the science, but they thought perhaps my theology needed some attention. They were probably right then; they might well say the same thing now.

Enthusiastic though I might have been, I couldn't see how I could fit writing a book on science and faith into my already busy life, until Margaret suggested that I devote Sunday mornings to the book instead of going to church. I could always go to church in the evenings. So I worked on the book most Sunday mornings and it soon began to take shape. I gave it the title *Does God Play Dice?*, which was actually a question posed by Albert Einstein when faced with the uncertainty principle in quantum physics. That little book was eventually published in 1988.[1] In it, I explored the wonders of creation, and considered what might lie behind it all.

I wanted the book to convey my sense of awe as I explore the wonders of what we might call "the big picture". The phrase "big picture" is in itself rather misleading because pictures have boundaries and frames, whereas the picture I'm exploring, through both science and faith, has no such boundary: it is bigger than we can possibly conceive. We humans have an awful tendency to think we know a great deal as our scientific knowledge continues to expand. But this is not sensible. Our knowledge of the universe, and of our own planet's atmosphere and oceans, is still limited, and consistently we discover that the more we find out, the more there is to find out. The greatest scientists who have lived have often been the most humble, experiencing humility before the facts of science. In a letter to Charles Kingsley, the English biologist Thomas Huxley suggested that without this "you shall learn nothing".[2] Known for his aphorisms, Huxley is also credited with the observation: "The known is finite; the unknown infinite."

The Royal Society of London, one of the world's oldest scientific academies, has as its motto *Nullius in Verba*, which translates loosely as "take nothing for granted". All scientific theories, in fact all theories of any kind, need to be given the most rigorous examination. Indeed, investigation of the unexplained is one of the major methods of scientific advance. When faced with puzzling information, one of the most important statements a scientist can make is "I don't know". Similarly one of the most important statements a theologian can make is "I don't know".

As I have experienced throughout my career, we may often miss something or fail to understand a vital part of a picture, resulting in a flawed conclusion. As scientists, we learn to pay attention to apparent anomalies or gaps in our knowledge, in case there is something of importance we have missed. Science is about looking at the unusual and asking why it's unusual; it's a very powerful way forward. Dismissing things just because we can't see how they happened is not good science. They are the very things that should be examined most closely.

Many scientific breakthroughs have been made this way. Henri Becquerel discovered radioactivity when he was about to throw away some photographic plates which had become fogged. Instead, he wondered how they had become fogged. The discovery earned him the 1903 Nobel Prize in Physics. Like Becquerel, scientists should keep an open mind towards the unusual or the unexpected, asking, "How has this happened?" and, "Is this important?" There are so many things we don't know and so many things to find out, which is why the universe is such a fascinating place, and why the quest for the big picture is so compelling.

Science is a very honest pursuit. Not only are we pursuing truth, but we have to be absolutely honest about what we find, otherwise it is not science. Scientists search the "how" of all things that happen. Some parts of science are open to absolute proof. For instance, in physics there is no doubt that a molecule of water consists of two atoms of hydrogen and one of oxygen. Similarly, in mathematics, there is no doubt that $2 + 2 = 4$ or that the angles of a triangle add up to $180°$. However, many parts of science are investigated by collecting evidence, weighing the evidence, and interpreting it in the most truthful and balanced way possible.

However, "how" questions are not the only questions I find myself asking. There are also "why" questions. These ask about meaning or value judgments: Why am I as I am? Why is the universe the way it is? Where do the laws of nature come from, and why? Should scientists be allowed to build deadly weapons for warfare? While a "how" question might identify all the ingredients in a cake, it doesn't tell us why it was made. Science on its own cannot provide answers to such questions. This is where other considerations come in, one of which for me is my faith, working alongside science. However, even now that I'm in my eighties, I cannot claim to have arrived at a full understanding of either how or why. Far from it. My lifetime's exploration has brought me great joy and wonder at times, but it has also presented difficulties. Nobody's life is free from pain, from doubt and, certainly if you're a scientist, from constant questioning and wondering.

Many of the most celebrated scientists have expressed belief in, or at least open-mindedness to the possibility of, an intelligent creator behind the universe, including those who laid the foundations of modern science around 300 years ago; for instance Isaac Newton, Robert Boyle, Michael Faraday, James Clerk Maxwell, Louis Pasteur, Albert Einstein, and Neils Bohr, to name but a few. Like me, they felt that there was something that defied scientific explanation. These scientists considered their pursuits to be an exploration of the wonders of creation, some of them, like me, feeling that they were exploring the works of God. The idea that the vastness of the universe, in all its complexity and fine-tuning, could exist without a creator, has never made sense to me.

In the time taken to write this sentence, the furthest galaxies that we can see with our strongest telescopes have travelled a million kilometres further away from us. This process of the universe expanding began about 14,000 million years ago. To gain a sense of the universe's immensity, consider that one million earths would fit inside our sun, which is 150 million kilometres from us. Our galaxy, which is about a million million million kilometres across, contains a thousand million stars. Breathtaking, awe-inspiring, mind-boggling vastness – and that's just our galaxy. There are upwards of a thousand million galaxies out there. Counting the stars provides even bigger numbers: a total of about 10^{23} (revised recently from 10^{22}). That is 100,000,000,000,000,000,000,000 stars: a quantity impossible to conceive.

Over the centuries, physicists, astronomers, and cosmologists have combined their sciences to reach an impressive level of understanding of how things began with what has become known as the big bang, and of what has happened since. The evidence is very strong that, some 14,000 million years ago, the entire mass and energy of the universe was all concentrated in a tiny volume of extremely high density, pressure, and temperature. This dense concentration suddenly began to expand. What is even more impossible to comprehend is that the minute volume of space in which it was contained also began to expand. Imagine the surface of a balloon expanding as it is blown up for a two-dimensional model of that expansion.

Immediately after the big bang, simple atoms of hydrogen and helium were formed. In what has been a continual process ever since, the action of gravity concentrates these atoms into stars at high temperatures and densities. Within these stellar furnaces, hydrogen and helium nuclei fuse together to create nuclei of elements in the periodic table, all the way from helium to iron. Groups of stars become galaxies. Even more extreme conditions are generated as some stars blow themselves apart in events know as supernovae. In these gigantic explosions, heavier elements are formed, completing the periodic table of 92 stable elements. The debris from such explosions mixes with gases to form second-generation stars, of which our sun is one. Around these stars, planets form, probably from the gas and dust clouds surrounding the young star. Our earth was born 4,500 million years ago, with its rich chemical composition and conditions suitable for the development of life: everything from which all life on earth is made and upon which it depends.[3]

For life to exist and develop on earth, very precise conditions were needed. The universe needed to be old enough, and therefore large enough, for at least one generation of stars to have evolved and died to produce the 92 elements, and then for there to be enough time for our sun and its system of planets to form. Not only that, but conditions at the beginning of the big bang itself had to enable expansion at just the right rate for matter to evolve. This is fine-tuning to such an incredible degree that it is the equivalent of shooting an arrow towards the furthest object in the universe and accurately hitting a target 1 mm across. Even more amazing is the conclusion derived by the Oxford mathematician and cosmologist Roger Penrose, regarding the entropy (or orderliness) of the early universe, that the probability of it occurring with the order necessary for its present form is 1 in $10^{10^{123}}$ (1 in 10 to the power of 10 to the power of 123).[4] The number of 0s needed to write that number down is far greater than the number of atoms in the universe.

Furthermore, if we then consider the conditions on earth itself, which have allowed life and the evolution of its many forms, the fine-tuning is just as remarkable. The average temperature of the earth's surface and the chemical composition of the atmosphere are awe-inspiringly near the optimum for life. From such a wide range of possibilities, from the big bang to the present day, we have conditions close to perfection for life. It is amazing that we can discover and understand all of this. Albert Einstein once said that "the most incomprehensible thing about the universe is that it seems to be comprehensible." In spite of its vastness, it is orderly: there are rules within it that we can discover and comprehend.

So I find myself continuously wondering just what is behind all of this creation. Science has discovered the beauty of the universe's complexity and has found ways to understand it more clearly, but it existed far, far before it was discovered. To me, explaining away as "chance" such elaborate, complex mechanisms for fine-tuning and for optimization as are built into our universe, is not very scientific at all. It's like answering a child's question of "Why is…?" with the non-committal answer "It just is." This is never a satisfactory answer; any curious seven-year-old will attest to that.

There are two important ways in which physics and indeed most sciences move forward. One is by reducing what is under study to its constituent parts – for example, into its basic atoms and molecules – explaining how these parts behave and interact. The other is to explore the behaviour of the whole that is under study and consider how it differs from or is greater than the sum of its parts. Scientists use both of these methods.

We might break a human body or even a brain into its constituent parts, but we will find neither consciousness nor free will. We don't understand human consciousness, even though we know it is there. For me, the possibility of God's existence is the same, and presents a similar mystery. The thought that there is a creator God who shares our consciousness and with whom we can have a meaningful relationship is one of the most exciting areas of human existence to explore.

Jumping ahead, in 1992 I was invited to give the Oxford Templeton Lectures. In these, I explored again the compatibility of science and faith, and God's place in creation. I once again gathered my ideas into a book, which I called *The Search for God: Can Science Help?* Eventually published in 1995, this contained many of my ideas from *Does God Play Dice?* with an increased focus, as the title would suggest, on the search for God.

In *The Search for God*, I explored the idea that we tend to look for God in the wrong places. I do not think that our failure to find a physical God within the universe or within the mechanisms of the universe in any way renders the creator obsolete. That just isn't sensible. The Selective Chopper Radiometer and subsequent instruments are all, like the universe, comprehensible; they all have abilities to self-maintain, and their mechanisms operate entirely independently of my team, the creators. However, no matter how hard you might search for me and my team within the instruments' mechanisms, you would never find us. But surely this would not lead anybody to conclude that we do not exist, or that we have never existed at all. You would simply have been looking for us in the wrong place.

In considering the question of where God might actually be, and whether any scientific pictures or analogies could help my thinking, I was gripped by the idea of God in another dimension. I had recently read *Flatland*[5] by a nineteenth-century Oxford mathematician called Edwin Abbott. His book is actually a satire on class, not a religious book at all, but his idea of "Flatland" provided the analogy for which I was searching. Abbott imagined life in a world of only two dimensions, in which everything was flat. Nobody could conceive of another dimension until a sphere flew through Flatland, from one side to the other, appearing first as a small dot, then growing larger, then as a dot again before it disappeared, turning the Flatlanders' understanding of their world upside down.

Of course, unlike the Flatlanders, we are familiar with the three dimensions of space, which are often conveniently described as length, breadth, and height: the dimensions of the visible, physical world. We are also familiar with the more complex, intangible dimension of time. When Einstein published his theory of relativity in 1905, it was a great leap forward in thought. Einstein was able to make time look like space through a mathematical formulation, so time could be envisaged as a fourth dimension. This revolutionized physics, just as the fictional sphere revolutionized life in Flatland.

To me, it is helpful to think about God in a similar sort of way, to imagine him present in a fifth dimension, beyond but including the normal dimensions of time and space. I have used this powerful analogy in numerous talks and presentations, and

I have seen faces light up as the idea is grasped. It seems to help people to imagine God as both transcendent – that is, apart from the universe – and immanent – that is, present within the universe.

These ideas are not mine and they are not new. In fact, they are expressed in Hebrew and Christian thought from the earliest times. Many Jews and early Christians thought of God as a spiritual being, both outside the universe he had created and present within it. In Isaiah, we read of a God who "inhabits eternity".[6] Isaiah goes on to say that God is with people who are humble and lowly, thereby emphasizing that while God is vast, he is also intensely personal. In Exodus 3, God describes himself to Moses as "I AM", and Jesus, God in human form, repeats this idea with a fascinating blend of tenses in John 8:58: "Before Abraham was born, I am."

In the Song of Solomon, the king says of God: "the heavens, even the highest heaven, cannot contain you" (1 Kings 8:27), conveying a sense of the awe, wonder and mystery that are as strong components of the scientific enterprise as they are components of faith.

Such awe, wonder, and mystery have always been driving forces for me.

9

CLIMATE CHANGE IN THE 1970S

Back in 1967 I gave my first lecture on global warming to the British Association for the Advancement of Science, pointing out that the greenhouse effect had been known for over 200 years. I observed that we were now putting carbon dioxide into the atmosphere in large quantities, so warming the earth and its atmosphere, but not enough to clearly stand out above the level of natural variability. We had no firm observations of this at this stage, but it was certainly a matter of scientific interest, and something on which I urged the scientific community to keep a watching brief.

Thanks to the revolutionary scale of space observations during the 1970s, the decade was one of great significance in international atmospheric research. The world of meteorology was now wondering how much more we might be able to learn about the climate. Rather than just forecasting the weather, could we look ahead over longer periods and even perhaps make long-term projections?

A group at Princeton University in the United States had started developing computer models of the climate, producing the first maps of possible changes in world temperatures due to the increase in carbon dioxide. Crude though they were by later standards, their results suggested that all this carbon dioxide we were pumping up there really was going to affect the atmosphere. So, climate questions were beginning to be asked internationally. Precisely how, and to what extent, was human activity influencing the climate?

In 1967, the World Meteorological Organization (WMO) and the International Council of Scientific Unions had developed a Global Atmospheric Research Program (GARP). Throughout the 1970s, GARP's work stimulated international cooperation in data exchange and computer modelling of the atmospheric circulation. Collating data from so many different sources revealed a far more detailed view of the big picture, and sharing results from the first global climate models led to significant advances in this important area.

Running in parallel to GARP, during the 1970s I had a seat on the committee reviewing research at the Meteorological Office, and for two years (1976–78) I held the position of president of the Royal Meteorological Society. In this latter role, I had the honour of hosting Queen Elizabeth when she opened a meteorological exhibition in Bracknell. Over lunch, I very much enjoyed her informed conversation and her warm sense of humour. A delightful lunchtime companion, she showed genuine interest in our work. At the end of her visit, we presented her with a rain gauge for Balmoral. We both enjoyed the pun on "reign". I imagine that gauge might still be in use at Balmoral today.

Through the roles described above, I was able to witness science's gradually emerging awareness of the potential effects of increasing levels of atmospheric CO_2. It now seemed to be more than something on which we should keep a watching brief. Much more detailed research was clearly necessary.

In 1979 I attended the first World Climate Conference in Geneva organized by the WMO. By this time, GARP's success in bringing the international science community together was recognized and greatly appreciated, but it was important to move on to concentrate on all the factors that influence the longer-term climate. In order now to bring into play other key components of the climate system, and in response to increasing concern about the potential impact of human activity, the Climate Conference decided to replace GARP with the World Climate Research Programme (WCRP), with which I would become increasingly involved.

Further evidence of increasing international and political engagement with the potential problem of climate change came in 1980, when I made my first visit to China. I was one of four scientists invited to give a lecture tour. Our hosts laughingly called us the "gang of four", reflecting the Chinese Communist Gang of Four from the late 1960s and early 1970s. We had the privilege of meeting some people in prestigious positions, including sharing a formal Chinese tea ceremony with one of the vice premiers, a man called Fang Yi.

Vice Premier Fang Yi gave a speech, which I still remember. "We have four problems in China," he said. These he identified as population growth, food production, science and technology, and bureaucracy. He described briefly how the Chinese government was trying to meet each of these challenges. In relation to science and technology, he explained that they had lost so many scientists and technologists during the Cultural Revolution that they feared falling far behind the rest of the world. China, he admitted, needed help in rebuilding its expertise, particularly in meteorology and climate science. This was why we had been invited. For a politician, he struck me as a very practical fellow, interested in doing things in a practical way. While I might have questioned some of China's means towards their ends, Fang Yi's speech gave me hope that pragmatism might outweigh political ideology. I still feel optimistic that China can meet the challenges of curbing CO_2 emissions in a practical way, and that the rest of us, including America, will be able to match it.

There was another, and to many more pressing, international concern than global warming at the time. These were the years of the Cold War, with the very real possibility of a worldwide nuclear exchange. This was frightening in the extreme. Many scientists were exploring the potential effects of the fall-out of a nuclear attack. Scientists and politicians alike were alarmed that the vast amounts of dust and debris released into the atmosphere could block the sunlight, creating a nuclear winter lasting several years and possibly even ending all human life. Frightening though this was, it seemed to me rather odd that we should be trying to prove a meteorological case against nuclear war, when the moral reasons against it were extremely strong anyway. Nevertheless, the studies were serving to raise further interest in the climate and the potential of humans to influence it by our behaviour.

By the end of the 1970s, many things seemed on the brink of change. What would happen to Margaret? What would happen to the Oxford space programme without NASA? Where would the global scientific community's early work on CO_2 and climate change lead us all? What was next for me?

10

LEARNING ON THE JOB

At the beginning of 1979 I invited Sir Geoffrey Allen, who was then head of the UK Science and Engineering Research Council (SERC), to dinner at Jesus College. I already knew Sir Geoffrey quite well and intended this to be nothing more than a social invitation. I had no idea that I was inviting change into my comfortable Oxford life.

During dinner, Sir Geoffrey asked whether I might be interested in working for the SERC as director of the Appleton Research Laboratories in Slough. The Appleton Lab, established in 1924, was a very well-respected radio research station, with an impressive record for investigating how radio waves travel through the ionized region in the high atmosphere, where they are reflected, making possible radio propagation around the earth. The Appleton Lab was also where Watson Watt had invented RADAR in the 1930s; a discovery that was to prove essential during the Second World War. They had had other excellent scientists there in their time, such as John Ratcliffe, a world-leading ionosphere scientist who had been their director in the 1960s. By the late 1970s, however, they had completed most of their pioneering work. Science had moved on, and their area of expertise was becoming less significant.

The Science Research Council had fairly recently acquired the Appleton Lab and, as Sir Geoffrey explained, they planned to turn it into a space science support laboratory. More significantly, they wanted to move the work from Slough and merge the lab with the much larger Rutherford Laboratory, the SRC's research lab for physical sciences, in Chilton, just outside Oxford, thereby creating what would be called the Rutherford Appleton Lab. This would mean relocating and dramatically changing the working lives of up to 300 scientists.

In one respect, Sir Geoffrey's invitation was exciting. I'd be able to introduce a major new programme of support for space science both in astronomy and geophysics. However, the challenge of relocating so many people was not to be underestimated. My immediate thought was, "Why on earth would I want to do something crazy like that, when I've got all this wonderful work in Oxford?" I loved Oxford and the students, and I knew it all so well. Why would I want to manage a difficult transition in a laboratory I didn't know? Sir Geoffrey left me to consider his suggestion.

In spite of my initial reaction, this wasn't an opportunity to be dismissed without further thought. Reflecting upon my present situation and on what might lie ahead, I realized that my involvement in NASA's space programme was, at least for the time being, ending. Although I anticipated that Oxford would continue making observations from space because we still had our expertise, it was going to be some time before there were any new instruments going into space on NASA satellites. As it turned out, the next NASA satellite with an Oxford instrument aboard was not launched until 1991.

I also thought about my situation in the university. Apart from my four years at Farnborough, I'd been there since I was 16 years old; I was now 48. I looked at people who had, like me, become heads of department at a young age, and then stayed for the rest of their working lives. At first, they'd grown and developed quickly, but then sometimes they'd run out of steam.

People who stay in the same job for too long tend to lose their edge, I reflected, so maybe I should consider this new challenge. Besides, it would only be a temporary post.

Contributing to the balance in favour of the move to Appleton was the courage with which Peter had embraced change when he went away to boarding school. Change had been the right thing for him; perhaps I should learn from my son.

When I discussed with the university the possibility of taking up the new job, they allowed me a three- to four-year leave of absence, during which I could retain 20 per cent of my responsibilities in the department. It wasn't to be a clean break. Fred Taylor, my research student who had left Oxford to go to the Jet Propulsion Labs in California in the early 1970s, and who had put the Oxford-built PMR on the satellite to Venus, returned to Oxford to take on my role, leaving me free to become director of the Appleton Laboratory.

My first visit to my new office within the Rutherford Laboratory didn't actually go very smoothly. I arrived early in the morning to settle myself into the grand new office I had been allocated. A colleague came in to discuss a particular matter. Our brief discussion over, he turned to leave my office, but couldn't. Nobody had fitted a handle on the inside of the door, which was now effectively locked from the outside. I looked to my desk to discover that I hadn't yet been equipped with a telephone. Not only was this embarrassing, but I had an appointment with union representatives at 9 a.m. My new colleague and I spent some 15 minutes hammering on the door before somebody kindly let us out.

It was very much a case of learning on the job, and the initial learning curve was steep. Even before I assumed my position, I was involved in the process of recruiting key staff. Aware that I would have to work very closely with the appointed people, I did some homework on the shortlisted applicants. During one particular recruitment, I learned an important lesson about people management. The first of the two shortlisted candidates was a very good scientist who had prepared himself well for the interview. Answering questions thoroughly and articulately, he gave an impressive performance. The second candidate, in contrast, had just flown home from a holiday, and was therefore less well prepared. He didn't perform at all well in the interview.

As a result of the interview performances, the better-prepared candidate was appointed. However, in a decision that was soon to prove very important for me, the losing candidate decided to stay in his present role at the lab. I soon found myself relying enormously upon him when the man we had appointed turned out to be quite a disappointment. I have since tried to ensure that I take into account what people actually do, not what they say they do.

I found many of the scientists in the Appleton Lab rather demoralized. To them, the proposed merger implied that they had been wasting their time and that government agencies no longer needed them: they sensed that their work was no longer valued. The Rutherford Lab was so large and prestigious that my scientists felt that they were about to be gobbled up by the great Rutherford tiger. Furthermore, few were keen to move, and few wanted to change the nature of the work in which they had developed such expertise.

My job was to look after these people, not do exactly what the SERC wanted. I knew that I had to present them to Rutherford as a great outfit and fight their corner in this merger. However, finding out more about their work served to confirm that although it was perfectly good stuff, much of it was becoming outdated. I would have to find a way of persuading the Appleton scientists to move on to new programmes in which their skills would allow them to flourish, rather than forcing anybody reluctantly into new roles. This would require a carefully thought-out approach.

How could I inspire, rather than push people into doing new things? Aware that I mustn't talk their work down in any way, I presented them with exciting new programmes, which really would need good people like them. The fact that I was genuinely enthusiastic about the programmes myself probably helped. "We have all these new jobs to do," I explained to my slightly interested but apprehensive team. I outlined the exciting programmes we'd be working on and gave an open invitation to them all to come to me as individuals and tell me what part they'd like to play.

This approach worked well. People are not pawns. I knew, from my management of the space project, that I had to employ the people I had in a way that made the best use of their talents and their enthusiasms. Any other strategy would be hopeless. I was also able to bring in external help. An experienced and capable scientist, John Harries, came from the National Physical Laboratory to contribute his expertise to managing a programme involving all aspects of earth observation.

Nevertheless, the early days of my job at Appleton were made more difficult than they might otherwise have been by the management style and techniques that had, over the years, become engrained in its culture. On the whole, people had been treated quite badly, leaving their confidence damaged. My new secretary was a prime example of this. Upon my arrival I had been warned that her level of competence was low, but all that I found was limited confidence. I quickly found that the more responsibility I gave her, the more she blossomed, and within weeks she was invaluable to me. Once again, my belief that you have to allow people the opportunity to bring their own strengths to a task was vindicated.

I had an awful lot to do and an awful lot to learn, so I needed to be able to rely upon the people around me. I remember once asking one of the senior managers for some advice about a difficult situation. I simply wanted to know what he thought I should do. He went away and thought about it before giving me an answer that surprised me. It just didn't make sense to me. I looked at him and I said, "You don't really believe that's the right thing to do, do you?"

He reddened and said, "No, I don't actually."

"Then why did you tell me to do that, if you didn't believe it was the right thing to do?"

"I thought it was the answer you expected to hear."

"I'm not sure that I was expecting a specific answer actually. I just wanted to know what was the right thing to do. Please never tell me what you think I want to hear; always tell me what you know or believe to be right."

This experience with the senior manager serves to illustrate an important point, relevant to management, to science, and to everything in life. Sometimes we have to tell truths that people might not want to hear, and sometimes we have to be told truths we don't want to hear. Without these truths, which might at the time seem inconvenient, how can we possibly get an accurate big picture?

Science in particular is about searching for the truth all the time; the integrity of science depends upon this. What you say about your science has to be absolutely right, even if others would prefer not to hear it. However, it's a sad truth that, in many areas of life, money talks, and science is not exempt from its power. There will always be a few scientists prepared to shape their science to please their paymaster. To me, such dishonesty is a betrayal of science itself, and can be very damaging. It is certainly a problem, as we will later see, in the unnecessarily over-controversial world of climate science.

Our eventual relocation and merger with Rutherford was a success. Of course, merging with a larger lab meant we couldn't just do what we liked. The role of the new Rutherford Appleton Lab (RAL) was to support the space work going on in UK universities and to help to organize their programmes and join people together. The largest space programme already underway in the new joint laboratory was in support of the Infrared Astronomical Satellite (IRAS) being built jointly by NASA in the USA, the National Aerospace Laboratory (NRL) of the Netherlands and the RAL.

Our task was the design and development of the ground operations software. This was part of the first space-based observatory to survey the entire sky at infrared wavelengths. Another important project involved working with my old Oxford team and some other labs in developing a new instrument for earth observation, called the Along Track Scanning Radiometer (ATSR), which made global measurements of sea surface temperature more accurately than previous instruments. First launched in 1983, the ATSR has continued to fly on satellites ever since. Today, the Rutherford Appleton Lab is very well established in its crucial role at the forefront of UK space research.

In 1979 and 1980 I had further developed my earlier contact with the European Space Agency (ESA), so it was appropriate to invite the new director of the ESA to visit us at Appleton. He was a Danish businessman called Erik Quistgaard, who had been brought in to make the ESA more efficient and businesslike. With little knowledge or experience of space science, Quistgaard was keen to hear my thoughts on how the agency's programme might develop over the next 10 years. Apart from Meteosat 1, the first European meteorological satellite launched in 1977 which took cloud pictures from geostationary orbit, the ESA hadn't been involved in looking down at the earth or its atmosphere, having focused more on looking up. I urged Quistgaard to consider a major space mission to observe the oceans, because they were still such an unknown area. New technology was becoming available, with much potential for gaining important information. I explained to him that sea surface temperature is a very important meteorological and geophysical quantity because the temperature of the ocean surface determines how much water vapour is in the atmosphere, which greatly influences the greenhouse effect and therefore climate.

Partly as a result of this conversation, I was given the job of chairing the Earth Observation Advisory Committee of ESA. This committee's remit was to oversee the development of an ambitious new European satellite mission in earth observation, known as ERS-1. This was a fascinating role and once again necessitated close liaison with my friends in Oxford, who would eventually be involved in designing one of the instruments for ERS-1, launched in 1991.

It's a good thing I thrive on being busy. In 1981, I was appointed as the second Chair of the Joint Scientific and Technical Committee for the WCRP, the body succeeding GARP. My predecessor in the post, Joe Smagorinsky, was a distinguished climate modeller at America's Princeton University, who had done an excellent job of establishing the committee. Being asked to follow Smagorinsky was both surprising and daunting. I think I was seen as somebody who was involved particularly in the space science that was providing much of the data required for climate science to progress, and I seemed to be gaining a reputation for being able to drive things forward. I was asked to move the programme forward, which was quite a task.

It didn't start well. At the beginning of my first meeting, the director of the programme, a Swede called Professor Bo Döös, handed me his letter of resignation. I can't now remember too well his reasons for resigning, but he assured me that it was nothing to do with me, which was a relief. Nevertheless, it meant that we had a significant problem, so the whole of that first meeting was devoted to discussing a potential new director. That hadn't been my plan at all.

We eventually appointed a Frenchman called Pierre Morel, a very dynamic scientist who, among other things, had been a driving force behind the programme for the first European meteorological satellite in geostationary orbit, providing cloud pictures continuously over about a quarter of the world, centred on Europe.[1] Pierre was a great person for setting new projects in motion. Like many people with strong personalities, he liked to have things his own way and he could be impatient with people who saw things differently. There were certainly occasions where it led to difficulty, which is a pity because international cooperation between climate scientists and meteorologists was becoming increasingly important.

Pierre and I discussed at length how the programme should develop. As the many areas of climate science could not all be addressed at once, it was necessary to provide some focal points around which attention could be concentrated. GARP had already provided an example that we could follow, having organized the GARP Atlantic Tropical Experiment (GATE) in 1974, a very successful experiment focusing on the tropical Atlantic between Africa and South America. Over a period of three months in that year, scientists took special observations of the atmosphere at different heights and the ocean at different depths, as many as were possible. This resulted in increased understanding of the connections between the tropical oceans and the global atmosphere. But, as with many scientific experiments, new knowledge led to more questions being asked than answers found.

Pierre therefore proposed to the committee overseeing the WCRP two new sub-programmes concentrating on key parts of the world climate system. The first was the Tropical Ocean Global Atmosphere (TOGA), a follow-on programme to GATE but covering all the tropics. TOGA's role was to study the links between the ocean and atmosphere, especially over the Pacific where the El Niño phenomenon is dominant and was poorly understood. If we didn't understand that, Pierre pointed out, we weren't going to understand much else. The second major sub-programme was the World Ocean Circulation Experiment (WOCE), which recognized the central importance of the oceans in determining weather and climate. Big changes occur from time to time in the very large ocean currents, moving enormous quantities of heat around the climate system. The particular aims of WOCE were to observe the oceans in as much detail as possible from space, ships, and floating buoys, and to develop computer models of the ocean circulation that could assist in understanding the strong interactions between ocean currents, weather, and climate.

Globally, research into the earth's climate was now really gathering momentum. By the early 1980s meteorologists and climate scientists around the world had developed excellent international bodies and projects through which we were able to get together and share our work. GARP had stimulated further advances in numerical weather prediction, and even the UK's Meteorological Office, whose priority was traditionally weather rather than climate, had begun to do some climate modelling. Although the Met Office was quite a way behind Princeton in the sense that they didn't have the same resources and their models weren't as sophisticated, they were doing some good work.

The Met Office's director, Sir John Mason, explained to me that the Ministry of Defence was encouraging and supporting their climate work because they were worried about the possibility of climate alteration being used as a military weapon. It was increasingly acknowledged that human activity was already, albeit unwittingly, altering the climate, which of course gave rise to the possibility that humans could also alter it deliberately. The work of the Meteorological Office and the work in which I was involved were gradually moving closer together.

Between 1979 and 1983, the four years encompassing my time at the Appleton Lab, I was privileged to have many opportunities to develop my knowledge and experience. At the Appleton Lab, I managed a large team of committed scientists through a difficult period of transition, for which I was honoured with a CBE. Through my work with large international bodies I gained skills in working with scientists and scientific organizations all around the world.

This climate science in which I was increasingly involved was relatively new; rapid advances were being made in both modelling and measuring techniques. I was fortunate enough to be in the darkroom as the first shades of the picture were becoming visible. It was all tremendously challenging and exciting.

11

THE WEATHERMAN

In 1983, with Appleton and Rutherford successfully merged, my four-year term as director was over, and I was looking forward to returning full time to my former position at Oxford University.

However, I wasn't the only one for whom things were drawing to a close. Sir John Mason was retiring after 18 years as director general of the UK Meteorological Office. He urged me to apply for his job. Just as when I was invited to go to the Appleton Lab four years earlier, my first reaction was negative. I didn't think I wanted the job at all. It struck me that it was fundamentally a civil service role, and as such it would be largely administrative. I was concerned that I would be moving away from the science I loved.

On the other hand, I reflected further, Fred Taylor was installed happily at Oxford, running the department with great efficacy. Programmes there had moved on, and they were no longer mine; Fred was in charge now. Going back is not necessarily as easy as it might seem, nor is it always comfortable for other people who may have grown used to being without you. To go back and try to return to the way things were is difficult for everybody. The long-term forecast being uncertain whichever decision I made, I decided to follow the lead I had been given by Sir John Mason's invitation. And so began my next adventure.

As the Meteorological Office was part of the Ministry of Defence (MOD), my appointment would have to be approved by the Secretary of State for Defence, Michael Heseltine, who, quite understandably, was keen to interview me before he signed any papers. Just before my interview, somebody told me that Mr Heseltine was unhappy that the Met Office had selected me without consulting him. Apparently, his response to the news was far from positive. "Who is this Houghton fellow?" he asked.

"He's a scientist."

"Why does the Met Office need a scientist? We need a businessman."

With this reported conversation ringing in my ears, I approached the interview with trepidation. It turned out that I was right to do so because as I opened Mr Heseltine's door, I walked into a very intimidating experience. Having entered the grand Whitehall office, I was still walking across the room when he leant across his desk and said, "Tell me: why does the Meteorological Office need 2,700 people?"

I was completely taken aback; I hadn't even reached my seat yet. I didn't answer immediately because I didn't know what to say. I later learned that this was a typical Heseltine tactic: he loved to throw people off balance. In silence, I tried to gather my thoughts. It was actually Heseltine who spoke first. "Perhaps that is not a fair question," he admitted.

"That wasn't a fair question at all, Secretary of State," I agreed, "because I'm not yet in the Met Office and I don't know enough to answer it."

It seemed that I had passed my first test, and I was invited to sit down. Heseltine now changed the subject completely, asking me about my involvement in the work of ESA. As he had actually been quite instrumental in setting up the agency, my space work interested him. He had many questions about my work with NASA and my more recent work with the ERS-1. I was able to tell him about the latest instrument we had devised. I now felt more comfortable. I was on my own ground.

"Tell me," he asked when the space talk came to an end, "how do you make a weather forecast anyway?"

Again, this for me was safe territory and an enjoyable conversation ensued. Nevertheless, exiting the ordeal I reflected that it could be risky to invite this potentially confrontational politician to the Met Office. I actually managed to avoid doing this on all but one occasion, which, in spite of my fears, actually turned out to be a success, with him showing a great deal of interest in our work.

Heseltine is a remarkably bright man. Every time I've met him I've been impressed by the speed at which he assimilates new knowledge. But back then he was an ambitious politician, and I suspect he thrived on political games. The political world seems to have its own culture, and with my new appointment I was taking my first steps into this unfamiliar territory.

With Michael Heseltine's signature on the appropriate piece of paper, I was appointed director general of the Meteorological Office, and later became chief executive. I was now a senior civil servant working for the Ministry of Defence, answerable to the Permanent Secretary for Defence, who in turn was answerable to the Secretary of State. That one signature handed me overall responsibility for more than 2,000 staff and all weather information, forecasting and its applications, and for a wide range of meteorological research. In short, I had full responsibility for Met Office activities.

Sir John Mason had done a fine job. After his 18 years in the post, the Met Office was now recognized as arguably the best of its kind in the world. He would be a hard act to follow. Nevertheless, there were financial difficulties, caused largely, I soon realized, by the Met Office's financial dependence on the Ministry. I was probably quite anxious when I arrived at our very large 1960s building in Bracknell on my first day in my new job. Of course, I had been there many times before so I was familiar with the building and hardly noticed its state of disrepair. However, a large notice in the doorway caught my attention: "Beware of falling masonry."

I thought at first that this was a rather corny pun alluding to Sir John Mason's retirement, but I was wrong. The problem was genuine. The building was crumbling: huge chunks of concrete were dropping off it and the reinforcing rods were rusting. It cost about £3 million to restore the building to a safe condition, at a time when government purse strings were being tightened. That building was eventually condemned, and in 2003 the Met Office moved its headquarters to Exeter.

But this was the end of 1983, and the economy was on a downward turn. On my first day in post, I learned that I was expected to get rid of 100 people immediately. Sir John Mason had been dragging his feet over that instruction, and I suspect the view now was that I, the green new boy, could be beaten into doing what the MoD wanted. They were mistaken. I resisted the instruction very strongly, saying, "I've only just come – how can I possibly do that?" I turned to the Second Permanent Secretary for help. Eventually we devised a civil-service-style strategy whereby we were able nominally to lose 100 staff without anybody actually losing their jobs. I was learning the art of politics and thankfully I had won my first battle. This had been a good, early opportunity to demonstrate that I would do what I believed to be the right thing to do, rather than simply what I was told to do.

My title was director general and there were two directors answerable to me. On my first day, they took me out for lunch. "Now John," they said, "don't imagine you're going to come here and run the place. We don't need anybody to run the place. We run the place, you know." It might not have been in exactly those words, but that was the message, loud and clear. They said that they expected me to play a similar role to that of my predecessor, going around giving excellent lectures and being a wonderful front man for the Meteorological Service.

I listened, but I doubt that my reply pleased them. "That's not my style," I told them. "I've not come here just to give lectures and things. I want to know what's going on and I want some part in how we move forward." It was only fair to let them know.

For the rest of that week and beyond, I did as I had done at Appleton. I walked around the building, in and out of offices without invitation, asking people what they were doing and trying to establish a clear picture. It was nice to see a few familiar faces, such as Phil Goldsmith, who had undertaken the higher level Farnborough flights on my behalf during my DPhil, and was now one of the Met Office's senior scientists. Interestingly, our paths would cross again in the future when we were both involved with ESA.

I needed to learn from the people at the workface, not just the top people. I needed to get to know them all to a certain degree. This of course also meant that I had to travel. The Met Office has many outstations all around the country that I needed to visit; for instance city weather centres and RAF stations. It was a very interesting time during which I soon discovered that a particular strength of John Mason's had been his recruiting of excellent people, absolutely the top people for their jobs. Feeling fortunate to inherit such an outstanding team, I knew that I must endeavour to maintain these standards.

From the beginning I found my role at the Met Office enormous fun and very interesting. One thing that always amused me was the fact that, as we were so closely linked to the RAF, I actually carried the equivalent rank of an air marshal. In my early days there, one of the people responsible for the military side of the service advised me, "When you go to meet people in the RAF or any of the other armed services, you are to behave appropriately for your rank and act like an air marshal." I think they were worried that this rather scruffy academic from Oxford would let the side down. Quite often, when I went to an RAF station, I would be the most highly ranked person on the site, and as such I would have to enter every room first, with somebody behind me saying, "Turn right, turn left," making me feel like a Monty Python extra.

The main problems I faced in my early days were systemic and financial. As I said earlier, the government was tightening its purse strings. As our budget was controlled by the MoD, and as I had no formal financial responsibility in my job description, cuts seemed imminent. The most surprising thing was that the Met Office budget was not decided in prospect, but put together in retrospect, so there could be no overall financial planning or forecasting. If we wanted something, we had to ask the MoD for money and justify our request. This meant that we had to wade through the treacle of bureaucracy every time we needed something. It seemed to me a crazy way of running an organization, and I wondered what I could do about it.

The only sensible way to proceed was for us to make our own budget, which could be agreed annually by the Ministry. I put this to the Permanent Secretary and soon found that I was not alone in making such suggestions. The prime minister herself was pushing for the establishment within government of bodies to be called executive agencies. At an early stage the Met Office was seen as a strong candidate for such treatment. Nevertheless, it took several years of hard work before the Met Office actually became an executive agency with financial autonomy and an annual budget agreed with the MoD. Along with the budget there were performance criteria and targets also to be agreed. Achieving our new status was by no means an easy process: there were many challenges along the way.

Considered the most reliable meteorological organization in the world, our forecasts were in some demand. The potential to grow our commercial services was clearly large, and I was keen to exploit this opportunity. An early challenge was to identify our customers, the most obvious of which were the Army, the Navy, and the Royal Air Force. Being dispersed around the world, the armed forces may require forecasts of detailed weather for any global location, at any time. Other significant customers were the Civil Aviation Authority of the UK and the International Civil Aviation Organization (ICAO), who required forecasts for civil aviation. In 1984 a new coordinated world forecast system was established specifically for aircraft. The US Weather Service in Washington and the UK Met Office in Bracknell were to share the important responsibility of providing these forecasts, upon which aviation safety would depend. These are large international tasks demanding the collation of detailed information from around the world and the provision of forecasts wherever in the world they might be required.

The third group of customers we identified was a very eclectic group from whom there was a rapidly growing demand for both general and specialized weather information. In this group we included commerce and industry; those involved with offshore oil drilling; farmers and others involved in agriculture or forestry; those organizing sports or other outdoor events, and many more.

The fourth, and a most important customer for Met Office services, is the public at large, for whom the day-to-day weather really does matter. Public forecasts based upon detailed information from the Met Office are usually delivered through radio, TV, or other media outlets. Included within the BBC's public service are also shipping forecasts covering seas and oceans, for which the Met Office also provides the information. One of the first visits I made in my new post was to the BBC, which was at that time developing new TV weather presentations. Recognizing that these represented our most important public outlet, we assigned some of our most able staff to assist the BBC in this development.

As I learned more about the service we offered and the way in which we offered it, I noticed that people who worked with a commercial vision tended to present their forecasts and our whole service more professionally than did the people who were just handing out information as a matter of course. Commercial activity acted as a stimulus to the improvement of standards, not just in those service provisions but also throughout the Met Office. My elder brother David had quite recently been head of the London Weather Centre, where he had been selling forecasts to offshore oil companies. I discussed with him the increasing potential for the Met Office. This led to me setting up a commercial marketing wing within the Met Office and appointing David as its commercial director.

I was a little worried that this smacked of nepotism, but he really was the man for the job. I was even more worried about the effect it might have on our relationship as brothers. How would David feel being answerable to his little brother? We had a good, honest talk about it, and he was still keen to do the job. It worked very well actually: he was always very respectful, in the office at least. Not only did David have more commercial experience than me, but he also knew a great deal more about routine weather forecasting than I did. He was a real weatherman.

Having identified our main customers, we opened discussions with the MoD as to how the new executive agency should be set up. A key consideration for us was that if we wanted to remain the best meteorological service in the world, which it was absolutely in our interest to do, we needed continued investment in research and development. We already had a sizeable research department, which constantly needed to develop new instruments and measurements to support our observational network from the surface, from balloons or aircraft, and from satellites in space. We also had one of the biggest civilian computer complexes in Europe for weather forecasting and climate modelling, but it was necessary to continue to develop our capacity further, thereby constantly improving our forecasting ability. I argued that the cost of holding our position as number one in the world was not great, but it would require an effective and efficient programme of continued research and development.

"Oh, the Met Office doesn't need to do research," some within the MoD argued back, "and even if it does, that research should be paid for by our customers."

In response, I talked about Rolls Royce. Like us, they were a high-tech, commercial organization. Did their customers pay for their research? No. But they bought the excellent products resulting from it. Fourteen per cent of Rolls Royce's annual budget was devoted to research and development, and I argued that ours should be the same. I was ignored for a very long time, but I kept battling and eventually won through. I think we eventually managed to maintain the level we currently had at that time of about 12 per cent of our budget for research and development.

Another argument developed around setting performance criteria. I've never been a fan of these as I think they can lead to a distortion of work in order to meet particular targets. One day a letter arrived on my desk asking me to sign a commitment that we would increase our efficiency by 2.5 per cent per year. I suppose I could have signed it and then invented measures of efficiency which were inevitably going to increase by 2.5 per cent, but that would be crazy. Why should I accept such nonsense? I got in touch with those who had sent the letter. "How do you propose that I measure efficiency?"

"Oh, that's easy," they breezed. "That's output over input."

"Fine, so what's our output and what's our input?" Measuring the output of weather forecasts isn't easy. Is it the number of forecasts? Is it the accuracy of the forecasts? Or is it the content of the forecasts? What exactly would we be trying to increase by 2.5 per cent every year?

The MoD's response was that I still had to sign or they would stop us being an agency.

I responded, "Well, if it's like that, maybe we can't be an agency." I've never been in the business of signing things that are trivial, meaningless, or phoney in any way. It was a real eye-opener to see how civil servants are prepared to play all sorts of silly games in order to satisfy the seeming demands of government. We managed to find a way through and keep our agency status. The Met Office as an executive agency within the MoD was formally launched with appropriate celebration in April 1990.

However, it wasn't long before a message came down the system saying, "The MoD has taken certain cuts, so the Met Office budget will be cut by a million pounds as from now." They couldn't do this, could they? We had an agreed budget and agreed performance criteria. Surely I would have to be consulted on any budget cuts? I called and said as much. The message came back to say that the Permanent Secretary would be writing to enforce these cuts. I said I didn't believe that he would write that letter, but if he did I would write back immediately and say, "Well, if I've lost a million pounds, that's the end of the agreement under which we have been set up, including the need to satisfy all the performance criteria." Of course, I never got that letter, but this approach exemplified how MoD civil servants were still trying to keep the Met Office within their control.

Managing our own resources proved a great boost to Met Office morale; it was the sort of challenge that brings out the best in people. Commercially too our move to executive agency status was a success. In the year 1990–91, the Met Office's budget was £107 million, of which £67 million came from the MoD for the Public Meteorological Service and forecasts for the armed forces; £22 million from the Civil Aviation Authority; £13 million from commercial services; and £5 million from the Department of the Environment for work related to the environment and climate change. In his *History of the Meteorological Office*,[1] Malcolm Walker asserts that becoming an agency was one of the most significant turning points in the office's history.

Knowing that our work – or output, to use civil service speak – was assessed twice a day by the 100 million people who listened to and sometimes depended upon our forecasts was one of many reasons to get as close to the truth as we could… every single day. The storm with which this book begins provides a good illustration of the demands, the pitfalls, and the variety involved in the job. Of course, I was there primarily as a scientist and, aside from the managerial and military matters, the science itself was always very challenging; looking at how to make better forecasts of something that is beset with a lot of uncertainty. So far, it has been true to say that developing and improving the science leads to more accurate forecasting. But will this always follow, or is there a limit to the number of days ahead over which prediction is possible, however thorough the science may be?

Scientists describe the weather as "chaotic" in scientific terms. This doesn't mean that it is entirely without order or predictability, but that the evolution of weather over periods of a few days is dependent on processes that are extremely sensitive to disturbances so small that they defy description by normal scientific calculation. Because of its chaotic nature, there is a limit beyond which forecasts of detailed weather cannot be made. The limit for most places in mid latitudes is generally accepted to be about two weeks. Our forecasting work at the Met Office was scientifically very demanding, and it was about to be made even more so… thanks to climate change.

Climate is defined as average weather, averaged over months or years, decades, centuries, or millennia. Large changes in climate are known to have occurred in the past: over the past million years, ice ages have occurred at intervals of around 100,000 years, triggered by regular variations in the geometry of the earth's orbit around the sun. Astronomers can predict with great precision how the earth's orbit will evolve in the future and have calculated that the next ice age is due to begin in around 50,000 years.

Changes in climate have also occurred on much shorter timescales, caused by factors such as changes in the solar radiation or in the concentration of carbon dioxide or other greenhouse gases in the atmosphere. The big question that has been vigorously addressed by climate scientists over the past 30 years or more is the extent to which changes in climate can now be predicted, particularly those due to the increase in greenhouse gases caused by human activities.

In the 1980s, because of the perceived future danger of climate change being used as a military weapon, the Met Office's numerical weather forecasting model was also being applied to climate forecasting. When I took up my post I encouraged this modelling work, widening its application to other factors that might cause significant climate change. However, some people were sceptical. If the weather is difficult to forecast just two weeks ahead, surely the climate must be even less predictable, and attempts to forecast climate change far less realistic.

Not only was this a fascinating scientific problem, it was also an area of expanding practical importance. When in 1991 I was invited by the Royal Society to give the Bakerian Prize Lecture, I chose as my subject "The Predictability of Weather and Climate".[2] In that lecture I concluded that studies of past climates, and of the processes influencing them, provide evidence for a largely predictable response regarding changes in climate because of increasing greenhouse gases.

However, it was also clear that to predict climate with acceptable accuracy, a great deal more understanding of certain factors would be required.[3] Finally I stated that

Climate Change research presents an enormous challenge to the world scientific community. The international scientific programmes underway or planned to address climate change are the largest ever undertaken. The challenge is not only to provide prediction of future climate with adequate accuracy but also to apply that information for the benefit of the whole world community.

Throughout the 1980s, both within and outside the Met Office, my own personal and professional involvement in the climate issue increased steadily, until in 1988 I became heavily involved in the Intergovernmental Panel on Climate Change (IPCC), of which more in later chapters. The point here is that by early in 1989, the IPCC needed a well-informed, capable support unit. Although the Met Office was the best place to look for the skills, knowledge, experience, and equipment required, we did not have formal responsibility for climate change work nor the funds to support it on the scale required. Not only did a few of my staff think I must be off my head to have taken on any IPCC role personally, many of them could not see how such a demanding programme could be introduced into the Met Office's system without additional resources. In the second of these concerns, at least, they were right.

I shared their concerns, both for them and for myself. How could I manage both my IPCC and my Met Office roles simultaneously? I discussed these challenges at length with David Fisk, who was then chief scientist at the Department of the Environment. In a surprisingly short time, the Department quickly agreed to sufficient funding to create the support mechanism that the IPCC would need. At an annual cost of about £250,000, they set up, equipped, and staffed a Technical Support Unit (TSU) at the Met Office in Bracknell; its remit was to support all aspects of IPCC work. This meant assigning entirely new roles to three or four key people. Things were moving forward.

The TSU has been absolutely vital to the success of IPCC work ever since, in ways to be explored in more detail in Chapter 13. Those involved have, right from the beginning, been excellent people, absolutely superb, and thanks largely to them the establishment of the TSU has opened opportunities and vistas that people wouldn't otherwise have seen.

During the 1980s, the UK government's commitment to supporting research into climate change was invaluable. Not only did the Department of the Environment provide support for the TSU to develop its future IPCC role, but they were also keen to support further Met Office research, particularly that associated with the computer modelling of climate. They provided substantially increased funding to allow the necessary growth of both computer capacity and staff numbers. This support soon put the UK at the forefront of international climate change research, something Margaret Thatcher had personally encouraged.

In response to this development, I brought together the various parts of the Met Office's climate related work, particularly that of the TSU, within a new centre called the Hadley Centre, named after the eighteenth-century British scientist George Hadley, who was the first to explain how the trade-winds circulate in the atmosphere. Officially opened in 1990, the Hadley Centre has since developed into a leading world centre in climate science. That it is part of an organization responsible for operational weather observations and world weather forecasting has been a major factor in developing the Hadley Centre's leading position: there are many synergies both of technology and purpose between the two activities.

Progress within the Met Office also served to stimulate progress overseas. The development of the Chinese Meteorological Service has run in interesting parallel to that of our own. During my years at the Met Office, my Chinese equivalent, Zou Jing Meng, was appointed president of the World Meteorological Organization, and eventually I became one of his three vice presidents. We spent significant time together. A delightful and determined man, Zou used his excellent persuasive powers and his connections with powerful people to develop the Chinese Meteorological Service into a very modern service, now one of the world's foremost.

Zou often expressed concern about what climate science was discovering. Working in parallel and meeting frequently through the WMO, we had regular opportunities to exchange ideas. Zou eventually established a climate research centre, similar to the Hadley Centre, within the Chinese Meteorological Service. As a result of his clear vision, the Chinese government now has access to excellent information on climate change. With a good understanding of what the resulting floods, storms, and droughts are likely to mean to their population and economy, they are working towards adaptation and making some efforts to influence world opinion to take appropriate action.

When I retired from the Met Office at the end of 1991, I was able to look back on a very enjoyable and rewarding time there. I felt that I had played a role in moving things forward and in equipping the Met Office for the future. I felt honoured to receive a knighthood for my work. Peter Ryder, my deputy director, spoke generously at my retirement, saying that despite the many problems we'd had to face, it had been fun. He could not have said anything that I would have appreciated more. I had enjoyed enormously the years working in the Office, with its wonderfully dedicated team of people. I do indeed remember those years as fun years.

12

LOSS AND OPTIMISM

It seems rather strange now to find myself describing the 1980s in such a positive way, as in my personal life I encountered loss beyond any I had experienced before, and challenges for which no husband or father can ever be prepared.

During the years of the Tamoxifen's effectiveness, Margaret was able to sustain her part-time job as a medical officer working with physically handicapped children in Oxford, a role she found immensely enjoyable and fulfilling. The centre in which she worked was a great testimony to the positive effect she was having on these children's lives. A place full of fun and laughter, I never once saw a sad face among the 30 or 40 children who would be there at any one time, in spite of their heart-breaking physical problems.

Gradually, however, it became evident that the Tamoxifen, which had been helping to slow the growth of Margaret's cancer, was becoming less effective, so we sought other answers. By now, Janet was approaching the end of her long period of study to qualify as a doctor at Guy's Hospital, London, and in July 1985 she married Paul, who had recently graduated in medicine and who later became a consultant radiologist. They married on a beautiful sunny day in my old college, Jesus College, in Oxford. The day is still a wonderful memory for me. Margaret, who had put a great deal of maternal love and effort into its planning, enjoyed it very much.

Continuing our research into potential treatments for Margaret, I talked with a scientist I knew in the Oxford Physics Laboratory who was exploring the use of lasers on cancerous cells. Early in 1986, Margaret decided to give this a chance. While it had the positive effect of slowing down the now persistent growth of her cancer, its effects were short-lived. In mid May, we were devastated to learn that the cancer had reached Margaret's liver. She immediately embarked upon a course of chemotherapy, the outcome of which was by no means certain. Margaret opted to go into a hospice during this treatment, where she received wonderful palliative care.

One of Margaret's most frequent prayers during this time was that she might live long enough to see Janet qualify as a doctor, and be well enough to celebrate with her. Her prayer was answered when we all gathered together in the warm June sunshine outside the hospice and celebrated Janet's hard-earned success.

However, within days of that happy family event, doctors decided to stop Margaret's chemotherapy. We had to accept that they could do nothing more to help her struggle against the cancer. On 10 July 1986, just one day short of 10 years after her initial diagnosis, Margaret lost her courageous battle. She had come within one day of proving the doctor's prognosis wrong. Janet, Peter, and I were all there together for Margaret's last day, although we had no idea that it was going to be her last. That evening, we all kissed her goodnight and then we went home. In the middle of the night, I was stunned by the dreaded but unexpected phone call telling me that she had passed away. I felt and I still feel so sorry not to have been by her side.

Margaret's spiritual strength towards the end in particular had been truly amazing. She experienced inspiring peace of mind, her faith growing and growing during her illness. When I look back on her final weeks, I might describe her as having been unusually happy: not happier than usual, but happy in an unusual way, perhaps triumphant. This had a remarkably positive impact on the people around her, including the nurses and the doctors. Even in her own suffering, Margaret was able to offer comfort and inspiration to others. She explained that healing, to her, wasn't about living longer; she believed that complete healing involves the whole person: our mind, our body, our relationships with others, and our relationship with God.

Margaret felt that she was moving towards the presence of God where pain, suffering, and evil are no more and where love reigns supreme. Her example has given me the strength to share her belief in the reality of that place. I believe that God really did answer our prayers during Margaret's illness. I rejoice and find comfort in my belief that Margaret is now with the Lord Jesus who meant so much to her and whom she had learned to know so well.

The hole torn into the very heart of my life by the loss of Margaret's cheerful presence and strength was indescribable. For Janet, Peter, and for me, life as we knew it had ended. This was undoubtedly the most difficult time I have ever had to endure. Of course, I knew and accepted that suffering and death are part of life, and I knew that far worse things happen in the world on a far greater scale, but nevertheless, this perspective did not ease my pain. Like many other people who suffer loss, I found myself asking why the world is as it is. As a Christian, I asked why a caring God would let terrible things happen.

Time, faith, and the blessing of loving support from family, friends, and colleagues all played important parts in the healing process. Over time, the size of the hole left by Margaret has gradually reduced, but there's always a scar. While I find joy in the memory of her life, there's always some pain in the memory of losing her.

Shortly after Margaret's death, with some friends and colleagues I established the Margaret Houghton Memorial Fund. The fund aimed to support understanding and cooperation between healthcare professionals and Christian ministers in the care of the unwell, the dying, and the bereaved. One of the fund's early projects was to organize and host a series of discussions between medical practitioners and theologians with a range of views. The contents of the discussions were collected in a book, *Christian Healing: What Can We Believe?*[1] Part of the book's conclusion (see Appendix 2) is that health and healing should be addressed in as *holistic* a manner as possible, combining the practice of medicine with caring and counselling, both physical and spiritual.

In 1986 I would never have imagined it possible that in 1988 I would be marrying again, but that is the way things happened. It's strange how one thing can lead to another, life being often even more difficult to forecast than the weather. During the 1970s and 1980s, Margaret and I used to organize an annual Christmas carol concert in the recently established North Oxford Overseas Centre (NOOC) described earlier. Every year, some singers came together from our church in Kidlington, just outside Oxford, to join the NOOC residents for this stirring concert. A key soprano in that choir was Sheila Thompson, with whom Margaret and I were friends. At the beginning of the 1980s, Sheila's work took her away from Oxford to Coventry. Although she returned at Christmas for a few years in the early 1980s for the concert, she then experienced a period of ill health and we largely lost touch. Little did I realize that she would one day come back into my life, and in what circumstances.

Sheila and I met again at Margaret's funeral in 1986. Remembering her beautiful voice, I invited her to join us again at the NOOC carol service the following Christmas. After that, I found myself persuading Sheila to return more frequently, until I finally found myself asking her to marry me. We were married in 1988.

Sheila and I share a love of music and of the countryside. As well as sharing our Christian faith, we also share a sense of responsibility for the world and the drive for an active rather than passive approach to the world's problems. Extremely interested in my work, Sheila has accompanied me on many of my international trips, when I have always truly appreciated her cheerful, supportive, and understanding presence.

For Janet, Peter, and me, and indeed for Sheila, the end of the 1980s had been an intense period of sorrow, of change, of challenge, and of development. I like to think that, as I entered the 1990s with Sheila at my side, Margaret would have been pleased to see our strengthening faith and optimism for the future.

13

THE FORMATION OF THE IPCC

The beginning of the 1990s marked an important new stage in global efforts to explore and understand the nature of climate change. The journey to reach this point had been gathering momentum throughout the 1980s. First, scientific progress had been considerable. Observations from space were now giving us a great deal more information on the global climate, and computer modelling of climate was growing in capability thanks to more powerful computers, thereby allowing more accurate forecasting. Secondly, international bodies and research programmes were facilitating collation and sharing of data and cooperation in tackling the big problems.

Running parallel to my work with the Meteorological Office throughout the 1980s, I had been privileged to be involved in some of the progress mentioned above; progress which eventually resulted in the formation of a new international scientific body supported by all of the world's governments: the Intergovernmental Panel on Climate Change (IPCC).[1]

As I explained in Chapter 9, the end of 1979 saw the establishment of the World Climate Research Programme (WCRP). Within the programme's remit was the task of developing understanding of climate processes, and considering how far climate could be modelled and predicted, as well as considering the potential impact of human influences on climate. From an early stage, the work of the WCRP caused the whole climate science community to sit up and take notice. What this work seemed to present was an emerging picture of unprecedented rapid change. Of serious significance was a growing body of scientific evidence that pointed to human-related CO_2 emissions as a major driver of this change. Aware that the rate of such emissions was on a steadily upward trend, scientists felt that further investigation and monitoring was imperative.

In 1985, an important conference took place in Villach, Austria, called SCOPE 29.[2] Organized by the International Council for Science (ICSU) and the WMO, SCOPE 29 was chaired by Bert Bolin, an eminent Swedish scientist, probably the most respected climate scientist at the time, perhaps ever. During the conference, a suggestion was made that nations should consider moving towards a global climate convention. It suddenly felt as though climate science was moving into a new phase, becoming an issue in which policymakers as well as scientists were taking an interest. However, for the scientists, the work in hand was still the pursuit of the truth. SCOPE 29's findings, summarized in a 500-page report, warned of a global average temperature rise in the twenty-first century that could possibly be greater and more rapid than any in human history.

In 1987 the matter was given some of the attention it deserved when it was brought before the UN General Assembly. The Assembly's discussions were based upon a further report by the UN Commission on Environment and Development, called "Our Common Future".[3] This report stated: "There are environmental trends that threaten to radically alter the planet, that threaten the lives of many species upon it, including the human species."

It went on to describe a scenario that might today be seen as very clear-sighted:

The burning of fossil fuels puts into the atmosphere carbon dioxide, which is causing gradual global warming. This "greenhouse effect" may by next century have increased average global temperature enough to shift agricultural production areas, raise the sea level to flood coastal cities, and disrupt national economies.

In spite of these alarming possibilities, the report looked optimistically to a future of global economic growth, which it believed could be "based on policies that sustain and expand the environmental resource base". The authors stressed that such growth was "absolutely essential to relieve the great poverty that is deepening in much of the world".

However, that particular report, foresighted though its words were, had only a limited impact. A sad truth is that, by and large, people are rarely excited by UN reports. They're not often written in layman's terms, and are not commercially distributed. Most end up in piles on busy people's desks.

Among those of us aware of climate change, there was by now no doubt at all that this was a global issue needing global study and global action. Fortunately, the meteorological community already had a strong international network of cooperation through bodies such as the World Meteorological Organization, through which we were well informed of each other's work, and in many cases we knew each other very well. Indeed, in the same year as the UN report, the WMO released one of its own, which was more effective because it suggested a way forward. The WMO identified a pressing need for further progress towards formal global research programmes, building upon the SCOPE suggestion of a global climate convention to propose the creation of a systematic exchange of information between the scientific and the political communities.

The secretary general of the WMO was a Nigerian called Professor Obasi. Upon his appointment in early 1984, I was

Above: Sir John's maternal grandparents and family, 1935. On the far right of the picture is John's mother and brother, David (7); his father stands behind. John (3), is between his two grandparents.

Left: Leaving Colne Parish Church, Lancashire, after wedding his first wife Margaret. Sir John's parents can be seen just inside the church, 1962.

Below: Sir John as a research student, using liquid nitrogen to cool the test equipment for his radiometer.

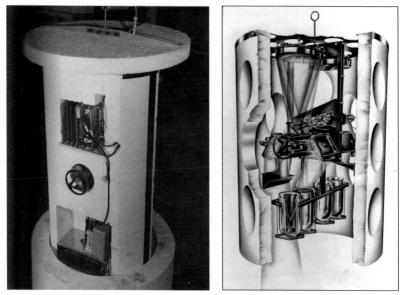

"The Dustbin", launched from a large balloon in 1966; these images show the outside insulation and some of the electronics (left) and the optical system inside (right). Full explanation on pp. 62–64.

Members of the Oxford Department of Atmospheric Physics in Leningrad, 1974. From left to right: Rebecca Kaplan, Lillian Kaplan, Lewis Kaplan, John Shaw, David Pick, Margaret and Jim Williamson, Clive Rodgers, Anthony Wilson, Sir John, Peter Abel, and Desmond Walshaw.

Sir John at the Royal Meteorological Society event in 1978 presenting Her Majesty the Queen with a rain gauge for her Balmoral Estate. John's wife Margaret is at the extreme left.

Above: With Prime Minister, Margaret Thatcher as she opened the Hadley Centre for Climate Prediction and Research of the Meteorological Office, Bracknell, 11 May 1990.

Left: Sir John with his wife Sheila at Buckingham Palace to receive his knighthood, 1990.

The old farmhouse on a hillside overlooking the Dovey Estuary in West Wales that Sir John and Sheila restored in the 1990s, and which became their much loved home.

Cartoon, publishied in *Nature* magazine, depicting the IPCC Science Working Group meeting in Madrid, November 1995 taking the Earth's temperature. From left to right: Bert Bolin the IPCC chairman, Sir John, Gylvan Meira co-chair.

Sir John speaking at the opening of the IPCC Science Working Group meeting to approve the 2001 Report, Shanghai.

Sir John at his 70th birthday celebration lunch with Desmond Smith, 2001.

Below: Sir John and wife Sheila celebrate the award of the Japan Prize, 2006.

Above: Sir John and Sheila relax in Kyoto after the Japan Prize celebrations with Dr Akira Endo and his wife.

Group from IPCC Scientific Working Group with the Nobel Peace Prize Medal presented in Oslo to the IPCC in 2007. From left: Dahe Qin (China), Sir John, Susan Solomon (USA), Robert Watson (UK), Daniel Albritton (USA), and Richard Wood (UK).

Sir John's son Peter, his wife Kendra, and their two boys, Max and Sam; the family live in Annapolis, USA, 2010.

Sir John's daughter Janet, her husband Paul, and their five children (from left to right): Hannah, Daniel, Jonathan, Esther, and Jemima, 2009.

Sir John and friend Donald Harris on their yacht on the
Irish Sea.

Sir John with his younger brother Paul on the summit of
Cader Idris in South Snowdonia on 6 May 2013, the day
before Paul's 70th birthday.

pleased that somebody from Africa had been found to fulfil the role, rather than a European or American.[4] Pierre Morel and I were keen to talk to Obasi very early on. Because WMO services at the time were mostly concerned with weather rather than with climate, we wanted to ensure that Obasi understood the importance and significance of climate work, and that he would encourage support for further research.

In Geneva, just after his appointment, we went to congratulate him, which I believe he appreciated; we also took the opportunity to discuss work on climate science. From then on we developed a very positive relationship, and Obasi's ensuing support for climate science was immensely valuable during the many years of his leadership of the WMO. Jim Bruce, a Canadian and formerly head of the Meteorological Service of Canada, was appointed as Obasi's deputy. Obasi trusted Jim 100 per cent, which meant that Jim was free to push forward with issues he himself considered important. Obasi's commitment to climate research and Jim's operational freedom were to prove absolutely instrumental in the establishment of what was soon to become the IPCC.

In my capacity as chief executive of the UK Meteorological Office, I attended the four-yearly WMO Congress in Geneva in 1987. In preparation for this conference, Jim Bruce had given a lot of thought to how information might be exchanged between scientists and politicians. He suggested the skeleton of a system whereby the necessary objective and independent scientific research and exchange of ideas could take place, and the results could be conveyed to governments worldwide. We all recognized the potential value of such a structure. The WMO and the United Nations Environment Programme (UNEP) agreed to set up what was to become the Intergovernmental Panel on Climate Change. The IPCC had been conceived.

In informal discussion about the way the IPCC might work, we identified two key factors. First, there had to be a more stringent approach to the assessment and sharing of scientific knowledge. Reports summarizing the science, while they had to be written by renowned and respected scientists, would also have to be written in a style and language that would be accessible to the public, to stakeholders, decision-makers, and politicians; in short, non-scientists. Secondly, in what was to prove crucial to our effectiveness and integrity, we realized that there should be a clear distinction between the scientific assessment and the political negotiations on policies and measures.[5] We scientists would deal with the science and with the task of making it clear and comprehensible for policymakers; we would steer clear of involvement in political debate.

These are the foundations upon which the IPCC was eventually built and our role defined. Much more work and many detailed negotiations lay ahead of us all, not least of which would be further defining of the IPCC's role. Many of us were to become heavily involved in the process, but there is no doubt at all that Jim Bruce's energy and influence, along with the support of Professor Obasi at the WMO and Dr Tolba, the head of UNEP, were absolutely instrumental from the start in making the IPCC happen. Eventually, the newly formed IPCC's first meeting was timetabled for November 1988 in Geneva.

In June 1988, along with representatives of the Department of the Environment, I attended an international ministerial conference in Toronto, organized and hosted by the Canadian government. Keen and somewhat impatient at that time to lead the world forward, the Canadians' ambition was to bring together ministers from many of the world's governments to discuss what should be done to cut the emissions causing climate change. They hoped to gain agreement from them all to cut CO_2 emissions by 20 per cent of 1988 levels by 2005.

Although the conference's suggested target was laudable, it was too ambitious. For many of the delegates, the idea of global warming was completely new. To achieve agreement on such a reduction in emissions would have required immense political will from all of the countries represented, but the robust science was not yet available to convince politicians that such measures were necessary. Without solid scientific evidence, it was too much to ask of societies whose economies had grown dependent upon fossil fuels, and in which there was considerable political and corporate ignorance and inertia.

Nevertheless, the Toronto conference was not a failure, because it performed the crucial role of raising political awareness of the problem. It also clarified two things, both of which justified our IPCC vision. First, it was clear that a great deal more scientific research was necessary, and that different areas of climate science needed to be brought together. Secondly, the meeting identified the need to formally bring together the scientific and political communities to consider climate change in an objective and effective way. Without this, politicians would remain ill-informed and action would be impossible. The IPCC's role was becoming more defined.

At the same time as things were hotting up metaphorically in the scientific and political worlds, they were also hotting up literally in the USA. The summer of 1988 saw widespread drought and crop failure in many states. James Hansen, a climate modeller in NASA's Goddard Institute for Space Studies, said that "global warming is now sufficiently large that we can ascribe with a high degree of confidence a cause and effect relationship to the greenhouse effect".[6] However, some respected scientists disagreed with this assessment. It was beginning to look messy. Again, the need for robust scientific study was apparent.

It was now time for the world's politicians to jostle themselves into position and declare their own stances on this emerging global issue. Noises coming from the US administration under Ronald Reagan were very different from the arguments we would hear from the Republican Party decades later once George W. Bush was in power. In 1988 Reagan's USA argued strongly that the time had come for political action on climate change. It might surprise the reader to learn that in his bid for the US presidency, George Bush Senior supported action on climate change, promising to "meet the greenhouse effect with the Whitehouse effect".[7]

In the United Kingdom, Prime Minister Margaret Thatcher was showing keen interest. She was an Oxford-educated scientist, which probably led to a natural curiosity about and understanding of this issue, but I suspect that her desire to be respected as a scientist was an additional driving force. Her interest became public in September 1988, when she made an important speech to the Royal Society, the UK's Academy of Science and a fellowship of many of the world's most eminent scientists, in which she made her own priorities clear.[8]

During a speech in which she addressed many scientific matters, Mrs Thatcher gave considerable prominence to global warming. She suggested that "we have unwittingly begun a massive experiment with the system of this planet itself". She referred to melting ice caps, rising sea levels, the hole in the ozone layer, and acid rain. Her speech was an optimistic one, referring back to successful public and political responses to scientific discoveries of the past. It was also an important one in raising public awareness. The following day, the headline in *The Times* asserted unequivocally that global warming was a problem.

Perhaps even more significantly, Mrs Thatcher indicated that she was thinking along the same lines as we were in preparing the IPCC. She identified some key needs:

- To identify particular areas of research that would help to establish cause and effect.

- To consider in more detail the likely effects of change within precise timescales.

- To consider the wider implications for policy: for energy production, for fuel efficiency, and for reforestation.

This, as she said, was "no small task", and she further insisted that whatever we did should be "founded on good science". This public endorsement and the subsequent commitment from Mrs Thatcher's government were to prove invaluable.

Globally, there were similar calls for political action, but to carry weight they needed to be grounded in appropriate scientific analysis. This would be the role of the IPCC. With a great sense of purpose and determination, we made the necessary preparations for the first IPCC meeting in November 1988. When November duly arrived, I travelled to Geneva full of anticipation.

Mostafa Tolba and Jim Bruce had prepared very effectively for the meeting, enabling us to make rapid progress. They suggested a well-considered IPCC structure, which still largely endures today. They proposed that there should be three working groups with clearly defined roles:

- Working Group 1: The assessment of available scientific information on climate change.

- Working Group 2: The assessment of environmental and socio-economic impacts of climate change.[9]

- Working Group 3: The formulation of response strategies.

They also suggested candidates for key roles within the new structure. Bert Bolin was the obvious choice for overall IPCC Chair. As well as being an influential and respected scientist, Bert had the political and diplomatic experience and skills to persuade the world to manage this immense undertaking. He was well liked, with infectious enthusiasm and energy. I had already come to know Bert well and thoroughly enjoyed working alongside this astute man.

When Jim invited me to chair Working Group 1 – the Science Working Group – I accepted without hesitation. Not only would this be a privilege, but it seemed a marvellous, exciting opportunity. Soon after our respective appointments, Bert confided in me that he would have preferred my job to his own; he thought it would be more fun. There was no way I was going to swap. I had no doubt at all that Bert would fulfil his role better than I could ever have done. Besides, what interested me most of all was the science.

Privileged though I might have felt, I wasn't naive. I saw clearly that my workload would be immense, and that I would need some sort of support if I were to be effective in both my IPCC role and my work at the Met Office. The UK Department of the Environment's chief scientific adviser, David Fisk, was also at that November meeting, and I lost no time at all in discussing with him how the government might support IPCC work. This was the beginning of the negotiations that led eventually to the establishment at the Met Office of the Technical Support Unit (TSU) for Working Group 1 mentioned in Chapter 11. Both the formal and the informal discussions at that IPCC preparatory meeting were remarkable. Had I returned from Geneva without having taken the first steps down the path to the creation of the TSU, I would have been facing an impossible task.

Nevertheless, it was inevitable that the IPCC would have a few teething problems for us to sort out. We were a little disappointed that only 28 countries sent representatives to Geneva, and only 11 of those were developing countries. For the IPCC to be truly international, the participation of developing countries was essential. It was clear that many of these developing countries might need financial help to enable their participation in the IPCC. One of our first actions was to establish a trust fund for this purpose.

All of us involved accepted that the IPCC's work was to be a substantial challenge; there was no way around that. Even so, as Bert Bolin has since written, none of us fully realized the far-reaching implications and struggles of the tasks that lay ahead.[10] We immediately set ourselves a tough deadline, accepting a suggestion from the delegate from Malta that we should produce a detailed report in time for the UN General Assembly meeting in 1990. This gave us less than two years. While an intimidating target, it seemed an important one.

For most of the scientists involved, our work was voluntary and unpaid and additional to our day jobs. I already had a very busy job at the Met Office, and to do the work required by the IPCC was a significant organizational task. Even before we began, I would have to find and communicate with many of the best scientists in the world and ensure that all countries were involved. It wasn't a case simply of getting a few scientists together in a room and asking "What do you think?" We would need hundreds of scientists from as many nations, backgrounds, and disciplines as possible, all of whom must have the ability to review the available science and to collaborate in writing the chapters. There would be language difficulties and logistical difficulties. In the face of these challenges and a complex structure, they would have to deliver their report with absolute clarity and precision within a tight timescale. We would have to find people in whose ability, integrity, and conscientiousness we had absolute faith.

Clearly, right from the outset we would need to establish systems and support mechanisms to facilitate their work. We would also need to create suitable procedures. Although many of us were accustomed to collaborative work, never before in the scientific community had this been done on such a large, international scale.

I couldn't have done any of it without the support of the TSU in Bracknell. The people working there would have to be of the highest calibre. Accordingly, Geoff Jenkins was appointed the first head of the TSU. A superb organizer and leader, Geoff did a wonderful job, leading a small team of talented, dedicated staff, some drawn from other countries, to make the first IPCC report possible. Other countries also contributed staff to help the TSU; Bob Watson, an Englishman sent as a representative of NASA, was a particular strength. Geoff's successors are also worthy of mention here, because Bruce Callander and David Griggs did equally invaluable work for the Second and Third IPCC Reports respectively. The potential workload of the TSU was and still is, in fact, unmanageable. They have to deal with issues raised by people from all over the world, and the whole world is interested in their work. They have to arrange meetings, make travel plans, collate and distribute scientific material, and share technical information. For the first IPCC report they had to ensure that the report was structured and written at an appropriate technical level, and build an overview of the science so that they could help me prepare the first draft of the Policymakers' Summary.

Working in a job where you can't conceivably do everything you'd like to do is always a strain. You have to decide and focus upon the important achievable tasks, a task which itself requires great sensitivity and skill. I feel grateful and privileged to have been able to work alongside such capable people. However, even with a highly effective TSU in place, IPCC work, with its global input and global relevance, was still going to be an enormous challenge for everybody.

The basis of the procedure we would follow had been agreed in Geneva. It was crucial that the science should be a *world* scientific assessment. Our eventual product was to be a detailed scientific report, broken into chapters. We also made the decision to produce a summary of the report, in which the science of each chapter was summarized accurately and written in language accessible to policymakers. Each chapter would require between two and four lead authors, one of whom would be a convening lead author with overall responsibility. All lead authors must already have earned the respect of the global scientific community. Within each chapter group there must be sub-groups of many contributing scientists, some of whom would become involved in the working meetings and engaged in the consideration of all the science. Any science contributed would have to be peer-reviewed, which would demand an extensive formal reviewing process managed and coordinated by the TSU (see Appendix 3).

Although the IPCC would by its very nature be intergovernmental because all members of the World Meteorological Organization were members, in order that all governments should feel ownership of the reports, especially of the Policymakers' Summaries, it was essential that their representatives at the plenary meeting agreed them. There would therefore be a final intergovernmental IPCC meeting for each working group, the purpose of which would be to go through the report sentence by sentence, word by word, until the representatives of all governments felt able to agree the document as an accurate summary of the science. Only by this tough and demanding process would the world's governments have ownership of IPCC reports. To the best of my knowledge, the IPCC has never received a complaint from any government about a document that has been subjected to this rigorous process.

The Science Working Group's first meeting was to be in January 1989, only two months after the Geneva meeting. From the start, I had a clear sense that the Science Working Group had a responsibility to tell the world what we knew. To keep such knowledge to ourselves in language to be understood only by fellow scientists would be irresponsible. We had to ensure that our research was done accurately and properly, and we had to start with a clean slate. We had to start from scratch. The importance of teamwork in every step of this undertaking cannot be over-emphasized, and I am grateful to every member of this almost unwieldy global team for the valuable contributions they made.

First we needed to find the scientists. We needed experts in oceanography, in the atmosphere, and in the cryosphere,[11] land surface and more. In trying to identify the best lead author for each chapter, we needed to keep the scope global, but ensure that the people we invited were competent in English and able to manage the task. We therefore needed people who had experience of previous involvement in international programmes, and who were sufficiently known and respected by the atmospheric science community.

Fortunately, thanks to the long tradition of international cooperation in climate science, identifying these participants was a fairly straightforward task. Along with my colleagues in the TSU, I already knew many of the leading climate scientists through the WMO. We also invited governments and the global scientific community to nominate appropriate scientists. To ensure that the process was sensible and objective, decisions were overseen by a body called the Working Group Bureau, set up and nominated by the IPCC, itself consisting of five or six representatives from different countries. The bureau too could nominate lead authors, and we had to agree all final nominations with the bureau.

Identifying lead authors was one matter; persuading these people, who were the world's best scientists, to join us was another. The task of a lead author is formidable. They have to manage the scientists within their group, manage the review process, and assimilate all of the reports, and then deliver something in clear English within a set deadline, while involving the whole working group in the process. Nobody was to be paid, so there were no contracts to tie people to deadlines. We therefore needed people who were absolutely reliable. What we were offering was a tremendous amount of work for no financial reward at all.

Why do we scientists give so much of our already busy lives to help to write a chapter for an IPCC report? The answer is simple. It's because we love the science. Meetings such as those held by the IPCC present an unparalleled opportunity for learning. As scientists, we are all engaged in a quest for truth, but we often work so closely within our small areas of expertise that we can lose sight of the bigger picture. Other scientists around us are working on their own areas, all of which are interrelated. International meetings enable us to see a bigger picture; we change our zoom lens for a wide-angle lens. It's a marvellous way of keeping abreast of neighbouring subjects and disciplines, which always increases our understanding of our own. The contributors are all experts. The discussion is mostly friendly, honest, and robust, with the occasional exception when matters grow heated. The reward you get is being there. Fortunately, many very good people saw this as adequate reward for the work we were inviting them to do, and so the Science Working Group of the IPCC could move forward.

14

THE FIRST IPCC ASSESSMENT REPORT 1990

We needed to get going quickly if we were to have a report ready for the UN General Assembly in 1990 and so, in January 1989, just over one month after we were formed, the IPCC's Science Working Group held its first meeting at Nuneham Courtenay near Oxford. About 70 scientists from around the world gathered to discuss the style, content, and organization of our first report. Aware that this had to be a scientific assessment, and fully recognizing the important responsibility we had been given to provide an honest, accurate, and comprehensive report, we set about our task.

We had to settle on the areas of concern for the chapters. We quite quickly agreed on divisions, which led finally to the following headings within the Policymakers' Summary:

- What factors determine global climate?

- What are the greenhouse gases and why are they increasing?

- Which gases are the most important?

- How much do we expect climate to change?

- How much confidence do we have in our predictions?
- Will the climate of the future be very different?
- Has man already begun to change the global climate?
- How much will sea level rise?
- What will be the effect of climate change on ecosystems?
- What should be done to reduce uncertainties and how long will this take?

A question of immense importance was and still is, "How much are humans affecting the climate?" The climate changes for all sorts of reasons, known as "forcing factors", many of which are external to the climate system itself and beyond human influence; they are well known and have been studied for many years, such as variations in the sun and volcanic eruptions. There are also unforced changes, which occur within the climate system independently of any external influence. These were still early days in the study of anthropogenic (human-induced) climate change. We had to estimate the extent to which the human burning of fossil fuels was influencing climate, and compare this to other factors.

The fact that human behaviour was increasing CO_2 concentration in the earth's atmosphere had been firmly established. The CO_2 from the burning of fossil fuel is distinguishable from naturally occurring CO_2 because the carbon has a different isotopic composition.[1] By 1989 there was no doubt at all that human activity since the industrial revolution had increased the amount of CO_2 in the atmosphere by about 30 per cent.[2] But was that contributing to climate change, and if so, how significant was this contribution?

The 1985 SCOPE 29 Conference in Villach presented further information about human influence on climate change, which indicated that average global temperatures could increase by somewhere between 1.5 and 4.5 °C in the next century, should human behaviour and CO_2 emissions continue unabated. If this were to be the case, it was potentially serious. To give a sense of scale, bear in mind that globally averaged, the difference between the ice ages and the periods between them was only 5–6 °C, and those changes occurred over tens to hundreds of thousands of years, allowing nature and species to adapt to the changes. The possible change we were looking at could feasibly take place within one human lifetime.

While our scientific judgment and experience might have enabled us to anticipate certain conclusions about the effects of human activity on the climate's variability, many of us in Working Group 1 were concerned that we did not yet have enough scientific evidence. To what extent had we really seen the effects of increasing CO_2 levels, and therefore of human activity on the climate? With so much variability, how could we with adequate confidence identify trends and write about them? As a result, our biggest debate concerned how to deal with and how to present scientific uncertainty.

It is too simplistic to assert that scientists can never be absolutely sure about anything, because there are certain mathematical truths. However, beyond that, certainty is rarely absolute. Prediction is particularly difficult. When it comes to predicting events, we can never be 100 per cent confident that what we believe will happen will happen. It's the same as in our daily lives; we always have to face the possibility that what seems to be true may not be right at all. That is OK, because constant questioning is what science is all about, but how to convey this to non-scientists can pose a problem. And now it posed a problem.

Some scientists on the working group argued the case for extreme caution. "How can we say anything definite about climate change?" they asked. "There's so much uncertainty here, we really don't know very much at all." Some went as far as to suggest that there was little point in doing this assessment when so little was known for certain. These were difficult concerns to address. What could we possibly say about the influence of continuing and growing greenhouse gas emissions on future climate? How indeed could we say anything at all?

As Chair, I had to be clear about what we were there to achieve. Our task was to evaluate all the evidence and to give the clearest possible summary of the science so far, complete with all its uncertainty. It was not about expressing opinion. I illustrated to the group the responsibility we had been given by referring to the task of a weather forecaster. If a forecaster appeared on the television and said, "I'm sorry, but I'm too uncertain about tomorrow's weather to present any forecast at all," they wouldn't be doing their job. What would be the point in doing that? The viewers would be left clueless when, in fact, the forecaster is never entirely without scientific information, which is more useful than nothing at all.

The storm of October 1987 had brought this issue to the fore. The forecaster's job is to present his best story about tomorrow's weather, and to acknowledge when there is a degree of uncertainty. A forecaster has to warn of the possibility of extreme weather even if there is uncertainty about how, when or indeed whether it will happen at all. Besides, the public has enough experience of weather forecasting to know that conclusions aren't always definite or indeed correct. Of course, there are times when we'd all love to know exactly what the weather will do tomorrow, but we often have to accept a picture of what it is likely to do, in the knowledge that some of it may not turn out to be correct. Our barbecue might be rained off.

Concerning projections about climate change, I believe our responsibility to be similar. At that first meeting I argued that we should provide our most accurate climate story based upon our science, but because people are not familiar with climate forecasts, we should also describe as clearly as possible our estimation of its certainty. I reminded the meeting that we'd been given a job to do, and if we didn't do it well, there were people out there who knew little or nothing about science who would pontificate about climate change and get away with it because we were unwilling to speak of what we actually knew. Little could I have suspected at that time how many such ill-informed voices would eventually speak, how loudly they would do so, and how much damage they would cause. But the severity of that particular problem was still a few years in the future.

The group began to gel with the sense that we must do as much as we could. Everybody agreed that of prime importance for our report was the need clearly to distinguish what we knew with reasonable certainty from those areas where uncertainty was much greater. If we did this, we could move forward. After a great deal of discussion both in that meeting and afterwards, we decided, following a suggestion from John Mitchell, my senior climate modeller, that the Executive Summary of our 1990 report would include quantifying statements such as "we are certain of the following", "we calculate with confidence that…", "our judgement is that…", and "there are many uncertainties in our predictions that…". Recognizing these distinctions from the start would provide a valuable basis for progress, and ultimately a precedent for the summary of this and future reports.

We were now free to consider all the data available. Over the next 12 months or so, the IPCC chapter groups held many meetings at locations all over the world to review all of the available science, carry out meticulous peer reviewing, and assess the significance of it all. (For details about how scientific peer review works, please see Appendix 3.) Once the science was thoroughly reviewed, the chapter groups worked hard to absorb the necessary changes into accurate, logical, and coherent chapters.

The strength of the IPCC has always been that it looks at all the data in detail, not just little bits of it, the object of course being to see the big picture and to reach informed, balanced conclusions, coming as close as possible to the truth. According to the agreed procedure, comments and questions were submitted by scientists, governments, and interested non-governmental organizations (NGOs) and dealt with by the authors, who were obliged to address every single one, keeping an accurate record of how or whether the comment had affected the chapter. It was quite a tortuous process. I firmly believe that no assessments of any other scientific topics have ever before been so thoroughly researched and reviewed by such a large body of the world's community of scientists as they have been for all of the IPCC reports.

The Science Working Group had two further meetings for the 1990 report, one for the chapter groups in Edinburgh, in March 1991, the purpose of which was to put the chapters into their final form and discuss and agree a draft of the Policymakers' Summary. The Plenary in Windsor in May, involving lead authors and government representatives, would agree the final version of the Policymakers' Summary. More recently, the IPCC would, quite rightly, never get away with two successive meetings in the same country, because of the geopolitics involved.

From the very beginning, I thoroughly enjoyed the rigours of the IPCC process. It's a wonderful thing when you get a group of scientists together with a particular aim. The discipline of science is very strong. You're there to say what you know from the point of view of the science; you're not there for your own personal or political or any other agenda. The remarkable thing was that even when we had some very distinguished people involved, their personal egos were subservient to the needs of the IPCC. The question was never "Who are you and what is your position?" but "What's your science?" Together, we were searching for the objective scientific truth about the detailed workings of the natural world.

In spite of this, difficult interpersonal situations did sometimes arise. I have always been saddened by a conversation between myself and Mikhail Budyko, to which I referred briefly in an earlier chapter. Early in preparing the first IPCC report, we were examining how historical evidence of climate might be used to inform us about future climate. This was Budyko's area of expertise, on which he had published numerous papers and books. However, his studies had failed to take sufficiently into account such matters as variations in the earth's orbit around the sun and changes in the tilt of the earth's axis, both of which have influenced climate over hundreds of thousands of years, contributing to ice ages and warm periods. Because of these, it is essential to exercise a great deal of care when trying to use climates of the past as templates for climates of the future. Budyko did not accept this.

Budyko was powerful and influential in Russian science, his work and his name carrying great weight. The Russians were therefore keen to push the Budyko line, but it just wasn't right. We held a meeting in Bristol specifically to discuss this whole area of science. Listening to other presenters and being made aware of other published papers, Budyko's people, of course, had their eyes opened to other opinions about the science. They were excited by it. Suddenly, poor Budyko was left out in the cold, even by his own people. He was, understandably, upset.

Budyko and I sat together for dinner one evening in Bristol. "You know, Professor Houghton," he said, "I never thought I would come to hate you so much."

I was shocked. "Professor Budyko, I don't hate you at all," I replied. "All I'm doing is trying to do some science and come to the truth. That's the whole business of the IPCC, and what we're doing here." I explained that our friendship should not be in any way disturbed by the direction of the science, and that we should move forward together. However, Budyko insisted that I had undermined him in setting up a meeting which, in his view, killed his reputation. Understanding his anger, I felt sorry that his area of science had, to an extent, left him behind.

Because it is a continuous quest for truth, the process of scientific search and discovery is an ongoing one. Important discoveries and breakthroughs regularly add to or even challenge our knowledge and understanding. This makes science exciting, as we have to remain always aware that our already incomplete knowledge might at any time be turned upside down. We have to keep our minds open to new possibilities all of the time, even when we think we have a tidy answer.

Another example of this occurred at the Edinburgh meeting in March 1990, where we were going through the almost completed chapters. Syukuro Manabe, a scientist from Princeton and a pioneer in computer modelling of climate, brought to the meeting some very new and important research results: the first credible results from an atmosphere–ocean coupled model. We would, for the first time, be able to look at the whole interrelated system of atmosphere and ocean. These results hadn't been available when the relevant chapter was drafted.

One major problem with climate modelling is the large variability from time to time and from place to place, sometimes due to external factors we understand, sometimes factors we can't fully identify. Until Manabe's work, all climate models had treated the ocean as part of the system but essentially as a "slab" or still ocean with prescribed properties, dynamic only in predetermined ways. The models made no provision for changes in ocean circulation or other dynamic factors. It had been a crude way of considering the oceans because the necessary computing capacity had not been available. Therefore, the detailed exchange and interaction between ocean and atmosphere was not yet built into modelling systems, even though ocean circulation and atmospheric circulation both strongly influence each other. Manabe's computer model for the first time allowed for more detailed exchange and interaction between ocean and atmosphere. It represented a significant, exciting breakthrough.

However, this research was brand new. There had been no time for a formal peer review process, and the IPCC was supposed to use only peer-reviewed material. The chapter to be most affected was Chapter 6. A few people felt that it was too late at this stage to include new material anyway. Conversely, the majority felt that Manabe's work was too important to ignore. What should we do?

My job as Chair was to ensure that the system ran entirely fairly, and that IPCC guidelines were followed. So far this was happening quite easily, but here was a new challenge. Most of us agreed that as we were a large group of the world's leading climate scientists, we were in effect capable of doing a very good peer review of Manabe's work ourselves. We still had two months before we had to submit our final report to the IPCC in May, which easily gave us time for thorough peer review and revision of Chapter 6. At the end of that Edinburgh meeting, Hans Oeschger, a distinguished Swiss climate and environmental physicist, said, "You know, John, I've never been to such an exciting scientific meeting."

I laughed, "It isn't supposed to be exciting – we just have a job to do." But it was exciting, and this scientific excitement and stimulation persists within the culture of the IPCC.

In Windsor a few months later, with a revised Chapter 6 into which Manabe's work had been absorbed, we all felt inspired. It was important that we had been able to include these new results. We couldn't have done that with the later reports, as the process has since become tighter regarding peer reviews. Nevertheless, the passage of time has confirmed that we were right, at that particular point in time, to include the groundbreaking results from Manabe's model.

The purpose of the three-day meeting in Windsor in May was to formally accept the chapters and agree unanimously that the Policymakers' Summary was an accurate summary of what the chapters said. It is crucial that the working groups are confident that their final reports are scientifically accurate, clear, and comprehensible, and relevant to the policy-making process. This means gaining agreement from the representative of every government involved. In 1990, this was about 60 governments. For subsequent reports, this number has been closer to 100.

Agreeing the Policymakers' Summary at a plenary meeting is an exacting, painstaking process. The lead authors and some of the scientists who have contributed to the report are present at the meeting, prepared to be quizzed. The majority of countries send scientists as their representatives, one or two send lawyers or politicians, but as ever, the focus is always on the science: it is a scientific meeting, not a political meeting at all. Only comments on the science, or questions relating to the science, are permissible. Delegates can request clarification, or point out any inconsistencies or confusion in the material, and we have to address each point, amending where necessary. In the end, all delegates and the lead authors have to agree unanimously every sentence of the document. It might seem to be an impossible process, but it works. This process of agreeing the summary is unique and quite remarkable in science.

Rather like a United Nations meeting, with delegates from all around the world we need simultaneous translation into six languages, which in itself has the potential to cause confusion. In that Windsor meeting, discussions were interesting, intricate, and at times very intense. A minority of the delegates seemed to have their own agendas. The oil states, for example, seemed to be trying to weaken the report in any way they could. Delegates from Saudi Arabia and some other oil states opposed any mention of CO_2 in the report at all, trying to insist instead that the less specific term "greenhouse gases" should be used. Of course, they didn't succeed, and they conceded gracefully. This was only the mid 1990s; the issue of climate change was still quite new and they hadn't got their act together so were far less determined and less effective than they were to be five years later.

Conversely, there were representatives of governments with green agendas, who would have liked our statements to be stronger. They tended to argue that we should state with greater certainty that climate change was a big issue. But all argument had to be based entirely upon the science. For most delegates, the priority was that the science should be accurate and presented clearly. Determined not to exaggerate, our aim was to convey with absolute honesty what we knew.

The process of creating a clear, comprehensible report was aided a great deal by some of the delegates from developing countries who didn't really know a lot about the science. They would say, "We don't really understand this – tell us what it means," thereby forcing us to address the clarity of the point in question. I was under no political influence at all. My job was to act as an independent Chair free of political affinity. That was and still is very important in order to maintain the integrity of the IPCC's work.

We eventually succeeded in producing a summary that satisfied all of our concerns about levels of certainty and uncertainty, and which accurately reflected the science available. In addition to the previously agreed statements about levels of certainty, the report contained numerous discussions of our levels of certainty within different sections. In short, the whole of the 1990 report was very cautiously written. Not wanting to be in any way alarmist, we erred on the side of cautious statements. Scientifically, this was absolutely the right thing to do. In spite of the uncertainty, there was still a great deal we *were* able to say, which *did* grip people. The things that we could calculate with confidence *did* add up to something essentially valuable at the time.

In the end, all the delegates went away feeling that they owned the final document. They were able to go to their respective governments' ministers and say with confidence, "Minister – this is the result of our meeting and this is what we've agreed." The wonderful thing was that when I sat down with the document and looked at the results of this very demanding meeting, it was considerably better than the initial document we had started with. This was also true of the subsequent IPCC reports with which I was involved, compiled when there was much greater controversy and disagreement in the meetings. The accuracy of IPCC reports results from the toughest scrutiny possible.

At the end of the Windsor meeting, we held a press conference in a sun-filled, glass-roofed room, aptly named "The Greenhouse". The room was packed with press representatives who showed positive and lively interest in what we had to say.

Although pleased with the accuracy of the report, many of us were still concerned about the gap between our emerging awareness as scientists that the problem of human-induced climate change was significant and urgent, and the limited scientific evidence so far. This gap led us, quite rightly, to proceed with great caution, but our own knowledge and experience made us uneasy about what the science might show in the future.

In an interview with the *Financial Times* five years later in 1995,[3] I commented: "People haven't seen global warming yet. It's all in the future. We can't expect them to take drastic action in the face of these uncertainties." In the same way, we couldn't raise too great an alarm in the face of the uncertainties. Later in the same interview, I reflected: "I sometimes wonder whether I should be shouting louder." This was true then and it's true now. But by shouting I do not mean exaggerating; I mean the clear and strong communication of facts.

Box 14.1 IPCC 1990 Report: Some extracts from the Executive Summary

We are certain of the following:

- There is a natural greenhouse effect, which already keeps the earth warmer than it would otherwise be.

- Emissions resulting from human activities are substantially increasing the atmospheric concentrations of the greenhouse gases: carbon dioxide, methane, chlorofluorocarbons, and nitrous oxide. These increases will enhance the greenhouse effect, resulting on average in an additional warming of the earth's surface. The main greenhouse gas, water vapour, will increase in response to global warming and further enhance it.

We calculate with confidence that:

- Carbon dioxide has been responsible for over half the enhanced greenhouse effect in the past and is likely to remain so in the future.

Based on current model results, we predict:

- Under the IPCC Business-as-usual scenario of emissions of greenhouse gases, a rate of increase of global mean temperature during the next century of about 0.3 °C per decade (with an uncertainty range of 0.2 °C to 0.5 °C per decade) – this is greater than that seen over the past 10,000 years – and an average rate of global mean sea-level rise of about 6 cm per decade over the next century (with an uncertainty range of 3–10 cm per decade).

Our judgment is that:

- Global mean surface air temperature has increased by 0.3 °C to 0.6 °C over the last 100 years, with the five global average warmest years being in the 1980s. The size of this warming is broadly consistent with the predictions of climate models, but it is also of the same magnitude as natural climate variability. The unequivocal detection of the enhanced greenhouse effect from observations is not likely for a decade or more.

There are many uncertainties in our predictions particularly with regard to the timing, magnitude, and regional patterns of climate change, due to our incomplete understanding of: sources and sinks of greenhouse gases, clouds, oceans, and polar ice sheets.

The week in which the report was approved was one of the most remarkable weeks of my life. The meeting opened on a Monday. That afternoon, having received an invitation from Downing Street, I went to present the report to Margaret Thatcher's Cabinet. Geoff Jenkins, who had been project managing the report in the TSU, came with me. We took along an overhead projector (OHP) to show our slides, unaware that we were breaking new ground: this would be the first time an OHP had ever been used in the Cabinet Room.

Just before I entered the Cabinet Room, one of Mrs Thatcher's ministers gave me a friendly warning: "You've been given 20 minutes. You mustn't worry if she interrupts you." I wondered how much of the report I would manage to present before I was dismissed. As it happened, the prime minister didn't interrupt me once. In fact, she listened with a great deal more interest than anyone else around the table. Immediately after the meeting, the minister who had warned me of interruptions shook my hand. "Well done," he said. "You kept her quiet."

I happened to walk out of the room with Nicholas Ridley, the Secretary of State for the Environment at the time. "Well," he said, "when are we really going to notice this climate change that you've talked about?"

"Hmm, well, in 10 to 15 years I think we'll be able to see enough evidence to be rather sure about it," I replied.

He laughed. "Oh, it'll see me out then."

As he died in 1993, I suppose he was right, but that's not the point. I thought his response both a sad and most unsatisfactory one from the man with responsibility for the environment in which my children and grandchildren, and indeed his own, would have to live.

Back in my day job at the Met Office, we'd been working to develop further the work and facilities of the TSU. With the government funding I had secured, the Hadley Centre for Climate Prediction and Research was now ready for its grand opening. The appointed date was that Friday, 25 May. Margaret Thatcher was going to open it with a speech.

On the Tuesday, the day after my presentation to the Cabinet, I received another invitation to Downing Street. Margaret Thatcher apparently wanted my assistance. "She's decided that this is going to be one of her special speeches," I was told, "and she'd like your assistance in writing it. Can you come back this evening?"

And so, on Tuesday and Wednesday of that week, I spent the daytime in Windsor chairing IPCC meetings, and the evenings visiting Margaret Thatcher in Downing Street. This bizarre timetable led my wife Sheila to complain that I spent more time with my "new lady friend" than I did with her.

Working alongside the prime minister was a fascinating experience. The majority of her speeches were scripted by her speech-writers, but occasionally she would select one for more personal input. This was to be one such speech. As a result, several hours of prime ministerial time were spent in constructing that speech. I found it very interesting to see her in action in that way, with her pencil and eraser in hand. "I'm a scientist," she said a few times. "I've got to get it absolutely right."

I was keen that she should say positive things about our aspirations for the Hadley Centre, which were essentially to move climate science forward by bringing together all the different parts of the whole; all the different specialisms. I really wanted people to understand how rapidly science can advance when you put its different parts together. Her usual speech-writer, Charles Powell, was in the room most of the time, helping with phrases here and there.

There is no doubt that Mrs Thatcher had a dominating personality, but she also had tremendously infectious enthusiasm and determination. Her attention to this speech was almost obsessive. I was surprised at her commitment, spending two hours on each of two consecutive evenings on a speech she could easily have got someone else to write. She was a very impressive person. The 2011 film starring Meryl Streep is brilliant in Streep's accurate portrayal of Thatcher's mannerisms, behaviour, attitude, and energy. Watching the film brought it all vividly back to my mind.

Finally, on the Friday of that exhausting but exciting week, with the IPCC report agreed and signed off, I had the privilege of welcoming the prime minister to the Hadley Centre. A very gracious guest, she delivered her speech with her usual assured persuasive powers. I was extremely satisfied with the end result. I also felt privileged to have had the opportunity, not only of influencing the content of the speech, but of spending some intensely productive time with the prime minister. Looking back on that speech now, almost a quarter of a century later, is rather like reading a science fiction novel written years ago, and finding that you live in the future therein described. Box 14.2 paraphrases some of Margaret Thatcher's main points.[4]

Box 14.2 Prime Minister's Speech, Opening of the Hadley Centre, Friday 25 May 1990

- The 1990 report provides an authoritative early warning system, confirming that greenhouse gases are increasing substantially as a result of human activities; that this will warm the earth's surface, with serious consequences for us all, and that these consequences can be predicted.

- The changes identified in the report will occur at a faster rate than anything our natural world has known in the past. This could lead to migration of animal and plant life and possibly the loss of some of them altogether.

- Changes in the sea level could also affect our lives considerably.

- There will be mass migration from areas of the world liable to flooding and from areas of declining rainfall and spreading deserts.

- By 2005 we should have a much clearer picture.

- Man's activities are adding greenhouse gases to the earth at an unprecedented rate, with inevitable consequences for our future climate. At the same time we are destroying tropical forests, which are a vital way of taking CO_2 out of the air and storing it.

- This effect will increase as the world's population increases.

- We have a full repairing lease on this earth. We would be taking a great risk with future generations if, having received this early warning, we did nothing about it or just took the attitude: "It will see me out!"

- We need a giant international effort with a fair distribution of the burden. Provided others are ready to take their full share, Britain is prepared to set itself the target of a reduction of up to 30 per cent in presently projected levels of CO_2 emissions by the year 2005, returning emissions to their 1990 levels.

- Action will mean significant adjustments to our economies and better management of energy in general.

- Changes we can expect in the future will be so much greater than anything we have hitherto experienced that we shall need to rely much more on computer models which take in the full complexity of the climate system. That is the purpose of the Hadley Centre.

- Discharges of CO_2 and CFCs, if unabated, will go on accumulating in the atmosphere and could not easily be reversed. Even the most urgent measures now cannot fully repair the damage of the past but action now will prevent the problem from becoming acute and give us time to improve our predictions and enlarge our understanding. We should start without delay.

Whatever her motives may have been, Margaret Thatcher's message was loud and clear.

Reading her autobiography, however, I find that her more recent comments about climate change were not quite so unequivocal. This is disappointing, and I wonder whether it might be due to the influence of prominent climate change sceptics whom she continued to count among her friends. Such dangerous voices, I fear, are still influencing leading politicians even now despite the much increased information and certainty in the science today.

Interestingly, 22 years later, I was invited by the WWF and Tear Fund to talk at a side-event during the 2012 Conservative Party Conference. Although my allocated slot was on a Sunday evening, the room was very full. This reassured me that some Conservatives are taking climate change seriously and are prepared to listen to the science, whichever side of the fence they may be sitting on. I took a number of questions from the floor, questions which showed people earnestly trying to inform themselves.

Greg Barker, a Conservative MP and Minister of State for Energy and Climate Change, spoke positively and eloquently about the climate change problem, about what the government was doing and what they could be doing. His proposals were good, but I think a lack of similar enthusiasm throughout the government means that he had a tough time. Unfortunately, even with all the science now available, climate change simply is not safe ground in current political games, and I have little doubt that vested interests are at work.

The Hadley Centre officially open and the working group report agreed, our next task was to publish it. I felt strongly that such an important document should go out to the world in the most effective way possible. If we had followed precedent, the WMO would have published it as an official-looking document with limited appeal and distribution. Feeling certain that we needed a commercial publisher on board, I negotiated terms with Cambridge University Press (CUP), for which I had Obasi's agreement. With help from the TSU, we prepared all of the finishing touches for CUP. It was published in August 1990 and the IPCC's First Assessment Report began to spread around the world.

We awaited the world's reaction. We'd succeeded in publishing the report in time for October's WMO Second World Climate Conference. An important "Earth Summit" was going to take place in Rio de Janeiro, Brazil, in June 1992. Largely because of the IPCC report, climate change was taken sufficiently seriously to become a significant part of the Earth Summit's programme, which really began the political world's attempts to address the problem. I thought this was an excellent result of our work. There was now a sense of urgency and purposeful optimism.

I did not attend the Rio summit. As a scientist, I had handed the results of the science to the politicians: I would have no involvement in political negotiations or decisions. Nevertheless, Maurice Strong, who had instigated the Rio summit, did once tackle me about the political angle of the IPCC, suggesting that as we were intergovernmental, we were by our very nature a political body. He felt it would be better if we were a purely scientific body. I argued back that we were in fact an expert scientific body with no political responsibilities, but that a major strength of the IPCC was its intergovernmental nature, because there was global ownership of our work by all governments and scientists of all nationalities. The actual physical climate change problem was global: its recognition needed to be so, as did the solutions. If we had worked in isolation as scientists, we could have come up with good reports but they would never have been seen by anybody. This message had to be discussed in the political arena, and that was a major aim at Rio.

The IPCC felt it imperative to ensure that the most up-to-date science should be available to delegates in Rio. It was to be the biggest such conference ever, attended by over 25,000 people, representing 172 participating governments, and including over 100 heads of state. Getting the very best, very latest information in front of these delegates should help them to agree sensible action. The Science Working Group therefore prepared a 1992 interim report to expand on the 1990 report. This significant-sized document confirmed most of the 1990 report in terms of the influence of greenhouse gases on temperature, although we also included some new material about science that had emerged in the two intervening years.

The Rio Earth Summit took the 1990 IPCC report and the 1992 interim report very seriously. Over several days, the world discussed the scientific case for immediate action, and how we might best tackle the problem. There was a sense of purpose; a belief among politicians and scientists that effective action could and would be agreed. Because of the clear messages about the reality and the nature of likely human-induced climate change, it was possible to discuss clear solutions and to suggest effective measures. It wasn't only politicians who were listening. It was industry, business, and the general public. Everybody, even future opponents, would agree that the IPCC was absolutely crucial in enabling the world to pick up the message. This was the real beginning of the political scene as far as the climate change business was concerned; the possibilities it presented were exciting and challenging.

A major result of the Earth Summit was the United Nations Framework Convention on Climate Change (FCCC), ratified by all participants, including George Bush Senior's American Senate, who ratified it unanimously within a week. This was very important internationally, raising climate change to a high political level. The agreement was that all countries would "take precautionary measures to anticipate, prevent or minimise the causes of climate change and mitigate its adverse effects". Very significantly for the future, they stated, "Where there are threats of irreversible damage, lack of full scientific certainty should not be used as a reason for postponing such measures."

Aside from its apparent impact on the political world, a very important spin-off of the IPCC process has been the creation of a world community of scientists who are really well informed about the climate. This enabled us to move forward again. In 1992, recognizing the vital importance of better observations of all components of the climate system, I led a move to set up what was to become the Global Climate Observing System (GCOS). I remember about five of us getting together over lunch during the World Climate Conference. We wrote our names on the menu at the restaurant, and that was the germ of GCOS. I became the first Chair of its organizing committee, with the task of designing a network of observations adequate for the needs not only of the climate science community but also of the community of national and international policymakers.

GCOS is now a major operation. It is essentially a scientific body, constantly trying to move climate science forward, thereby improving knowledge. It formally brings together all climate observing systems: observations from space; balloons, land stations, ships, marine buoys, aircraft, and from many other sources; observations concerning the atmosphere, the oceans, land surface, ice, vegetation, aerosols, wind, rain, and more. They are all coordinated, checked, calibrated, and recorded under the guidance of GCOS. The work is of an immense scale, and setting it up was a major operation. Such measurements had never been formally coordinated before.

I'm proud of what we set up all those years ago. It's quite remarkable to see how GCOS has developed into a body with an absolutely crucial role. Through bodies such as GCOS and the IPCC, we really are moving ever closer to being able to see the whole of the big picture regarding world climate, as each of its smaller parts becomes clearer. I was disappointed in 2012 when other commitments meant that I was unable to attend a party celebrating the twentieth anniversary of GCOS.

In 1992, after the success of Rio and with the formation of GCOS, it seemed that the world was building up considerable momentum to tackle the problems of climate change. Had agreement made then been firm, formalized, and acted upon, it could have led to effective measures to stabilize CO_2 in the atmosphere. Unfortunately, measures proposed in the Rio declaration, while good, were not binding, and have not been acted upon in the way agreed. CO_2 emissions on a global scale have continued to rise for the last 20 years and stabilization of CO_2 levels in the atmosphere is still a long way away. What could have gone so wrong?

15

THE SECOND IPCC
REPORT 1995

Between the publication of the 1990 report and that of the second report in 1995, my life was as busy as ever. Having had the privilege of being at the forefront of climate science for so many years and, through the IPCC, of having a good grasp of the most recent developments, I felt that I could and should write a textbook presenting the scientific and political situations as clearly and concisely as possible. This led to *Global Warming: The Complete Briefing*.[1] My aim was to write a book aimed at about undergraduate level, in which the science of global warming was both accessible and comprehensive. It also dealt with issues of adaptation and mitigation, as well as touching on moral responsibility and ethical issues.

When the publishers sent the manuscript out to reviewers, the comments they received were positive, as they have usually been ever since. A few reviewers even responded favourably to a chapter in which I referred to my Christian faith and the sense of responsibility it has given me. Only one reviewer objected, asking, "If Houghton believes all this mumbo jumbo, how can we believe his science?" Now about to go into its fifth edition, the book is still selling well. As in that first 1994 edition, the science will be objective and the most up to date available.

Both for my book and in order to do effective work for the IPCC, I had to ensure that I stayed right up to date with scientific progress. This entailed a lot of fascinating work for all of us involved. The early 1990s saw significant advances in some important areas of climate science, three of which were particularly important. First, we now recognized the significant influence of aerosols on the climate, and scientists were working to understand this more fully (see Box 15.1). Secondly, climate modelling capabilities had continued to improve, leading to increasing confidence in predictions. Thirdly, the science concerning the detection of changes in the climate and the attribution of these to different influencing factors had become increasingly robust.

Box 15.1 Aerosols

Aerosols are particles from dust, smoke, sea spray, and many other sources that deliver or create particles within the atmosphere. I have flown over India many times, usually unable to see the land surface even when there is no cloud. What is blocking the light? The answer is aerosols, particularly noticeable over a country like India but also having substantial effects over many areas of the world.

The most significant source globally is from sulphates from burning coal, which form aerosols in the atmosphere that reflect sunlight and tend to cool the earth. Since the 1950s, sulphate aerosols have increased and are most likely the cause of cooling found in global temperature records during the 1950s and 1960s. They continue to mask some of the warming from increased amounts of greenhouse gases.

Because of the polluting effects of aerosols, many industrial nations including China are bringing in controls on their emissions. For sulphate emissions, this implies less masking of the warming effect of greenhouse gases.

By 1995, Manabe's model and other substantial progress in computer modelling were improving our understanding of the factors influencing circulation.[2] Factors such as the reduced negative forcing by aerosols could now be taken into account when making climate predictions. We therefore had greater confidence in these predictions, which still pointed towards significant global temperature increase. Regarding the detection of the temperature increases already occurring, the improved coordination of observations from all sources had produced more firm evidence that the global average temperature had been increasing and was continuing to do so, and we were better able to identify the causes of this.

All of this meant that an ever-growing body of science was becoming available, attracting the attention and interest of more and more scientists, which in turn led to further rapid progress, of which we were all trying to keep abreast. We had to work hard in order to learn quickly and to assimilate all this new knowledge. As we prepared to start work on the second IPCC report, due in 1995, we were deeply immersed in the challenges posed by the advances since 1990.

Beyond science, another very significant change since 1990 was that the Rio Earth Summit had led to a rapid worldwide increase in awareness of the changing climate. Unfortunately, while increased awareness must, on the whole, be a good thing, it had some less positive effects. Besides helping to alert the world to the problems of climate change, the Earth Summit had also awakened the fossil fuel giants, particularly in the USA and in the OPEC countries, most notably Saudi Arabia and Kuwait. As it is very much in the interests of these companies, and in some cases governments, to keep us all dependent on oil, coal, and gas for our energy, so it is against their interests if we become concerned about the consequences of this dependency and try to find alternatives. As any child will tell you, waking a sleeping giant is dangerous, and these particular giants' instincts for self-preservation kicked in straight away, lending them immense drive and commitment. They began to work behind the scenes to discredit both the science and the IPCC. This was the beginning of what has continued to be a systematic, destructive, and dangerous misinformation campaign by giants with loud, scary, and persuasive voices... and lots of money.

At that stage, however, we in the IPCC's Science Working Group were largely unaware of this. Immersed in our science we were just getting on with our job, which was increasingly demanding anyway. We were scheduled to meet in Madrid between 27 and 29 November 1995 to agree our Executive Summary and our Summary for Policymakers. The IPCC process was to be almost identical to that of 1990, but time and experience had led the panel to tighten some of the rules, regulations, and guidelines. This was a positive move, reflecting the serious, official nature of our work. To balance the relationships within the working groups more successfully, each group would now be chaired by two people, one from a developed and one from a developing country.

My co-Chair was to be a Brazilian scientist, Dr Gylvan Meira Filho. A clever man who was delightful to work with, Gylvan is still very active in climate science, particularly in observations from space concerning the destruction of the Amazon rainforest and its effect on climate. He was to prove an excellent colleague: our abilities complemented each other. We shared between us the chairing of meetings, Gylvan chairing the more formal meetings while I chaired the longer debates. I also oversaw liaison with the TSU: a sensible and pragmatic way forward given my strong relationship with them.

Following the same process as the previous assessment, the chapter groups began their work preparing for Madrid, agonizing to assess and explain as clearly as possible just what the scientific evidence was saying. The task of getting the chapters consistent and correct was a tough one; tougher than last time. Although I was perhaps vaguely aware that oil-producing companies and countries wouldn't take any threat to their influence and to their wealth lying down, I could never have guessed the lengths to which they would eventually be prepared to go to protect their own interests. While they were preparing their plans, we continued meeting the challenges of carrying out the science and setting up the meetings for the second IPCC report.

Consistent with the IPCC process, governments and their delegates had received the drafted chapters about six to eight weeks ahead of the Madrid meeting and had been able to register their comments. The Summary for Policymakers had been prepared and we were ready to go through it line by line. We would, I was sure, be able to say a great deal more about the human impact on climate, and with a great deal more certainty than in 1990. To reflect the importance of this and other scientific advances, I had ambitious plans for a more detailed summary. Certain that we should produce a more detailed Executive Summary and Summary for Policymakers, I felt optimistic about what we might achieve in our three days in Madrid. I wasn't underestimating the difficult scientific discussions ahead: there would be more scientists and more material than in 1990, and not only was the science more complex, but we were more exposed. There was no doubt that differences in emphasis or interpretation would arise, and that scientific discussion would be thorough and complex. I was looking forward to the challenge.

However, there were to be some difficulties I did underestimate. I do not think I could have foreseen the effectiveness and the formidable organizational powers of those with vested interests. Led by the American giant ExxonMobil and the American coal industry, they had come together to form the euphemistically named Global Climate Coalition (GCC). Other contributing members of this GCC represented associated industries just as likely to suffer from emission restrictions; there were manufacturers of chemicals, automobiles, tyres, paper, and more. As an NGO, the GCC was permitted to attend IPCC meetings, alongside groups with an opposing viewpoint such as the Worldwide Fund for Nature and Greenpeace. This balance was important, and we had to be fair to all groups. The GCC's ostensible aim was to bring honesty and reliability into the climate change debate by ensuring the objectivity of the IPCC process. They were keen to ensure that the IPCC did not overstate the case against fossil fuels. There is no doubt that their questions and comments did in fact force us to consider carefully the wording of the report, resulting in a more accurate final product. However, I believe that their primary motivation was to protect certain financial and political interests.

A group very similar and closely related to the GCC was the Climate Council, represented by an American called Don Pearlman. An authoritative figure with a deep, impressive voice, Pearlman was a lawyer in a Washington legal and lobbying firm with the almost Dickensian name of Patton Boggs. Tremendously, admirably dedicated to his task, he quickly proved himself a formidable adversary. In preparation for the meeting, Pearlman had evidently gone through the draft with a lawyer's fine-tooth comb. His arguments were well prepared and he knew how to present them. Even then, it was clear that the GCC and Pearlman were working closely with Kuwait and Saudi Arabia. In fact, some of the reports we received in advance of the meeting from the Saudi government were written on GCC headed notepaper. They hadn't even bothered to change the document in any way; it was exactly as they had received it themselves. It was laughable really – disturbing, but laughable.

During the Madrid meeting, neither the delegates nor Pearlman tried to hide this connection. Pearlman was like a puppet-master pulling people's strings. Inevitably, there would be delegates within the meeting who would take notice of him. He hired a room close to our meeting, into which I believe he invited those delegates who might be persuaded most easily towards his point of view. He made his presence and his influence very clear during the three days in Madrid. Far from operating covertly, he would move among the delegates throughout the day, handing them notes and talking closely with them.

The first day of the meeting was slow, as is usual with such meetings. We scientists were trying to get things absolutely right, which led to great deliberation. We also needed to break into smaller working parties to consider different chapters before coming together again, all of which took time. However, this conscientious dialogue between committed scientists was not entirely to blame for the slow progress. The energy and commitment those mentioned above devoted to their work during all three days caused prolonged debates, which I had not foreseen, but it was important to let everybody have their say.

I have the privilege of having access to a transcript of the Madrid meeting, which I use to remind myself from time to time of the problems we faced, and which enables me to use here some of the words that were actually spoken, rather than relying upon my memory. During the first day of the meeting, the lead authors gave short presentations about their chapters. We then set up working groups to go through parts of the summary, ensuring that everything was in place for us to proceed efficiently when we reconvened the whole meeting. It should have been quite straightforward, and Gylvan and I were quite determined that discussion should stay within its allocated time.

However, when we eventually closed the first day's meeting just a little later than planned, we had not covered as much ground as I had intended. I told the meeting that I would consider our rate of progress overnight. That evening, I wondered whether my aim of producing a more detailed Executive Summary might prove unrealistic.

Of course, the majority of the discussion over the three days was absolutely essential and very helpful, but there were other moments when we lost valuable time. The Saudi delegate made the reasonable suggestion that the titles of the various sections within the report should be presented as questions rather than statements, as had been the case in the 1990 report. This gave rise to a short discussion in which delegates from the UK, USA, Tanzania, Norway, France, Australia, Germany, Canada,

Zimbabwe, India, Belgium, and Italy argued that questions would weaken the document. As the delegate from the United States said: "We are here to provide information and answers to policy-makers, not to pose rhetorical questions." They were right: questions, even rhetorical ones, would be weaker than statements. The Kuwaiti delegate's comment, "We agree with what was said by the Saudis", became a frequently repeated refrain. That particular point about the nature of the titles was debated at what I consider now to have been unnecessary length, until we agreed to stick with statements. Still dissatisfied, the Saudi delegate tried unsuccessfully to raise the point again on a subsequent day.

Deciding between questions and statements was child's play compared with the discussions ahead. It became quite evident on Day One that many of our problems were to centre on what was to prove a highly controversial chapter: Chapter 8. An extremely important chapter, it dealt with the detection of climate change and the attribution of its causes. The significant progress in detection and attribution since 1990 meant that there was now considerably more to say. In 1990 we had not claimed that there had been any significant detection of human-induced climate change in the scientific record. In fact, we had stated that unequivocal detection of human-induced climate change was "not likely for a decade or more".

However, by 1995, some evidence was already emerging. There was great scientific interest in the question of the extent to which any climate change we had seen was attributable to human influence. Through solely scientific debate, we were looking for honest answers to difficult questions. What truth was the scientific record showing us? This question was at the very core of the discussions ahead.

The lead author of Chapter 8 was Dr Ben Santer, an atmospheric physicist at California's Lawrence Livermore Laboratory. Ben is an excellent scientist and a lovely man. In what was to prove a terrible problem for Ben, while the science of Chapter 8 was thorough and sound, the draft hadn't yet been put together consistently from an editorial point of view. For instance there were two summaries, one at the beginning and one at the end, and the two didn't quite say the same things. It was in this unpolished form that it had been sent to delegates and governments. This really was a shame and, not surprisingly, many governments had commented extensively and helpfully on this chapter in writing before the meeting. Some asked for the chapter to be revised editorially before the working group could accept it. This was clearly necessary. The instructions as to how this should be done were agreed at various stages during the meeting. The US government in particular made many constructive comments.

Unfortunately, just as a crack in a bucket will always be found by the water within, so a weakness had become evident in the IPCC's work, a weakness that was later to be exploited. I have no complaints about the fact that mistakes and weaknesses were pointed out: that was the purpose of the meeting. The problem came later when the "crack" was incorrectly used to raise doubts about the credibility of the IPCC, and the unfortunate Ben Santer was in the firing line. The full extent of that problem was in the future. At the Madrid meeting, the regrettable inconsistency in Ben's chapter made it harder to express exactly what the science was showing.

This was a scientific problem, not a political one, and of course we had to sort it out. It was, after all, a scientific meeting in which science and the presentation of science were to be discussed. Accordingly, most governments had sent scientists to represent them in Madrid. The Saudi Arabian government, however, had sent a lawyer instead: a very good lawyer. Mohammed Al-Sabban, like many of his profession and just like Don Pearlman, was very clever with the intricacy of words.

The GCC's best bet was to play down the importance of any of Ben's evidence and cast doubt upon its reliability. If they could do this, they would win a significant battle. And so, with Pearlman's help, some of the delegates set to work on the structure and wording of Chapter 8. Their central strategy seemed to be to ensure that the levels of certainty expressed in the document were as low as possible. After our experience in writing the previous report, we had a system of indicating the balance between certainty and scientific judgment: a system which most delegates considered fit for purpose. We were well equipped for dealing with levels of uncertainty.

Ben Santer presented very clearly all the results of the relevant experiments and climate models, and explained the conclusions to which these pointed. I think he was right when he said that the chapter's conclusions erred on the side of caution, and that "stronger statements could have been made if you look at the totality of the evidence". He continued:

... there are uncertainties in our estimates of natural climate change variability, but the best information that we have suggests that there is a human component to be observed in the changes we have seen. That evidence comes not only from these statistical detection studies but also from our physical understanding of the climate system and the evidence paints a coherent picture.

Ben's chapter summary did not in any way shy away from acknowledging the existing uncertainties. However, not everybody felt that it went far enough. The first sentence for contention began, in its draft form: "More convincing evidence for the attribution of a human effect on climate change is emerging from pattern based studies..." The Kuwaiti delegate requested that the first three words be altered to "Some preliminary evidence...". This phrase, actually borrowed from another part of the report was not unreasonable, but in this instance it would place a misleading emphasis on the fact that the science was still in its early stages, implying thereby that little was known. Although the Kuwaiti proposal found little support in the meeting, it still led to prolonged debate.

After 90 minutes discussing this one point, we eventually settled, for the time being at least, upon "More convincing recent evidence...". This discussion of "preliminary" versus "convincing" would itself occupy 12 pages of transcript when the meeting was converted to paper.

Later in the chapter, we came across a similar sentence, which was to cause similar problems. In its draft form, the sentence read: "The balance of evidence suggests human influence on global climate." Again, we embarked upon a careful, very detailed scientific debate in our endeavour to achieve the most accurate and truthful statement we could find. None of the words we discussed seemed quite right. Al-Sabban argued that "balance of evidence" was far too strong.

The ensuing debate lasted well over an hour, during which various alternatives were proposed including *balance, weight,* and *preponderance*. Not only did we all struggle over how to describe as honestly as possible the evidence, we also had to agree on what this evidence actually did. Did it *indicate* or *suggest* that the climate is influenced by human activity? Not surprisingly, Kuwait and Saudi Arabia argued for *suggests*, which carries less conviction. Although Ben was prepared to accept *suggests*, he wasn't particularly happy. He felt that it was the "lowest common denominator word". He said that stronger statements "would be justified on the basis of the science and we feel that *the balance of evidence* and the use of the word *suggests* is a compromise solution to deal with the concerns of the Saudi Arabian and the Kuwaiti delegations and some of the NGO comments". Throughout all of this, our concern was to get the presentation of the science absolutely right.

However, the Saudis still weren't satisfied. Still on the same sentence, they and some others wanted to insert an adjective to quantify the level of human influence on climate, keen once again to emphasize uncertainty; this time that humans were having any significant influence on the climate. One of the lead authors argued that the human signal emerging was sufficiently large and distinct to be described as *sizeable*. We discussed using *appreciable*, *detectable*, *identifiable*, and *measurable*. Keen not to exaggerate, we were equally anxious to be honest. We settled eventually on *appreciable*. Or so we thought.

Most delegates agreed with Ben's preference for stronger statements. There was a great deal of concern that over-emphasizing the uncertainties was as bad as exaggerating, in that it would fail to present accurately the science and, worse still, might fail to say anything at all. Bert Bolin, in a rare interjection, pointed out that

> **if we pile a lot of uncertainties on top of each other it may look like very little is certain. I think it's really important to make clear that there are remaining uncertainties and they do indeed need to be addressed but it does not detract from the kind of results that we have presented here.**

Another contributing author said, "I think we need a couple of sentences to turn this back around to the level of concern that we're expressing here." Predictably, Greenpeace and the Worldwide Fund for Nature agreed, arguing that the existing text, if it had any fault, was not strong enough. They felt that the available science justified a more strongly worded text. In truth, so did I. Stephen Schneider, another scientist in Ben's chapter group, tried to clarify our role by drawing a helpful analogy of a GP having to diagnose a patient without access to a blood test or an X-ray. The GP would assess a collection of symptoms pointing to a certain syndrome, based upon which they might have to make a life or death decision, using their expertise and experience to make the best judgment of the evidence available. Like GPs, we were experts in our fields, and our judgment would be valid, as long as we were clear upon what evidence it was based. Similar in essence to my weather forecasting analogy, this helped to vindicate our discussion, but it still didn't provide the precise wording we needed.

As the end of the second day approached, I was concerned about all the material we still had to get through before the end of the day, never mind the end of the week. We had to find a way through these discussions. I suggested that we form a small working group to meet that evening to redraft one part of Chapter 8, based upon the day's discussion. Of course, the group would be led by Ben Santer. Keen to achieve a balance of opinion within the group, I invited the Netherlands, New Zealand, Kuwait, Canada, and Kenya to contribute. Mohammed Al-Sabban immediately offered to join, tipping the balance to the extent that I commented upon it, and asked the UK to join too. The USA offered to add to the number. I advised the group, "We must not, because we're frightened of what people might do to us, chicken out of saying what we believe is correct and accurate and sensible." I advised that the statements should not be so over-cautious that we ended up with a statement that didn't really do justice to the scientific evidence.

Having finalized the members of the working group and charged them with considering this point, I took the opportunity to remind them of something fundamental to their discussion:

We are here as a scientific body. This is a scientific document… comments must not be influenced by political motivation of any kind whatsoever. So the group has a very strong instruction – as indeed we all have in this meeting – to make sure that what we say is scientifically accurate, and uninfluenced by the sort of political concerns people have here. We have to try to put those on one side.

Our job was to inform honestly and accurately.

Important though it was to qualify and quantify as accurately as possible the human impact on climate, we needed to move forward.

We were all concerned. I could not suppress my smile when, at one point during the meeting, Al-Sabban suggested limiting the number of contributions delegates could make. I had to point out to him the irony of his suggestion. Should it be accepted, he would certainly find himself being constrained in some of our discussions in ways that he would not wish. Fortunately, Al-Sabban was, on the whole, a good-humoured man, so even the most awkward of exchanges could be handled with a smile. He was just doing the job he had been assigned to do.

There were similar moments throughout the three days when I was able to point out some arguments on behalf of the Saudi delegation, to the extent that Al-Sabban laughingly suggested I should be awarded honorary Saudi citizenship. This was a joke to which we both returned on several occasions, so much so that it possibly wore a bit thin, but it helped prevent people's patience wearing thin. There would be times on the third and final day when I would be grateful for any such opportunities to defuse the increasingly tense atmosphere.

Another significant point of contention was how we should describe the progress made in measuring and modelling the changing climate during the last five years. There had been progress – that was an irrefutable fact – but how much? During the meeting, delegates referred to this progress as *significant*,[3] *substantial*,[4] and *nothing short of stunning*.[5] However, we could not agree which adjective to use in the report. We seemed to be settling upon describing the progress as "considerable", even though most delegates felt that even this was a compromise, arguing that the statement could have been much stronger. However, in contrast to this, Al-Sabban wanted the word "considerable" removed completely, which would have weakened the sentence still further. Ben disagreed. After further wrangling, Al-Sabban addressed me in a friendly manner, but there was criticism in his words. "Mr Chairman," he said, "maybe instead of the word *considerable* we can use the word *shocking*. *Shocking progress*. Maybe that will satisfy most of our lead authors. But to be serious, Mr Chairman, *considerable* is a compromise and we go along with the compromise given that the word *shocking* may appear… this shows how flexible we are."

"Or how shocked you are, perhaps," I answered jokingly.

Al-Sabban looked across at Ben and smiled. "I can see that the lead author is laughing – finally, he's laughing."

"I think we're all laughing," I replied. But the laughter sounded rather weary. It had more to do with relief than with amusement. Unfortunately, the progress we were making was far from considerable, and certainly not shocking in a positive way.

Throughout the first two long days, we struggled on. I struggled on, probably clinging for too long to my plans for a more detailed Executive Summary and Summary for Policymakers, because that kind of obstinacy is a character trait of mine. In retrospect, I should have realized earlier that we weren't going fast enough to get through the material. Alone in my room at the end of Day Two, as I looked back on the day, I could see how effective Pearlman, the GCC, and the Climate Council had been. I had to think long and hard about how we might avoid the very real danger of a failed meeting. I saw a possible way through. I must have discussed the matter with Bert Bolin and others. I thought perhaps a practical way of getting through the final day's work would be if I reduced my ambitions for the Executive Summary, thereby making the document a little less unwieldy.

On Day Three, I put forward a proposal in which I relinquished my hopes for a longer Executive Summary. In the interest of completing the report, we all agreed to a pragmatic revision of the structure. We agreed to turn the Policymakers' Summary as it stood into a Technical Summary, which was written by the lead authors and didn't have to be agreed by the whole meeting. What I had intended to be the Executive Summary then became the Policymakers' Summary, which we all had to agree. There was no need for an additional Executive Summary. I felt a little disappointed with this compromise of my vision, but it proved to be the right thing to do. Interestingly, this new structure was to be used again in the Third and Fourth IPCC Reports.

By now, tired delegates were susceptible to tension as we continued to race against the clock without compromising the accuracy of the report. Ben's redrafting group had met as instructed. Working late into the night, they had endeavoured to consider carefully every single one of the concerns raised during the day, using them to improve the clarity and the accuracy of the chapter. But Al-Sabban was still not happy. He now complained that some of his comments had been "completely ignored" by the small group.

When he responded, Ben's voice was tight with restrained exasperation. The group had indeed met, but with one noticeable absence. "It was one of the most important sections of the document," said Ben. "I feel it would have been incumbent on at least one member of your delegation to attend." Having offered their help, the Saudi delegation had failed to send a representative to the meeting; now they complained about the results. In their defence, they argued that they were a small delegation, and that they had other meetings to attend. They tried to deflect the criticism, saying, "We are not here trying to say who has done what. We're not engaging in personal debate." Nevertheless, they had not played the part they had offered to play.

In response to continued criticism, Ben argued, "We have been charged with evaluating the balance of evidence and reaching a decision." He voiced his concern that too many compromises had weakened his document to such an extent that it no longer reflected what the scientists truly believed. Al-Sabban saw an opportunity to pounce. He was now really playing his lawyer's games, casting unnecessary doubt and piling unnecessary pressure upon Ben:

I felt very sorry to hear from the lead author that he is saying that this concluding summary is not a reflection of science. What is it if it is not a reflection

> **of science? And I'm very sorry to hear that from a prominent scientist like the lead author.**

This trick was unkind. I had to allow Ben to respond, which he did with considerable feeling:

> **The concluding section of Chapter 8 goes out of its way to stress the uncertainties... Now, if you want me to say that I'm stupid then I'm saying that here. The things that we wrote regarding quantification were attempts to be very, very cautious. I believe that those statements are no longer justifiable.**

He spoke of the diligent work of the hundreds of scientists who had contributed to and deliberated over the chapter.

To return to a more formal procedure and to restore a more cooperative atmosphere, I opened the floor to other contributors. They spoke unanimously in support of Ben, saying that he had done a "tremendous job".[6] The US delegate's words were particularly strong:

> **We believe that, if anything, the authors have bent over backwards to be conservative. In our judgement, and in the judgement of many scientists we have talked to in the US scientific community, this is a very conservative document... Our objection, if anything, would be that we've weakened the document too much.**

Denmark agreed, saying the documents were now a "compromise". He meant that we had compromised some of our certainty for something weaker.

The Saudis and the Kuwaitis continued in their efforts to introduce more and more expressions of uncertainty into the report. For example, when we wrote *these studies...*, they wanted to add the qualifier *which have very large caveats...* Similarly, when the text referred to *natural variability*, they wanted to add *assuming that the model estimates of variability were realistic*, and even when the text spoke of uncertainties, they wanted to describe them as *large uncertainties*. Each one of their points had to be addressed, which was all very time-consuming.

We had now reached lunchtime on the final day. Certain that we would not complete our work by the scheduled finishing time of 7 p.m., I had to consider the possibility of continuing into the night, for which I would need not only the agreement of the delegations and the interpreters, but extended hospitality from the conference centre. I managed to gain agreement from all parties, and we continued. Things didn't get much easier during the afternoon, and by dinner time it was clear that we couldn't afford time for a break. We allowed ourselves a few minutes to pop out for sandwiches. Everybody was remarkably cooperative. We really didn't want to give up or fail.

We were still having problems reaching agreement over specific words, with the Saudis bringing up previous bones of contention that the rest of us considered to have been settled. They and Kuwait were still unhappy with the use of "convincing evidence" rather than "preliminary". Bert Bolin offered what seemed to be the only way to break this deadlock. Eventually, it was agreed by all parties that a footnote should be included in the report, stating that Saudi Arabia and Kuwait dissented from the majority view. The World Meteorological Organization, whose rules and guidelines we were following, had precedents for this, so it was accepted as a solution – for the time being.

As the evening progressed, our numbers gradually dwindled as delegates left for their flights. The interpreters had kindly agreed to stay until 9 p.m. instead of 7 p.m., but when 9 p.m. arrived we were nowhere near finished. I really thought we were in trouble. Fortunately, no delegation objected to continuing in English only. They certainly could have objected, and I really thought somebody would, but they didn't, for which I was grateful.

Nevertheless, this meant that we couldn't address more complicated things. Besides, we were no longer sure that we had a quorum. The US delegate voiced his concern that, some of the delegates already having left to catch their flights, we might be facing a procedural problem. Not surprisingly, Al-Sabban agreed: "I think it is appropriate if we take a decision not to continue in this." Somehow, and with the cooperation of people I feared might choose not to cooperate, we agreed to continue.

Later in the evening, Saudi Arabia and Kuwait returned to the matter of being named as dissenters in the report. They really didn't want to be named, arguing instead for a comment such as "some countries" had dissenting views. Other delegates didn't like this at all. They would not like to be mistakenly identified as having a view opposite to the one they held. The US delegate was particularly, and correctly, adamant about this. In order to settle this particular matter, we needed to know exactly what the WMO rules stated. Bert Bolin offered to look into it, so we deferred the matter until the Rome IPCC meeting.

In due course, Bert was able to consult with WMO before we all met again in Rome. They confirmed that dissenting countries had to be identified in the footnotes. Bert wrote to explain this to delegates. Rather interestingly, the response of Saudi Arabia and Kuwait was to withdraw their footnote completely. If you hold a view strongly, why be ashamed to put your name to it?

Still in Madrid, we continued to work towards completing our document. Tired though we were, I felt uplifted by the process through which we had worked and the problems which together we had surmounted. The Saudis returned once again to how to describe the level of human influence on the global climate. David Warrilow, the UK delegate, spoke quietly to Bert Bolin, who then proposed David's suggested word *discernible* to the meeting. It was not generally considered permissible to go back later in a meeting to a decision made earlier, so it was appropriate that Bert, with his authority as IPCC Chair, should make this suggestion. It was met with grateful applause.

David Warrilow had saved the day. The contentious sentence now read: *The balance of evidence suggests a discernible human influence on global climate.* It's a good sentence: a positive result of rigorous debate.

Even at this late stage, Al-Sabban was proving to be indefatigable. He now seemed to be trying to make the whole thing into a game, offering to trade favour for favour, for example saying he would concede on one point if we would let another be used. I had to remind him that this was not a competition. "I'm keeping no score sheet," I said. "... The object is to get a balanced, good scientific document... It's not about whether or not we've managed to score points."

Very late in the proceedings, I noticed Don Pearlman walk across to Al-Sabban with a piece of paper. I can still see it in my mind's eye. They went into an intense huddle over whatever the issue was. I held my breath. Would this next obstacle be the one to break us? When I saw Al-Sabban shake his head quite vigorously I sighed with relief. "Wonderful!" I thought. "Wonderful! We've been saved that particular problem." In the end we finished at about 12.20 a.m. The building was due to close at half past. Looking back, it was a stimulating and exciting time, but we had come within a hair's breadth of failure.

I said at the beginning of this chapter that the challenge of presenting the science accurately, honestly, and clearly would have been difficult anyway. The GCC and OPEC delegates were not solely responsible for the problems we encountered, nor, in the end, did they succeed in weakening the report. The day after the meeting closed, I sat and read through the whole Summary for Policymakers and the Technical Summary. I was amazed. Despite all the problems, the report had actually come through as a much better document, because the painstaking process had made it clearer, and in many ways stronger. I reflected at the time and still maintain that we can attribute some of this success to Don Pearlman and delegates such as those from Kuwait and Saudi Arabia. Their attention to detail in pointing out weaknesses that really did need to be addressed had helped to make the report more accurate and more consistent than it might otherwise have been. Whatever their motivation, the result of their actions was more constructive than destructive. Wonderful.

The meeting might have been over, but our work on the document was not yet complete. The alterations decided and approved by the meeting still needed to be written up in full. It was upon the understanding that this was to happen that Ben's chapter had been accepted by the meeting. Ben and his group would have to revise their chapter in the light of the instructions given during the last three days. They would have to take into account all of the agreements we had reached. Ben would need support from both me and the TSU, and I as Chair would have to approve the alterations made. Unfortunately, the IPCC plenary meeting that would formally accept our work was scheduled to take place in just under three weeks. Because of the careful thought needed, it would not be possible to get all of the required alterations into Ben's chapter before the plenary, so we decided that I would report this fact to the plenary meeting, and we would, in the meantime, work on the chapter with the best possible speed without compromising its accuracy.

In describing the 1995 Madrid meeting of the IPCC Science Working Group I have concentrated on the debate that occurred in plenary sessions on Chapter 8 regarding the extent to which climate change due to human activities had yet been observed. A large proportion of the plenary sessions was taken up with this. Considerations of the other chapters in the report took place in smaller sessions of representative groups of delegates often meeting in parallel with the plenary sessions. The draft contributions from these groups to the summary document were then presented to the plenary for approval and took little of the plenary's time compared with the very lengthy debates on Chapter 8. The main conclusions of the final report are summarized in Box 15.2.

Box 15.2 Summary of the 1995 IPCC Science Working Group Report

There were two main conclusions of the 1995 report additional to those of the 1990 report. First, that the growing influence of aerosols in the atmosphere, in particular sulphate aerosols from burning coal, is leading to a cooling that is offsetting some, perhaps up to one-third, of the warming due to greenhouse gases. The second conclusion was that as the expected "signal" from human influence on climate begins to emerge from the "noise" of natural variability, the meeting was able to agree that "The balance of evidence suggests that there is a discernible human influence on global climate".

That memorable 1995 meeting in Madrid has since been identified by *Nature* magazine as one of ten "Meetings that Changed the World".[7] It was a significant step on the road from Rio to Kyoto. Had the science not come through unscathed, the integrity of the IPCC would have been seriously questioned, and governments would have faltered on taking urgent action on climate change, such as the signing of the 1997 Kyoto Protocol.

But not all of the fall-out from that meeting was positive. For Ben Santer, the trouble had only just begun.

16

DIRTY TACTICS

While I was pleased with what we had finally achieved in Madrid, there was still some work to be done tucking it all up into bed ready for the IPCC Rome Plenary in two weeks. Most of it, I was confident, could be tucked up quite cosily, but we would have to leave the troublesome Chapter 8 untucked for the time being, toes still sticking out.

We were duty and honour-bound to change the chapter, but we had made the decision not to rush it just to be ready for Rome. So what should we, or could we, put forward in Rome? What would be the best way to present and explain the situation? I wasn't particularly worried. The obvious decision was to include the unaltered draft of Chapter 8 in our report to Rome, so that the whole picture could be seen by the IPCC. However, I would make it very clear at the meeting that the careful editing demanded by the Working Group 1 meeting in Madrid meant that the draft could in no way be accepted as final. This seemed to be the sensible way forward in the imperfect circumstances. There shouldn't be a problem.

Accordingly, I went to Rome, where I reported to the whole meeting in the proper way that the available version of Chapter 8 was not and could not be the final version, and that further editing was needed to remove inconsistencies as instructed by the Madrid meeting before final publication in March. This was all crystal clear to everybody present. But unfortunately, we did not actually label the chapter with a big sticker saying "This is preliminary" or "Some revisions are still to be incorporated according to the meeting". Unfortunately, nothing was actually written on the report to suggest that it was not a final version. This was my big mistake. It allowed a weakness that could be exploited by Don Pearlman and his allies and was therefore to have serious repercussions. However, these future problems were as yet unforeseen, and the IPCC plenary in Rome was satisfied to accept our report on this basis. It was accepted in its revised form in prospect, providing we made the changes as agreed in Madrid.

As well as having been present in the Madrid meeting, Donald Pearlman attended the Rome plenary and therefore heard my remarks about changes and approvals still being necessary. Even if he hadn't been in Rome, he would have known this to be the case, having been very alert throughout that difficult Madrid meeting. Knowing his attention to detail, and his diligent approach to his work, I don't for a minute doubt that he took in every word that I said. After all, he prided himself upon such professionalism and thoroughness. And yet, it would appear, Don set to work preparing his anti-IPCC media blast. He knew that he could make a story out of the fact that the printed final version would be different. His ammunition was the difference, not any lack of clarity. He could see an opportunity to accuse the IPCC of major fraud.

In their book *Merchants of Doubt*, which gives eye-opening information about the scientists behind the attack which was to follow (of whom more later), Naomi Oreskes and Erik M. Conway accurately describe Ben Santer as "one of the world's most distinguished scientists – the recipient of the 1998 MacArthur 'genius' award and numerous prizes and distinctions from his employer, the US Department of Energy." They also say that he is "of moderate temperament, of moderate political persuasions... very modest, soft-spoken and almost self-effacing".[1] Again, this is all true. Furthermore, Ben is a man of utmost integrity with an impeccable scientific record. He carried out his alterations to Chapter 8 exactly as required by the Madrid meeting and within all the procedural guidelines.

On 12 June the storm hit with full force. Somebody alerted me to an article in the *Wall Street Journal* entitled "A Major Deception on Global Warming".[2] I immediately logged on to my computer and found the article. I couldn't believe what I read. In a shocking piece of writing, an American scientist, Dr Frederick Seitz, damned the whole IPCC process. It was a determined and potentially effective effort to kill the IPCC. It was also a terrible piece of journalism. Seitz began by stating, perfectly accurately, that the credibility of the IPCC rested upon our meticulous peer review process. Then, within the same paragraph, he wrote, "I have never witnessed a more disturbing corruption of the peer review process than the events that led to this IPCC Report." Within the same paragraph, he also took the trouble to list his own credentials, so that his opinion would be taken seriously. He wanted readers to recognize that these were the opinions of a credible scientist.

Indeed, Seitz, who died in 2008, had impressive credentials. An eminent physicist, in the 1960s he had been president of the American National Academy of Sciences. But he was never a climate scientist, and he played no part in the IPCC process. Alongside his science, Seitz had a history of other allegiances and priorities. From 1979 to 1985 he was very active in working for the R.J. Reynolds Tobacco Company in refuting the science behind claims that smoking and passive smoking could damage health. Asserting his scientific status, but ignoring his scientific integrity, he had also been vociferous in his denial of the effects of acid rain and denial of the effects of chlorofluorocarbons on the ozone layer. On all of these topics he had considerable influence on American public policy.

Among his several influential positions, Seitz was founder and subsequently Chairman of the Board of Directors of the George C.

Marshall Institute from 1984 to 2001, the years spanning this attack on Ben. Originally Reagan's think tank on the Strategic Defense Initiative, the Institute had, by 1989, turned its attention to climate change scepticism, where it was very effective. Seitz was an influential man with important contacts in the media and in Washington DC, including the White House. It wasn't difficult for him to get his message heard. Any forward momentum on tackling global warming in George Bush Senior's administration faltered after the presentation of the George C. Marshall Institute's 1989 report.

Interestingly, later, in 1998, apparently without a sense of self-irony, Seitz headed an article misleadingly designed to look like a National Academy of Science report, which claimed that CO_2 poses no threat to climate. None of the science was peer-reviewed, and serious doubt has since been cast over the scientific credentials of the 15,000 alleged "scientists" who had signed it. The National Academy of Science immediately disowned the report. In *Merchants of Doubt*, Oreskes and Conway argue that Seitz and others are "science-speaking mercenaries".[3] It is an apt description, although I wouldn't go as far as to accuse him of being motivated solely by money, and neither do they. I suspect his drive arose from a belief in free-market capitalism, which he might have felt was being threatened by what he mistakenly saw as liberally motivated science.

So, this was the man who now, in the name of science, was attempting to discredit the IPCC. He based his argument upon Chapter 8, comparing the report presented in Rome with the eventual published report. Citing some of the sentences removed from the Rome draft version, he publicly named and accused Ben Santer of deceiving policymakers and the public "into believing that the scientific evidence shows human activities are causing global warming". He wrongly claimed that the report presented in Rome was the approved consensus report, and that the report published in 1996 had been fundamentally altered by Ben without any consensus at all. In fact, Seitz's ally, Fred Singer, suggested in the *Washington Times* that I had prevailed upon Ben to make the changes.[4] Of course, both Seitz and Singer were quite wrong: all the changes had been demanded by the whole meeting without dissention. The conclusion Seitz then drew from his flawed argument was that "it would be best to abandon the IPCC process, or at least that part that is concerned with the scientific evidence on climate change".

We were all upset and angered by this article, particularly by its unfair attack on Ben. That same day, Ben wrote to all of the report's lead authors and to all contributors to Chapter 8. As he said in the letter,[5] he was "very troubled" and "deeply upset" by the implication that he was personally responsible for the alleged corruption, and feared that Seitz's article might have the effect of marginalizing the excellent science in the rest of the report. This, he said, "would be the biggest tragedy of all". After a paragraph strongly refuting any claim Seitz might have to scientific credibility on the subject, Ben wrote:

> **In short, Dr Seitz does not have the technical competence to judge whether there was or was not good scientific justification for the changes made to Chapter 8. He made absolutely no attempt to obtain the facts regarding IPCC procedural rules, and no attempt to ascertain who had made changes to Chapter 8 and why such changes were made.**
>
> **Science is intimately bound up with the exercise of critical judgment. Dr Seitz failed to exercise critical judgment, and failed to behave as a responsible scientist should. He obtained only one side of the story – the opinions espoused by the GCC – and accepted those opinions as being immutable fact. I believe that Dr Seitz's behaviour is a disgrace to the august scientific bodies he once represented.**

Ben was clearly finding it difficult not to be affected personally by the article. He rightly said that there was now a "concerted attack" on both the IPCC and his own reputation as a scientist, which was proving distressing and destructive to him and his family. He justifiably felt that he was being "taken out as a scientist" by "powerful interests". He was right. It was absolutely terrible.

The IPCC needed to speak in support of Ben and indeed of our own integrity and credibility. I wrote a letter to the *Wall Street Journal*, which was signed by Bert Bolin, by Gylvan, and by me. Our first sentence stated unequivocally that Seitz's article was "completely without foundation". We pointed out the fundamental error in Seitz's evidence, suggesting that, had he taken the trouble to consult us prior to writing, he would have known this. Offering a clear explanation of events concerning Chapter 8, we stressed that the report had been

carefully and honestly crafted to explain our understanding of the uncertainties and to express clearly the scientific basis for the conclusions stated in the Summary for Policy Makers, namely that our ability to quantify the human influence on global climate is currently very limited...

Making use of the sentence that had been the result of so much debate in Madrid, we reasserted that "the balance of evidence suggests that there is a discernible human influence on global climate." It had turned out to be a very good sentence.

However, when the *Wall Street Journal* printed our letter on 25 June, they edited out all of the above. They printed only one paragraph, which again threw the focus upon Ben and made our defence of him and of the IPCC seem more personal than scientific. On the same date, the *Wall Street Journal* carried a letter from Ben himself. In this instance, they included much more of the letter, which was a credit to Ben. However, they deleted the paragraph in which Ben pointed out that Seitz had failed to contact any IPCC officials to check his facts. More significantly, they omitted the entire list of 40 distinguished climate scientists who had been happy to add their names to Ben's letter. It might have appeared to the *Wall Street Journal* reader that Ben was on his own, and that the IPCC had issued nothing more than a personally supportive letter.

The *Wall Street Journal* is a phenomenally influential paper. Seitz's report was followed the next day by an item in the *New York Times*.[6] This article was much more balanced, quoting explanations from both Ben and me. I think my indignation was evident in my cited comment that Seitz's article hadn't "any basis in fact at all", and that such contentions were "just rubbish". However, the paper allowed Seitz the opportunity to respond to our comments. "Heavens, no!" he insisted, maintaining that the report had been "arbitrarily modified" for "public purposes".

On the whole, the balance of evidence suggested that there was a discernible Pearlman influence on the media climate – to borrow a phrase. I suspect that Seitz's misinformation about the proceedings surrounding Chapter 8 came to him directly from Pearlman. Pearlman certainly wasn't keeping quiet. In fact, in May 1996, Ben had presented his chapter to the American Meteorological Society on Capitol Hill, where Pearlman (note his presence at such a meeting) accused him of "secretly altering the IPCC report, suppressing dissent by other scientists and eliminating references to scientific uncertainties". Ben has since described Pearlman "screaming at me" and said that he kept "following me around".[7] Was he trying to intimidate Ben?

This was just the beginning of a relentless campaign against Ben. The GCC continued to harass him and tried to destroy him. They were very nasty. I spoke to Ben frequently at that time. I felt quite strongly that if the GCC insisted on going for anyone, it ought to be me, because I had been in charge of the meeting and the process. The attacks should never have been on Ben. I actually sent a message to that effect to Don Pearlman, but to no avail.

Ben had a terrible time of it. Not only was so much of his time taken up with the controversy arising from the article that his research began to suffer, but he even had some of his research funding withdrawn. Ben's a very sensitive fellow, but even a tough nut would have found it very hard to handle this battle of words by such powerful bodies accusing him of incompetence and dishonesty.

In the end, the American Meteorological Society, along with the University Corporation for Atmospheric Research, published a substantial piece in absolute support of both Ben Santer and the IPCC in their bulletin.[8] They made very many pertinent comments which actually showed considerable understanding of the problems behind the debate, and where they might lead in the future:

> There appears to be a systematic and concerted effort by some individuals to undermine and discredit the scientific process that has led many scientists... to conclude that humans are modifying Earth's climate on a global scale. Rather than carrying out a legitimate scientific debate, through the peer-reviewed literature, they are waging in the public media a vocal campaign against scientific results.

With considerable foresight, they observed that

> attempting to carry out scientific debate in the media is inappropriate... Letters and opinion pieces can be written by any individual, and one opinion piece can carry as much or more weight in the public's mind as a letter signed by forty scientists who have passed scientific muster over many years by publishing on the topic in peer-reviewed literature.

Alongside their article, they printed copies of Seitz's original article and uncut copies of our letters. Helpful though this letter was, the damage had already been done, and of course the readership of the American Meteorological Society is not the same, nor is it anything like as influential, as that of the *Wall Street Journal*.

Overall, our responses had very little impact. The *Wall Street Journal*, just like some British newspapers, still carries pieces by acknowledged climate science deniers, rarely with any foundation in credible climate science, and the "debate" can still be accessed on the Internet. Seitz's piece is still used when people need ammunition with which to try to kill the IPCC. A thorough account of the 1996 controversy is available in Bert Bolin's excellent book, *A History of the Science and Politics of Climate Change*.[9] Bert tells the story of strange personal letters he received from Seitz at the time. "I was," Bert writes, "indeed amazed about Dr Seitz's way of proceeding."

Fortunately, as Chair of the Science Working Group, my work usually ended with the science, although I would be involved in political discussions to some degree. I tried to avoid any personal confrontations with people such as Seitz and Pearlman. I still do. However, on one particularly memorable occasion, I couldn't avoid a confrontation. In Geneva for a meeting, I saw ahead of me Don Pearlman. He was right in my path, surrounded by a lot of serious, important-looking fellows, all ready, I presume, to do their dirty work. As I approached, Pearlman's hand was outstretched, offering to shake mine. I couldn't avoid him. What should I do? A handshake can be a tremendously symbolic gesture. I stopped. "I'm not sure I want to shake your hand, Don – not at all sure."

He looked astonished. "Why?"

"Because you've been so unprofessional."

He flew into a tremendous rage at me. I've already described Pearlman as an impressive man. As his deep voice lends him a certain gravitas, his rage could have been quite intimidating, but

I just walked away. Upon reflection, I think those words were the most effective I could have said to him, because he prides himself on professionalism above all else.

17

COMMISSIONS AND REPORTS

Throughout my career, I've been involved in many projects that have worked extremely well because, like the IPCC, all participants looked objectively at the science. My role in some of these ran parallel to my work with the IPCC, or arose directly from it. In all instances, the people involved were prepared to discuss the science in detail; the discussions were sometimes quite heated, but everybody's focus was always on the scientific evidence available to us.

One such body was the UK government's Royal Commission on Environmental Pollution, which I chaired from 1992 to 1997. The Royal Commission had been established back in the 1970s by the prime minister of the time, Harold Wilson. Assigned the task of researching and reporting on various important issues, the Royal Commission drew together a body of disinterested experts from fields such as science, economics, and social science, and had the potential to be very effective. Ostensibly answerable to the Queen, the Commission presented their completed reports to Parliament, which was obliged to respond. Although there was no legal obligation for Parliament to act upon the conclusions, the fact that they had to make a sensible response meant that they at least had to pay the report some serious attention. I use the past tense when talking about the Commission because in April 2011 it became one of the victims of the Coalition government's spending cuts. That's a shame, because the Royal Commission provided an excellent vehicle by which governments could gain expert, objective advice on complex environmental issues.

For me, the attraction of working with experts in a range of disciplines was similar in some respects to the attraction of the IPCC. Furthermore, it offered an opportunity to deal with issues of great environmental importance. I accepted readily. The first report I worked on was about the incineration of waste. In our 1993 report, we concluded that waste incinerators, if built and developed responsibly, could be entirely non-polluting and could provide sustainable energy. Although it's still sometimes difficult for the public to accept, incineration is a better option than landfill. The evidence shows that the very worst thing we can do with our waste is to bury it.

The second report, published in 1994, was on public and private transport. At the time, the Conservative government's approach was to encourage car ownership at the expense of public transport, which meant that roads had to be built to meet an ever-increasing and insatiable demand. "Predict and provide" seemed to be the motto of the Department of Transport: predict the number of cars and provide for them.

At the start of our work, we invited senior figures from the Department of Transport to give evidence to the Commission. Based upon my experience of other government departments, I imagined that there would be a think tank with responsibility for planning for the future. However, there appeared to be no such thing, and no mechanism for considering the consequences of different policies. The public transport infrastructure was not, for them, a priority. After our first meeting with Department of Transport officials, we felt stunned. This was ridiculous. We had a Department of Transport that had no serious plans for the future of public transport, and little imagination. This situation spurred us into addressing the issue. After a couple of years' work, we published a strong report, arguing in favour of planning for the future by integrating public transport into the roads system rather than simply responding to the continued, insatiable, and unsustainable demand for cars and roads.

John Gummer, the Secretary of State for the Environment, was in general supportive of our report but found it difficult to sell it to the government as a whole. However, through him and otherwise, our report did have some influence in beginning to change attitudes and put public transport back on the map.

Our third report under my chairmanship was on soil and soil degradation. This involved considering the impacts of organic as well as intensive farming. The conclusion of this report, in brief, was that farming methods, rather than whether or not a farm is organic, have the most impact upon a farm's sustainability. We strongly recommended the practice of integrated crop management, which includes greater control over the use of fertilizers and pesticides.

For the fourth report, we returned to transport to try to emphasize our earlier messages. By this time, Labour was in government, with John "Two Jags" Prescott as Secretary of State for Transport. Fearing that he might not be someone I would get on with particularly well, I wondered how Prescott would respond to our efforts to push public transport up the agenda. I was pleasantly surprised. Of all the Secretaries of State I've met in my career, John Prescott was probably one of the most effective leaders of a Ministry. From our first meeting, he took an active interest in our work. What he might have lacked in finesse and articulateness, he more than made up for in passion and decisiveness. During the meeting, he would bang out instructions to his staff, expecting immediate action. Rather than a polite "Thank you very much for coming; that's all been very interesting; we'll talk about it among ourselves", Prescott instigated action there and then. Again, the Commission's argument for improving public transport as the most helpful, sustainable option had, I believe, some impact.

The last report I chaired was on environmental standards, in which we articulated in detail the processes to be followed in identifying and tackling environmental problems. My involvement with the Royal Commission ended in 1997, but there was no time for rest.

In the late 1990s, probably just as my work on the Royal Commission was drawing to an end, the International Civil Aviation Organization (ICAO) approached the IPCC asking for a report on the effect of aviation on the climate, which was at the time largely unknown. We said we could do this if the ICAO itself was involved, because we would need their scientific expertise on matters such as the nature of particles emitted by engines; how engines might become more efficient; and how design or operations might change. Without their help, we would struggle to find the necessary science. After my recent experiences with the Royal Commission, I looked forward to working again with experts across a range of disciplines.

In requesting the ICAO's involvement, we didn't for a moment worry about possible vested interests on their part, and we were right not to do so. Our eventual findings showed for the first time that the impact on climate due to aircraft is between two and four times that due directly to the CO_2 actually emitted by the aircraft because of the effect of other factors such as particles and water vapour. Although these results were not to the advantage of the airline industry, the ICAO sought neither to hide nor to deny the results.

Working on this report was an interesting experience in many ways. The IPCC worked with the ICAO in mutual trust, looking objectively at the science so that we could come up with honest answers. We involved people from all parts of the airline industry: the airlines and airport operators, constructors, and more. We applied the IPCC process of research, peer review, and publication. The air industry representatives, upon being given huge piles of review comments on their chapters, had to address each review point and either agree, disagree or ignore, and annotate accordingly. As with all IPCC work, this thoroughness was an essential factor in the accuracy and integrity of the report.

At our final meeting, two aviation representatives said to me, "We've enjoyed these meetings much more than we anticipated. We've never been involved in a report before where we didn't know the answer before we began." As this was said with a smile, I realized it was an overstatement of what happens in industry, but it's a pretty damning indictment of what sometimes happens: reports might be commissioned, funded and written with a view to a political or commercial end. In those instances, the writer's job is to build an argument towards the predetermined conclusion, rather than to conduct open investigations and research to find the objective truth.

Reports by the Royal Commission, the ICAO report, and all IPCC reports have been the result of honest, objective searches for truth.

18

THE THIRD AND FOURTH IPCC REPORTS

The period of preparation for the third IPCC report, due in 2001, was fairly smooth, possibly helped by the fact that it fell within the years of Bill Clinton's presidency of the United States. Politics shouldn't really have made any difference to the IPCC, but it did make a difference to the pressures we sometimes had to face. Having said that, in my years as Chair of the Science Working Group, the UK government never tried to politicize me. Quite correctly and deliberately, they never involved me in any of their discussions about what they were going to do regarding climate change. I didn't want to be involved, and it was quite right that I shouldn't be. The IPCC's independence has always been of the utmost importance.

By 2001, a few things had changed in terms of personnel and procedures. My new co-Chair was Yihui Ding from China. Bert Bolin had retired, his position as overall IPCC Chair being filled by a distinguished English scientist, Dr Bob Watson (now Sir Robert Watson). Having worked for NASA, the American presidency, and the World Bank, Bob had scientific credentials and experience, which made him an excellent man for the job.

Once again, I was looking forward to working on this third report. There had been fascinating developments in climate science since 1995. Not only did the temperature record show further evidence of increasing global average temperatures, which was largely consistent with the projections made in the earlier reports, but attribution studies showed clearer evidence of anthropogenic climate change. We had also seen significant warming in the Arctic, with worrying loss of sea ice. We were ready to look into the research in all the specialized areas in detail to see what we could learn about the big picture when we put them together. It seemed likely that the IPCC would have some important new things to say.

The world meteorological community had grown still further since 1995. Globally, there were more scientists involved in this field, and therefore more scientists to choose from, and there was more science to consider. It was widely accepted that using different lead authors would be a healthy thing to do, so that no critic could claim that chapters were fulfilling an individual's fixed agenda. With more science, more scientists, and more chapters, a few of our processes had to be reviewed and, where necessary, tightened or improved. Expressions of levels of certainty were now to be quantified as percentages. Anything more than 90 per cent certain would be described as "very likely", 67 to 90 per cent certain was "likely", and so forth. I thought this should make discussions a little easier.

With so many more people involved, the work of the TSU would be even more demanding than before. There too a few key roles had changed. For the 1995 report, Bruce Callander had assumed Geoff Jenkins' role, and by the time of the third report, Bruce had in turn been replaced by David Griggs. They were all excellent scientists, with the key qualities of efficiency, organization, and patience. My job would have been unmanageable without any one of them.

This time, I was less naïve about the possibility of interested parties trying to cause trouble. Before the process began, I gave very careful consideration to the question of how best to deal with this. Again, I did not want to exclude any parties. Not only would such a move have played directly into the hands of our critics, but it would have deprived us of the valuable questioning voices which contributed, perhaps in spite of themselves, to the accuracy and clarity of the reports.

Having considered several options, I felt that it might be wise to involve a scientist called Richard Lindzen in the chapters for the IPCC Third Assessment Report. Lindzen is a distinguished professor of meteorology at the highly respected Massachusetts Institute of Technology (MIT) in Boston. He is a respected scientist with a good brain, but he has achieved a degree of notoriety within scientific circles as a man who loves to be on the opposite side of any argument: a contrarian. Thanks to his high profile in American science, Lindzen has been the most credible opponent that any opposition has managed to get hold of to line up against the IPCC, and he is frequently used in this capacity. Fortunately, his contrarian stance regarding climate change is no longer taken seriously in scientific circles, although, as the *New York Times* stated as recently as 2012, among determined climate change sceptics, he is still treated as "a star".[1]

So why did I want to involve such a man? My first hope was that his scepticism about climate change would help to make the report better, because he would have to criticize from the inside, during its development, rather than from the outside after its completion. This would allow us to deal with any of his points that had any genuine scientific basis. If our science was not sufficiently robust to withstand his questions, we would need to reconsider any results or conclusions. In this way, I felt certain his participation could be positive. Accordingly, I wrote to him, offering him a role as a lead author within the chapter on climate processes, which is very much his area. My second hope was that by playing an important part in the report, this talented scientist would experience at first hand the IPCC's scientific integrity, thereby becoming convinced of it. Unfortunately that was a hope too far.

I was surprised and pleased when Lindzen accepted my invitation and joined that particular group. However, it wasn't long before I realized that other members of the group were far from grateful to me. The leader of that group, a very fine fellow, came to me almost tearing his hair out, saying, "Lindzen is impossible. He tries to dominate the group and it's difficult to get him to write anything." The problem was that writing for a document of that nature entails going through all the relevant literature objectively. In his contributions, Lindzen failed to review the literature as required, concentrating instead on his own scientific contributions. He was evidently finding it difficult to take into account anybody's work but his own, which he cited generously throughout his piece. The rest of the authors recognized that his contributions were limited and needed to be made more accurate and more balanced. They eventually had to revise everything he wrote.

Years before, Lindzen had published interesting work suggesting that water vapour in the atmosphere has a negative, or cooling, feedback. At the time, it had been given due attention by the scientific community, but was eventually dismissed because there was in fact more convincing evidence to the contrary, namely that water vapour actually has a positive feedback, adding to the greenhouse effect. Lindzen refused to accept this evidence at the time, continuing to argue his case. Now, he wanted his opinion to be included in the report, but the chapter group came to the informed conclusion that water vapour has a positive feedback. In the end, this particular chapter group concluded: "The balance of evidence favours a positive water vapour feedback of a magnitude comparable to that found in simulations."[2]

My advice at all times to the Chair of that group was: "Whatever you do, don't let Lindzen resign; don't give him any reason whatsoever for leaving." If Lindzen had resigned, he could have used it as a platform from which to criticize the IPCC process. It really was quite a big risk taking him on, but it was a calculated risk, and thanks to the skill of that particular Chair in difficult circumstances, Richard Lindzen continued to participate in the report. Eventually, unable to deny that the balance of scientific evidence pointed to an overall positive feedback by water vapour, Lindzen signed his name to the completed chapter.

Nevertheless, ever since the report's publication, Lindzen's spoken statements on climate change have frequently been at variance with the contents of the chapter. He still questions the IPCC, his frequent remark being that the chapters are fine as they are written by real scientists, but the summaries are written by crazy, politically motivated people like me, who do not correctly represent the science of the chapters. Therefore, he argues, the summaries are unreliable. This is not correct at all. He has argued this groundless case so many times that it's almost funny. I've challenged him to provide examples of where the summaries disagree with the chapters, but he has failed to substantiate his argument with a single example. But because of his status and his connections, and because his voice and presence are naturally impressive, he carries a misleading air of authority. Just like Singer and Seitz, he has had the ear of Congress, and has presented his "testimony" and "evidence" to them on numerous occasions. I think he has been a significant obstacle to the IPCC and therefore to progress in global efforts to combat climate change.

My invitation to Lindzen to participate in the IPCC Third Assessment Report had been an attempt both to strengthen the report and to pre-empt some possible future problems. I foresaw other problems too. Feeling quite certain that the Saudi and Kuwaiti delegates would try to hinder the process as they had in 1995, I arranged a meeting with them just before the session began. "I don't want to waste a lot of time this year," I told them. "If you don't mind, could you please tell me what you'd like to achieve, what you're after, in so far as you can do that? It would be very helpful to me to know what you really want out of this meeting. I'm not promising you anything at all; I'd just like to know what's in your minds." They were quite open in response because they were essentially good people who knew that they couldn't argue for things that were manifestly unscientific. The things they mentioned were actually all manageable and reasonable. It was a pleasant conversation, and being forewarned, I could allow time for the necessary discussions. They were pleased that they would be able to address their points, and I was relieved. I could now proceed with greater confidence.

The meeting of the Science Working Group of the IPCC Third Assessment Report, the equivalent of the 1995 Madrid meeting, took place in Shanghai in January 2001. Although discussion was detailed, vigorous and challenging, and in spite of the increased amount of science, and even though we still didn't finish until 3 a.m. on the final day, it was an easier process than in 1995. This was my IPCC swan song, I suppose. I felt both relief and sadness to have finished work on my final report. At the end of the meeting, people said a lot of nice things about me, reflecting on the burden I had borne and the troubles I had met with. The meeting gave me a five-minute standing ovation, which I felt was very flattering at 3 a.m. when I'm sure they were aching for their beds. The end of the meeting coincided with Chinese New Year, and I remember standing on the balcony of the fourteenth floor of our hotel, watching the fireworks over the whole city in the early hours of the morning. It was extremely impressive, and felt somehow very apt.

Not only was this Chinese New Year, but the date was significant for another reason. George W. Bush had just been inaugurated as President of the United States. I felt an uneasy suspicion that those working on the next IPCC report might be in for a bumpier ride. I was handing the reins of the Science Working Group into the capable hands of Susan Solomon, a distinguished American atmospheric chemist who has won many prizes for her work.

Box 18.1 Main Points of the 2001 Science Working Group Report: Summary for Policymakers

An increasing body of observations gives a collective picture of a warming world and other changes in the climate system.

- The global average surface temperature has increased over the twentieth century by about 0.6 °C.

- Temperatures have risen during the past four decades in the lowest 8 km of the atmosphere.

- Snow cover and ice extent have decreased.

- Global average sea level has risen and ocean heat content has increased. Changes have also occurred in other aspects of climate.

- Some important aspects of climate appear not to have changed.

Emissions of greenhouse gases and aerosols due to human activities continue to alter the atmosphere in ways that are expected to affect the climate.

- Concentrations of atmospheric greenhouse gases and their radiative forcing have continued to increase as a result of human activities.

- Anthropogenic aerosols are short-lived and mostly produce negative radiative forcing.

- Natural factors have made small contributions to radiative forcing over the past century.

Confidence in the ability of models to project future climate has increased.

There is new and stronger evidence that most of the warming observed over the last 50 years is attributable to human activities.

Human influences will continue to change atmospheric composition throughout the twenty-first century.

Global average sea temperature and sea level are expected to rise under all IPCC scenarios.

Anthropogenic climate change will persist for many centuries.

Further action is required to address remaining gaps in information and understanding.

Source: *Climate Change 2001: The Scientific Basis* (Cambridge University Press, 2001).

The IPCC now had to look ahead to their fourth report, due out in 2007. Unlike me, the IPCC Chair, Bob Watson, was not ready to retire. However, even before the third report was published, we were aware of mounting pressure for a representative of the developing world to have a turn in the role of overall Chair. It was a sensible point, and one that Bob and I had already discussed. With Bob's continuing chairmanship now under threat, co-chairmanship seemed to me to be an ideal solution. Just as chairing and co-chairing the working groups was now shared between the developed and the developing world, so, I felt, could be the overall chairmanship of the IPCC. However, Bob wasn't particularly keen on the idea, and as he was doing such a good job anyway, I didn't pursue the matter.

As elections for a new Chair approached, it became increasingly clear that Bob did not have the White House's support. The oil industry was lobbying Bush's administration to push him aside. Greenpeace has a copy of a letter from Exxon to the White House asking them to get rid of Watson. Their ostensible motivation was to involve the developing world; their real motivation, I suspect, was that Bob was too effective. Bob's days as IPCC Chair were numbered. Of course, the process of deciding the new Chair was carried out in the proper way. The UK proposed Bob, while India proposed a scientist called Rajendra Pachauri. As we all acknowledged that the developing world was under-represented, the outcome of the selection process was clear from the beginning. I tried to encourage Bob not to take the result personally, but he was hurt by it nonetheless.

In spite of the unpromising political scene as we moved into the new millennium, climate science progressed, meetings took place, and preparations were made for the fourth IPCC report, which was to be published in March 2007. The work ahead of the IPCC must have been daunting. Not only were they moving into new areas of research, but they would have to bring together more scientists and more science than ever before in a bigger meeting than ever before.

I had little, if anything, to do with this report, other than being very interested in its outcome, and the outcome certainly was interesting. The IPCC now had enough scientific evidence to enable them to make a very firm statement on the human impact on climate: "Warming of the climate system is unequivocal..." (p. 2) and "Most of the observed increase in global average temperatures since the mid-20th century is *very likely* due to the observed increase in anthropogenic GHG [greenhouse gas] concentrations" (p. 5).[3] As "very likely" means more than 90 per cent certainty, this is a very strong statement. However, the report, while presenting the problem, is not a negative document. Although the Synthesis Report's section on "The Long-Term Perspective" acknowledges that "There is *high confidence* that neither adaptation nor mitigation alone can avoid all climate change impacts", it continues more encouragingly, "however, they can complement each other and together can significantly reduce the risks of climate change."[4] I doubt it could be stated much more clearly than that. That was in 2007. Time passes quickly.

Box 18.2 Summary of the 2007 Report

Global atmospheric concentrations of carbon dioxide, methane, and nitrous oxide have increased markedly as a result of human activities since 1750 and now far exceed pre-industrial values determined from ice cores spanning many thousands of years. Increases in carbon dioxide are due primarily to fossil fuel use and land use change, while those of methane and nitrous oxide are primarily due to agriculture.

The understanding of anthropogenic warming and cooling influences on climate has improved since the Third Assessment Report, leading to very high confidence [i.e. at least 9 out of 10 chance of being correct] that the global average net effect of human activities since 1750 has been one of warming.

Warming for the climate system is unequivocal, as is now evident from observations of increases in global average air and ocean temperatures, widespread melting of snow and ice, and rising global average sea level.

At continental, regional, and ocean basin scales, numerous long-term changes in climate have been observed, including in arctic temperatures and ice, precipitation amounts, ocean salinity, wind patterns, and aspects of extreme weather including droughts, heavy precipitation, heat waves, and the intensity of tropical cyclones.

Some aspects of climate have been observed not to change; for instance, Antarctic sea ice extent continues to show no statistically significant average trends consistent with the lack of warming reflected in atmospheric temperatures averaged over the region.

Palaeoclimatic information supports the interpretation that the warmth of the last half century is unusual in at least the previous 1,300 years. The last time the polar regions were significantly warmer than present for an extended period (about 125,000 years ago), reductions in polar ice volume led to 4 to 6 m of sea-level rise.

Most of the observed increase in global average temperatures since the mid twentieth century is very likely [i.e. greater than 90 per cent likelihood] due to the observed increase in anthropogenic greenhouse gas concentrations. Discernible human influences now extend to other aspects of climate including ocean warming, continental-average temperatures, temperature extremes, and wind patterns.

For the next two decades, a warming of about 0.2 °C per decade is projected for a range of emission scenarios. Even if the concentrations of all greenhouse gases had been kept constant at year 2000 levels, a further warming of about 0.1 °C per decade would be expected.

Anthropogenic warming and sea-level rise would continue for centuries due to timescales associated with climate processes and feedbacks, even if greenhouse gas concentrations were to be stabilized.

Source: Taken from highlighted sections in *Climate Change 2007, the Physical Science Basis*, Summary for Policymakers.

I rather miss my IPCC work. Demanding though it was, it was tremendously exciting to be leading for so many years such a large group of scientists, all sharing their knowledge and working towards a common aim of getting the most accurate information possible on such a complex and important issue. I feel grateful to have had the privilege of playing a significant part in science's quest for truth concerning the workings of the earth's climate system.

In 2007 the IPCC as a body was awarded the Nobel Peace Prize "for their efforts to build up and disseminate greater knowledge about man-made climate change, and to lay the foundations for the measures that are needed to counteract such change". For a scientific body to be awarded a prize for peace rather than for science was a remarkable thing to happen. The award tells us something about the nature and significance of climate science and the reasons for doing it. This, the greatest possible accolade the IPCC could receive, came as a complete surprise. My certificate hangs in my living room in Wales.

To accept the Nobel Prize, I travelled to Oslo with 20 other members of the IPCC in December 2007. It was a wonderful celebration; a joy to share with so many valued colleagues. Speaking on behalf of everybody involved, Pachauri cited the Hindu philosophy of "Vasudhaiva Kutumbakam", which means "the whole universe is one family". This philosophy, he said, must dominate global efforts if we are to protect the earth.

There was, however, sadness in the occasion. Bert Bolin was very ill with stomach cancer. We had all hoped that he would be able to accept the award on our behalf, but he was too ill to attend. Returning from Oslo, a couple of members went immediately to Stockholm to visit him and to show him the pictures and the prize. He appreciated the gesture. Bert died just two weeks later, aged 82. In spite of his sensitive, modest, and somewhat retiring nature, Bert is probably the most diplomatically competent scientific leader I've ever known. Many times he defended the IPCC from political interference, his diplomatic skills being just as strong as his scientific ones. Although he refused to exaggerate the evidence, he always felt that political progress towards addressing the problem of climate change was far too slow. Al Gore, who received the Nobel Peace Prize at the same time, honoured Bert in his own acceptance speech, saying rather movingly, "Bert, without you we would not have come to where we are today."

19

THE TRUTH WILL OUT

In Shakespeare's play *The Merchant of Venice*, the unfortunately named Launcelot Gobbo says to his father that "at the length truth will out". Of course, in 1597 Shakespeare wasn't writing about climate change, but nevertheless the phrase is remarkably apt. "Outing", or discovering and revealing truths about the earth's climate, is the end to which the IPCC has always devoted its resources. As we moved into 2009, the IPCC had two very significant challenges to face as it began work for its next report, due in 2014. The first was the continued growth in the amount of scientific literature available; the second, a marked increase in unwarranted hostility from some quarters: hostility towards the IPCC and, I would argue, towards truth itself.

The first of these challenges was an exciting one. Although no longer officially involved in the IPCC process, I was invited to attend a preparatory meeting in Honolulu, where I presented those of my IPCC experiences that might be helpful to those planning the 2014 report.

That Honolulu meeting was stimulating. IPCC members had devised a brilliant new way of organizing the meeting, which consisted of three days, with two sessions per day, so a total of six sessions. In each session, 20 people presented just one slide each summarizing their work. They were allowed to talk for only three minutes each, totalling one hour. They then each had an area of the room in which to display their work. For the next two hours, delegates could wander among the posters and discuss their contents with the scientists. That way we got through 120 reports in three days, covering all aspects of climate science. This efficient way of updating everybody provides further evidence of scientists trying to become as well informed as possible, constantly seeking understanding and truth.

In discussing the second challenge, the hostility towards the IPCC's work, I would like first to consolidate a few points about the honest way in which the IPCC operates:

• Set up by all the world's governments, the IPCC carries out scientific assessments with contributions by scientists from all countries and from all relevant disciplines. The science is collated and the chapters written by a similarly broad spectrum of scientists, nominated by a range of international bodies solely for their scientific credentials.

• Every piece of science is peer-reviewed.

• Science Working Group meetings are purely for the discussion of science. Scientists look properly and honestly at the science available and try to understand what it says about the past, the present, and the future.

• The substantial progress in both observation techniques and computer modelling over the past 30 years has much increased the confidence level of the IPCC. The projections of the first IPCC report in 1990 have been proven accurate within the ranges of uncertainty quoted, giving the IPCC and governments increased confidence in the skill and accuracy of scientists, systems, and projections.

• The IPCC has always endeavoured to express every statement in its reports as accurately as possible, taking great care to be honest at all times about levels of certainty.

- Summaries of the reports are subjected to the closest scrutiny possible, with the aim of achieving unanimous agreement of every sentence. This occurs within meetings of representatives of international governments, including those of the oil states who have been very active in ensuring that absolutely nothing gets agreed that hasn't got a very sound basis in science.

The integrity of the entire IPCC process has led to a very high level of credibility in IPCC projections. Of course, mistakes have been made, but no government has ever had grounds to object to any statement within any of the four IPCC Summary Reports published to date.

It has been suggested that bodies similar to the IPCC should be set up in other areas where there is controversy over the science and where various interests might be at play. It's a valid point, but in many such areas now there would be too much powerful opposition: it's an awful indictment of our time. Most of us realize that it's a good thing the IPCC started before the real controversy about climate change began; before the oil industry started their lobbying. Had we tried to establish the IPCC a few years later, vested interests would probably have blocked its formation in the first place.

However, not everybody appreciates this degree of integrity. In 2009, Lord Lawson, a former Chancellor of the Exchequer in Margaret Thatcher's government, published *An Appeal to Reason: A Cool Look at Global Warming*.[1] In his book, he writes that "what was intended by the governments who set it up and continue to fund the IPCC to be a fact-finding and analytical exercise, has mutated in the minds of those who lead it into something more like a politically correct alarmist pressure group" (p.12). Ninety-three pages later, he repeats his point: "The PC at the heart of the IPCC as it were, is the most intolerant form of political correctness in the western world today."

Lawson is sceptical about the science of climate change, arguing that reports such as those of the IPCC are exaggerated.

He fails repeatedly to provide sound scientific evidence to support such assertions. A politician and free-market economist, not a scientist, he argues also that even if we were to accept that climate change is a real problem, we should take measures to deal with its effects rather than addressing its causes. This shows his complete lack of understanding of the scale of the problem. Adaptation alone is neither practically nor economically a viable option. We have to address the root cause, the emission of greenhouse gases, as fast as we can. Unfortunately, Lawson's opinions carry considerable weight in certain circles, allowing him still to influence UK government policy, whose stance on the environment is getting worse.

Lord Lawson is founder of the Global Warming Policy Foundation (GWPF).[2] The GWPF claims to be "restoring balance and trust to the climate debate", thereby implying first of all that balance and trust have otherwise been sacrificed, and secondly, that their stance is the objective one. Neither is true. Thanks to such claims, and thanks to their clever name, which makes them sound disinterested, they are often used in UK news reports about climate change to give a counter-argument to the science, thus making it seem as though the news report is balanced and objective. In such a way, opinion is often presented as a viable alternative to scientific evidence.

I do not mean to imply that everybody who doubts or opposes the IPCC and its science is under external influence or has vested interests or a political agenda. There are good, able people as yet unconvinced that climate change has been influenced by human behaviour and that it presents a serious problem. It is undoubtedly more comfortable to believe this than to accept what science is showing us and consider the consequences. I sometimes wonder how many of these people have ever read an IPCC report. I suspect that their opinions are usually formed by reading newspaper columns or the Internet.

However, just as any scientist would ask questions before accepting something as fact, so it is always worth asking certain questions of those individuals or organizations with strong opinions on climate change. What scientific evidence do they present to support their case? Have they studied the IPCC reports in depth? How are they funded? What are the political leanings or ideologies of their founders and members? With which other organizations do they have connections? Disappointingly, such questions are rarely asked by the media, and the answers are often difficult to find. In contrast, details about the IPCC are available to everybody.

Unfortunately, media coverage of and opposition to the IPCC have been very effective in undermining public confidence in the science of climate change. This has created obstacles to progress in tackling the problems. We have seen how Fred Seitz and the *Wall Street Journal* succeeded in influencing the USA's response to climate change in the 1990s. Such a combination of apparently vested interests and a media apparently pliant to their demands continues to delay important progress today by their creation of white noise to drown out the strong scientific signals, particularly in the USA, the UK, and other Western countries. They have a lot to answer for, as I'm afraid the future will prove.

Still in 2009, further trouble arose in the UK just a few weeks before the UN's Copenhagen Summit on Climate Change. The story was first broken in *The Telegraph*, in an article by James Delingpole entitled "Climategate: the final nail in the coffin of Anthropogenic Global Warming?"[3] Delingpole had somehow gained access to a large number of emails between scientists at the University of East Anglia (UEA), in which they discussed informally the work in which they were involved. They used some casual phrases which would have been understood perfectly well between them, but which could be misinterpreted by others. The contents of these emails led Delingpole to accuse UEA scientists of, among other things, "manipulation and suppression of evidence". *The Telegraph* soon followed this article with Christopher Booker's column, in which the opinion columnist referred to climate change as "the worst scientific scandal of our generation".[4] It was awful for the scientists involved. The story immediately became headline news worldwide.

The scientific community's response was woefully and regrettably inadequate, because we didn't have knowledge of the emails concerned. Our professional lives being a pursuit of truth and facts, we are not in the habit of rushing to voice opinion. The media focused initially upon the word "trick" contained in the emails, failing to understand that, in mathematical and scientific terms, "trick" is a positive word, referring to a way of solving a problem. The scientists at UEA were beleaguered, with immense impact on their personal and professional lives.

The impact on international public opinion so soon before Copenhagen was of even greater significance. Eventually, a number of independent reports, one led by an ex-Chair of the oil company Shell, concluded unanimously that there was no evidence of scientific fraud or impropriety. The only mistake the UEA scientists had made was to fail to share all of their data, which would have been impractical anyway: they had such vast quantities of data in a form not easy to share that the time spent making it all available would have been impossibly large. It is perhaps of some significance that despite extensive investigations, the police have never been able to trace the original email hacker who passed the information to *The Telegraph* at such a crucial moment in world negotiations.

Of course, when the scientists were completely exonerated, the newspapers weren't interested. Besides, the damage had been done. The clearing of the scientists' names and of their reputations did not make the front pages, appearing instead in small, easily missed columns. It is scandalous that the newspapers are free to print something as front-page news, and when it is proven incorrect they have no legal responsibility to report the correct version with the same degree of emphasis, just as in our experience with the *Wall Street Journal*. It is thoroughly dishonest. Disappointingly, in the case of the UEA scandal, even what I consider to be the best newspapers failed to do this.

That was quite a year for anti-climate change arguments. In October 2009, the *Telegraph* columnist Christopher Booker, mentioned above, published a book entitled *The Real Global Warming Disaster: Is the Obsession with Climate Change Turning out to be the Most Costly Scientific Blunder in History?*[5] This has since become what *The Independent* newspaper describes as "the manual of climate denialism".[6] The book opens with a quotation Booker attributes to me. I'm supposed to have said, "Unless we announce disasters, no one will listen." He even claims that these words are found in the first edition of my textbook *Global Warming: The Complete Briefing*, published in 1994, but those words aren't there at all, because I neither wrote nor said them.[7] The quotation is completely fabricated. Nevertheless, it has been used repeatedly as a foundation for sceptics' arguments, with millions of references on the Internet, and has done a great deal of damage. In suggesting that I exaggerate when I talk about global warming, this fabrication implies that the IPCC exaggerates too. I hope previous chapters have demonstrated that this is far from the case.

The quest for truth should surely be as much the concern of a journalist as it is of a scientist. I find it ironic when journalists accuse scientific bodies or individual scientists of telling untruths. Less than a year after his "climategate" article, James Delingpole, again in *The Telegraph*, said of me, "I've never had the pleasure of meeting Sir John, but I'm sure I'd recognize him instantly by his extraordinarily long nose." My nose isn't actually very long, but that's not the point. By this allusion to Pinocchio, he was accusing me of being a liar. In the same way as he was prepared to judge me without meeting me or even talking with me, some journalists comment freely and ignorantly on climate science without taking the trouble to read it themselves. Why would a serious journalist fail to find out facts? James Delingpole eloquently answered this question in an interview for the BBC's *Horizon* in 2010:[8] he doesn't have the time. "It is not my job to sit down and read peer reviewed papers," he told the interviewer,

Sir Paul Nurse, the President of the Royal Society. "I am an interpreter of interpretations."

It doesn't take long to read an IPCC assessment report's summary, and they're all written in a language and style comprehensible to intelligent non-scientists. It's surely reasonable to expect a serious journalist to do his research, and to expect a responsible newspaper editor to demand it.

Such an irresponsible approach is dangerous because it has great influence on public, and therefore political, opinion. The climate change arena can be very nasty at times. In the past, when I found myself misquoted, maligned, and undermined, I decided not to fight back. I feared that I might give these people still more publicity and perhaps lend them credibility without successfully getting my own point across. Able only to tell the truth, together with careful judgments regarding its degree of certainty, while others can say what they like, I was aware that I might lose the fight. The variability of the climate and therefore the degree of uncertainty in projections is something people find hard to understand. Besides, most journalists and columnists are skilled and highly trained communicators and orators, whereas I'm a scientist. We're rarely renowned for our communication skills.

By 2010 I was beginning to change my mind. In March I wrote in *The Times*: "Perhaps there is a criticism that can be made of IPCC scientists: that they have been too slow publicly to defend their integrity… We scientists have facts on our sides – we must not be afraid to deploy them."[9] I deliberately chose the word "deploy", as facts are our only weapons.

When I became aware of the full extent to which the fabricated quotation in Booker's book was being used as ammunition against the IPCC, I decided that in order to limit the extent of any further damage, I should fight back, and speak up for the truth. Although I was blessed to be helped for free by a wonderful law firm, the ensuing legal battle consumed a considerable amount of my time and energy. Of course, the truth eventually won.

The Independent published a whole page on the verdict and on Booker's misrepresentation.[10] In response to a letter I wrote to the Press Complaints Commission, *The Telegraph* had to publish a short letter from me explaining the problem. Nevertheless, just like the UEA fiasco, we were shutting the door after the horse had bolted. The damage had been done.

In spite of this outcome, and in spite of the continued lack of evidence to support their views, the same journalists continue their battle against climate science. Early in 2013, in a blistering attack on the Meteorological Office, James Delingpole used a reduction in Met Office predictions of the rate of global temperature increase between now and 2017 to accuse the office of being "useless" and "a national joke".[11] He also referred to me personally as "a fanatical believer in the great global warming religion". Although tipping his hat to objective reporting with a brief comment in support of the Met Office by an unnamed "expert from the IPCC", he cited his old friends in support of his opinion: Christopher Booker and a spokesperson for the GWPF.

Just to put the record straight about the Met Office's change in figures, I'd like to outline the issue at the heart of Delingpole's misunderstanding. The Met Office is involved primarily in three areas of forecasting: short-term weather forecasting, midterm or decadal weather forecasting (i.e. 5–10 years ahead), and longer-term global climate forecasting. They run a decadal forecast from December every year, the results of which are published at the end of December on the Met Office research pages.

As Professor Julia Slingo, the Met Office chief scientist, explains in a recent report, changes over decadal periods occur through changes in the large-scale ocean circulation or large events in the oceans, such as the El Niño, which can strongly influence weather patterns around the world.[12] An unusually strong El Niño in 1998 caused an exceptional rise of global average temperature at that time, and 1998 still remains the warmest year (or equal warmest) on record in global average terms. Every year, Met Office scientists do their best to forecast as accurately as possible, within boundaries of uncertainty, the weather for up to 10 years ahead. Every year, these forecasts have to be adjusted to take account of events over the past 12 months. As Professor Slingo points out:

Decadal forecasts… do not tell us anything about long-term climate sensitivity (i.e. how much the planet will warm for a specified increase in radiative forcing related to greenhouse gases). There is no evidence that current estimates of climate sensitivity produced by the Met Office Hadley Centre have changed.

When the world is faced with a challenge that is potentially extremely damaging to us all, and when there is a very strong body of scientific evidence that has been well researched and peer-reviewed, and worked at so conscientiously, then journalists surely have a responsibility to try to explain to the public what the science is and what it means. That's not to say that they should ignore other opinions, but that these should be examined before they are given the forum. Maybe their opinions need to be subjected to a process of peer review like the IPCC. The public need to know, and in order to know they need the facts explained. How can they learn if they can't get the best information, carefully explained? The truth is going to be very important for the world to know, but at the moment we're being fed a diet of junk.

The IPCC exists to explore and to share the truth as we know it ourselves. We have put our evidence in front of all the world's governments, including oil states. We have had to persuade them that all we are saying is accurate and acceptable, and we can only do that with facts. The IPCC's one and only agenda is accuracy and clarity: nobody who has taken the trouble to inform themselves of the facts could conceivably claim otherwise. It is time the papers stopped printing opinions unsupported by evidence.

I still work as hard as I can to inform politicians and the public alike about the science of climate change. This book represents the first time I've written or spoken at such length about the struggles we climate scientists have endured. As Shakespeare said, "at the length truth will out", but it's now a matter of increasing urgency. We scientists are doing our best, but the media, industry, and politicians should all be more responsible.

20

TOWARDS A SUSTAINABLE WORLD

Perhaps due partly to the perspective my age lends to me, my focus on issues of sustainability is strong. Sustainable living is about far more than just climate change. To me, sustainable living is about living in a way that can endure: conserving resources, protecting the natural world, and having as little adverse impact upon the environment, both local and global, as possible. Living sustainably means not cheating on our children, not cheating on our neighbours, and not cheating on the rest of creation. After all, who would want to pass on to our children or any future generation an earth that is degraded compared to the one we inherited? Who could reasonably argue against the sharing of common resources with our neighbours in the rest of the world and caring properly for the non-human creation?

But how does living sustainably in terms of preserving the earth's resources relate to living sustainably by limiting our effect on the earth's climate? The two are inextricably linked. Science tells us that current emission rates of greenhouse gases, arising from our burning of fossil fuel resources, will change the climate at a rate too fast for nature and its ecosystems, or humans and our needs, to adapt adequately. Real damage is going to occur, for instance through the increased frequency and intensity of climate extremes and through sea-level rise. The earth, under such conditions, will find it difficult to sustain us all. More details of this are in Chapter 26.

To understand the issues at stake I often borrow the analogy of a spaceship, inviting my audience to imagine that we are the crew of a spaceship on a voyage to visit a distant planet. Our journey there and back will take many years. An adequate, high quality source of energy is readily available in the radiation from the sun. Otherwise, resources for the journey are limited. As crew members, a priority is the careful management of our finite resources. That the resources be sustainable at least for the duration of the voyage is clearly essential. Failure to manage our resources will result in failure to sustain our journey. Similarly, if we damage the environment within our craft so that it fails to be optimal for our survival, we will suffer.[1] I invite them to imagine the desperate struggles between the crew should necessities such as food, water, and clean air to breathe become depleted. It would not be a pleasant picture.

I'm not the first to use this analogy. In 1965 an American politician called Adlai Stevenson made a speech to the UN in which he said, "We travel together, passengers on a little space ship, dependent on its vulnerable reserves of air and soil."[2] Just three years later, Buckminster Fuller[3] borrowed the phrase, writing:

… we can make all of humanity successful through science's world-engulfing industrial evolution provided that we are not so foolish as to continue to exhaust in a split second of astronomical history the orderly energy savings of billions of years' energy conservation aboard our Spaceship Earth. These energy savings have been put into our Spaceship's life-regeneration-guaranteeing bank account for use only in self-starter functions.

Now, almost 50 years later, would Fuller say we have been foolish? Will we continue to be so?

Spaceship Earth is enormously larger than any spaceship. The crew, numbering about 7 billion, and rising, is also enormously larger. Nevertheless, the principle of sustainability should be applied to Spaceship Earth as rigorously as it has to be applied to the much smaller vehicle on its interplanetary journey.[4] The reasons why should be self-evident. It is not just about physical survival. Environmental sustainability is strongly linked to social sustainability; that is, creating sustainable communities, businesses, and economies.[5]

Perhaps central to the problem of our understanding of what could be a straightforward matter is that many of us in developed countries imagine that we will be OK, at least for the next few decades. We imagine that we have the resources and infrastructure to cope with any climate change or sea-level rise we might experience. We also imagine that any effect upon current ecosystems will be slow enough to see most of us out. We are mistaken. Our imagination is misleading. We are actually closer to disaster than we think.

Is there a reason to care about this beyond its direct impact upon us? I think so. Over the past 200 years, we in the developed world have become rich largely thanks to cheap energy from burning cheap and plentiful fossil fuels. We have only recently realized that the emissions from this are beginning to contribute to immense suffering, especially among poorer people in the developing world. Our failure to take swift action upon discovering this injustice is an appalling indictment of our times, and we're all part of this shameful mismatch. Of course, we didn't know the future impact of what we were doing, but now that we do know, the moral imperative for us in the developed world, whether or not we are people of faith, to care for the earth and for those less fortunate, and to reduce our carbon emissions as fast as we can, is very, very strong.

All around the world, early societies to which we now refer as "primitive" recognized their dependence upon nature. They had a deep sense of reverence for the earth. Their daily lives relating far more closely to nature than do our own, these people understood the importance of managing the resources upon which their survival, both immediate and far into the future, depended.

With this in mind, it is no surprise that the early days of most, if not all, of the world's major religions taught respect for the earth and for its resources. What might be more surprising is that, if we take the trouble to look, we find that this is still central to their theology. Regrettably, in the developed world we no longer live our lives in a close daily relationship with nature. As we have distanced ourselves from the earth and from our responsibility to look after it, so have the priorities of most of the major faiths.

Although my faith and my science always sat quite comfortably together, it wasn't until I started working more specifically on climate change that they began to interweave. What I was learning through science was of enormous significance, which for me brought with it moral responsibility. I wasn't alone in this. Among the people on the Science Working Group for the IPCC, people of all faiths and those of no faith at all felt the weight of this moral responsibility that came with our increasing knowledge. What should we or could we do with the truths we were discovering? Increasingly, I found myself examining more closely the principle of responsibility.

I often use the Bible for guidance, and the Bible tells us quite clearly that we are on the earth as God's stewards, a steward being somebody entrusted with management of another's property. This introduces accountability. I see the earth as belonging to God, and our job is to work with him in caring for it. This perspective has always influenced my approach to sustainability. It is difficult and I think unnecessary for me to try to distinguish what might be an instinctive, almost primitive urge to care for the earth from the responsibility I feel, based upon my faith, as a steward for God.

Some people argue, not without justification, that Christians are not doing enough to care for the earth. In many cases, I agree. However, I have encountered and worked with many good people who really are trying to be responsible stewards. This is true of both people of faith and people of no faith.

Stewardship of the earth in practice is beset by the problems of human selfishness and greed. We are also faced with the challenge of human impotence: we know that we need to act, but we're not getting on with it. Perhaps we lack the will or perhaps even the confidence to do anything. We may sometimes despair that it is beyond the capability of the human race adequately to remedy the damage we have done. This isn't a rational position, because in fact the scientific means to make the changes already exist, and are not expensive, as I will discuss later. In many ways, therefore, human-induced climate change poses as much of a spiritual and moral problem as it does political, commercial, and scientific.

To me this challenge reflects that set by Jesus, after whom my Oxford college was named over four hundred years ago. He is a towering figure in my life and I find encouragement in the support he offers. I frequently remind myself of his simple but enormously powerful message of love; love for God and love for our neighbours, coupled with his offer of forgiveness, friendship and, of great importance in this context, support.

The developed world has to take the first action in reducing greenhouse gas emissions, as is required by the International Climate Convention agreed at the Rio Earth Summit in 1992. We need to put less emphasis on wealth at any cost, and instead use our wealth in much better ways. In doing so, our lives could be enriched. Stewardship or long-term care for our planet, for its wonderful resources, and for those less fortunate than ourselves brings to the fore moral and spiritual goals. I'm optimistic that reaching out for such goals could lead to nations and peoples working together more effectively and more closely for the good of us all than is possible if we follow the more familiar, more self-serving goals of wealth and power.

21

PROGRESS AND
OBSTACLES

It is now more years than I care to remember since I was last involved in any of the hands-on science of my Oxford days. I miss it sometimes, just as I miss the intellectual rigours of the IPCC. However, I still have the privilege of reviewing and writing about science in numerous books and articles. Furthermore, I receive frequent invitations to attend interesting meetings and to talk about climate change to a wide range of bodies. This has presented me with opportunities to present the science to government committees on both sides of the Atlantic as well as to numerous Christian organizations, academic institutions, leading international banks, and even to the boards of two of the UK's major oil companies.

In 1995, Sheila and I were invited by the Greek Orthodox Church, along with the Patriarch Bartholomew of Constantinople, to enjoy a cruise around some Greek islands in celebration of the 1900th anniversary of the writing of the book of Revelation. This treat wasn't to be entirely leisure. We were just two of a remarkably diverse group of around 150 politicians, environmentalists, religious leaders, secular leaders, journalists, scientists, and others. Our object was to discuss environmental problems in that part of the world. At the time, the terrible effects of a heavily polluted Eastern Europe were still being felt in the Black Sea and further afield. In areas of Siberia the maximum life expectancy was 35 years, thanks to chemical pollution. There was an imperative to get to grips with all of this.

Sheila and I were to join the cruise in Istanbul. There was a delay in boarding, during which we discovered that our pre-planned luxury liner had proven unserviceable, and a reserve vessel had been commissioned. We eventually found ourselves boarding a roll-on roll-off ferry. This was rather disappointing. However, Sheila and I were fortunate in being among the few guests honoured with a cabin to themselves: many others had to stay in much more crowded quarters. Still, the food was marvellous and we all had a lot of fun, and the discussions themselves were very interesting.

Throughout discussions that week, John Zizioulas, the Metropolitan of Pergamon, and Chair of the cruise's scientific committee, kept emphasizing his belief that failure to care for the earth was a sin, not only against nature but also against God. His message struck a strong chord with the rest of us, even the atheists. Discussions led eventually to a series of principles we called the Patmos Principles, named after Patmos, the Greek island where the book of Revelation, the last book of the Bible, was written. The Principles declare that any activity leading to "species extinction, reduction in genetic diversity, pollution of the water, land and air, habitat destruction and destruction of sustainable life styles" should be considered a sin, or a crime, or just plain wrong.[1] The cruise concluded with a magnificent ceremony on the island of Patmos itself. Conducted entirely in Greek, it could have been an amazing experience, had it not lasted for four long hours.

Reflecting over the next few months on the discussions during that cruise, I considered how I might bring together in a helpful and purposeful way matters relating to the environment and faith, these two crucial areas in which my quest for truth has taken shape.

I shared my ideas with some friends, in particular an eminent zoologist, John Sale, who had recently retired to Wales after many years working in Africa and India, and Sam Berry, a distinguished professor of genetics at University College London (UCL), about creating a new body to connect environment and faith.

We eventually established the John Ray Initiative (JRI). An educational charity, the JRI's mission is to promote environmental stewardship and the wise use of science and technology in accordance with Christian principles. The JRI has hosted conferences, created a number of books, and set up a community of JRI associates throughout the country. Early on, we summarized the challenges we face (see Appendix 4). This helped to define our role. Now in its sixteenth year, the JRI seeks to support Christian thinking and action on the climate.[2]

In the more secular world of big business, I have found myself on occasions speaking about climate change before the boards of large companies. I always attend such meetings with prayer and optimism. You never know who might be listening and what the impact of your words might be. Perhaps one of the most remarkable occasions to which I've been invited was in 1997, when John Browne, then chief executive of BP, invited me and an economist from the Massachusetts Institute of Technology, called Jake Jakobi, to talk about the science and economics of climate change. Our audience was to be the BP Board of Directors. In my presentation I covered my now familiar ground of the dangers of climate change and what we have to do about it. Of course, given the nature of my audience, I spoke particularly about how we might get our energy in the future and the changes we would have to make.

John Browne listened carefully. "Tell me," he said at the end, "is this a real problem? Will it still be here in twenty years' time?"

Both Jake Jakobi and I said, "Yes. Absolutely."

"But is it a *real* problem?" he asked again. With his first class physics degree from Cambridge, Browne had to be convinced of the science.

"Yes, it's a real problem: there's real science behind it."

"Okay," he said. "We're an energy company; we must have a long-term view. We must pick up this issue and take appropriate action." A long debate followed, during which the members of the board asked us many questions. I remember one member saying, "You know, you've been talking about the cost of the damage and the cost of doing something about it in terms of perhaps a few per cent of world GDP. That's an awful lot of money."

Another member responded to this comment: "One per cent of world GDP and we're an energy company. What an opportunity!" With that optimism he switched the thinking of the entire board. All of a sudden, there was a whole new sense of purpose in the room.

Since that day, John Browne has been passionate about the climate. "We're going to take this on board," he said, and he was true to his word. In 2000, quite soon after the meeting, BP adopted a new corporate slogan, "Beyond Petroleum", reflecting perhaps at least the intention of a long-term shift in emphasis towards renewable energy.

Within a short time, thanks I'm sure to Browne's enthusiasm, BP set up one of the world's largest solar energy businesses, as well as an internal carbon trading system whereby if one part of the company wanted to exceed their allocated allowable CO_2 emissions, they had to acquire them from another part of the company. BP made some substantial savings this way: somewhere in the region of $500 million within a year; far from big bucks by oil companies' standards, but savings nevertheless. At a later date, John Browne invited me to address 30 or so of his senior global property managers at a meeting in Bath. He was introducing a policy whereby all new BP buildings worldwide should be carbon neutral. It was very interesting and impressive to see these representatives of enormous companies at work and beginning to take the environment seriously.

Unfortunately, Browne and his measures to help reduce damage to the planet had limited longevity within BP. In 2007, finding his private life under uncomfortably close media scrutiny, John Browne felt it necessary to resign. The "Beyond Petroleum" slogan gradually slipped out of use and the company's focus shifted away from renewables.

Nevertheless, John Browne, being a very able man determined to do good things, he has continued to give authoritative lectures on climate change. I haven't kept in touch with him, but I did bump into him once at Hull University, where we both found ourselves being awarded honorary degrees.

In 2005, although I had retired from direct involvement with the IPCC, I was still very busy with related work. On 21 July, I was among four scientists, including the president of the American Academy of Science, invited to present a testimony before the US Senate Committee on Energy and Natural Resources in Washington DC. When I'm given such an opportunity to speak to influential people, I feel an immense sense of responsibility. You never know who, like John Browne, might accept the truth about climate change, and what actions they might take in the future. I felt encouraged that such a committee was prepared to listen to the science.

Although the committee's main topic for consideration was to be nuclear energy, I was invited to talk on "Climate Change Science and Economics". The meeting was packed, and they allowed the discussion almost twice its allocated time, during which there was some rigorous debate. Beginning with a brief summary of the science, I went on to discuss the impacts of human-induced climate change, and I explained how the IPCC dealt with scientific uncertainty. I argued strongly for urgent action and the need for global leadership, stressing the results of recent studies on the economic impact of action or inaction: action would cost less than inaction. I finished with an assertion of my own optimism that this was still an issue the world could tackle.

Unfortunately, some senators' interest in nuclear power tended to derail discussions somewhat. While we four scientists agreed that nuclear energy does not contribute significantly to climate change, we voiced concern about other problems associated with it. I'm sure it would have pleased them more if we had given unequivocal support to nuclear energy as the solution to the climate change problem. I came away feeling that although I had managed to convey something of the urgency of addressing climate change, I perhaps had not convinced the meeting of the true strength of the scientifically based imperative for action. I wasn't surprised by my presentation's lack of impact on US energy policy.

That same year, but on this side of the Atlantic, I was honoured with an invitation to deliver the Prince Philip Lecture to the Royal Society of Arts. At the event in May, I took the opportunity to talk about "Climate Change and Sustainable Energy". I found Prince Philip a very engaging man with an active and intelligent interest in environmental issues. At various times over the years some of my work has led me to work with His Royal Highness Prince Charles the Prince of Wales. I have invariably found him, like his father, to be passionate about the environment and keen to keep abreast of related concerns. Prince Charles has the potential to influence significantly public opinion in the UK and possibly elsewhere; he has already spoken in public very eloquently on several occasions.

Just a few years after the Prince Philip Lecture, I attended a meeting of the International Energy Agency (IEA). Based in Paris, the IEA is an intergovernmental body representing the energy industries of the OECD (Organisation for Economic Co-operation and Development) countries. It provides logistical and technical support for energy use and development around the world.

The 2005 G8 summit in Edinburgh asked the IEA to report back about how it might be possible for the world's energy industries to reduce their CO_2 emissions enough to enable the world to succeed in limiting the rise in average global temperature to 2 °C above that of pre-industrial times.

The detailed, comprehensive annual IEA reports since then (the latest is 2012) assert that this would be possible between now and 2050.[3] Furthermore, they show that the subsequent savings in fuel costs over this period (even if discount factors were included) would more than meet the costs of switching to renewable sources of energy or of providing carbon capture and storage in places where fossil fuels are still used. The IEA reports also point out that moving away from fossil fuels will bring the worthwhile additional advantages of reducing pollution and increasing energy security.

A few years ago I attended an IEA brainstorming session, which took place in Paris before one of their meetings. Senior representatives from the world's energy industries and energy ministers from OECD governments gathered to consider the changes required to meet the problems of human-induced climate change. I was invited as an interested scientist. The debate was fascinating but disturbing. Industry representatives, including those of the oil industry, were quite outspoken, saying to the world's governments, "If you want big changes, we can make them. Just give us a planning framework including the price of carbon." This, they said, would enable them to move forward. However, the governments present, including that of the UK, failed completely to answer the question or to provide any adequate indication of policy to bring about the required transformation.

The presentation by the US government's representative was particularly disappointing. Grossly exceeding her allocated time, she made a great deal of the very little that the USA was actually doing, demonstrating how little her government understood about the scale of the problem. It was clear to me that if the world's governments would establish the rules of the game, industry was actually willing and, it would appear, able to make the necessary changes.

In 2010, I received an invitation to attend the third Lausanne Congress in Cape Town. The Lausanne movement began in

1972 when two of the most influential Christians of the last century, Billy Graham from the USA and John Stott from the UK, organized a world conference in Lausanne to discuss how the Christian message could reach the whole world. The 2010 Cape Town Congress was an inspiring gathering of over 4,000 Christian leaders from 198 countries, representing all continents, all ages, and with one-third women. The enthusiastic African hospitality was wonderful. Addressing audiences at a few of the event's smaller sessions, I spoke particularly about the urgent need to encourage the world to behave in a way consistent with Christian teaching, which includes the important component of caring for the whole of creation: the earth, its ecosystems, and its peoples, especially the poorest and most vulnerable.

Another interesting, more recent meeting with senior staff from one of the world's leading banks, together with some of their major investors, provided further evidence that the inaction of governments is the major obstacle to progress on tackling climate change. The meeting's focus was the need to provide investment in renewable energies. In his opening speech, the Chair stated that banks' *raison d'être* was not primarily to make money, but to serve people, and that to do so it was important to meet the challenge of climate change. I was amazed by the positive presentations by people from the world of banking. Again, just like the meetings with industry, the banks said they needed a long-term framework from governments in order to act. There are large sums of money, hundreds of billions of dollars, which investors are waiting to invest, but they need confidence in the structure. The question raised loud and clear by most of the speakers at that meeting was a very simple one: why can't governments sit down with industry and the banking sector to plan the future that is required? It's a good question.

I'm a scientist, so what I say about politics, economics, and the mysterious world of big business may come across as naïve; indeed it may be so. However, sometimes we need a degree of simplification in order to see a way forward. The same might be said of science. I have placed up-to-date climate science in front of politicians, business leaders, and religious leaders, trying to make it as accessible and comprehensible as possible. To them all, I have argued that living sustainably, or stewardship of the earth, needs to be a serious long-term commitment. We are entrusted with the earth in perpetuity, not just until tomorrow. This is not a comfortable idea within modern cultures interested in immediate gain, where a short-term view often predominates.

22

MAKING MONEY WORK

It is all too easy to dismiss big businesses, particularly oil companies, as being interested only in profit. However, my experiences with BP show that there are many concerned people within such companies, working to reduce the negative impacts of their work, or otherwise attempting to ensure that some good comes from their wealth. Similarly, there are wealthy individuals anxious to use their money to help others. Microsoft's Bill Gates is an excellent example. I'm not particularly interested in money, but when you're blessed with having enough of it, it presents an opportunity to have a positive impact in the world.

One of the most exciting recent projects in which I've been involved since the IPCC has been work with another oil company, this time Shell. As a trustee of the Shell Foundation between 2000 and 2010, I was involved in projects to bring sustainable energy and sustainable development to the developing world. Set up as a charity by the Shell company, the Foundation's mission is "to develop, scale-up and promote enterprise-based solutions to the challenges arising from the impact of energy and globalisation on poverty and the environment".[1] Surely a worthy goal.

When the Shell Foundation was established in 2000, three of the six directors were to come from Shell itself, with the other three, which included me, being independent. Shell's managing director at the time was keen to get the company involved in renewable energy. Mark Moody-Stuart, a man with a deeply held, intelligent interest in the environment, was one of the first high-profile people to drive a Toyota Prius hybrid car, which was quite a statement, given his position. With his support, the Foundation presented an opportunity for positive action.

As the Foundation considered the contribution it could make to meet needs in developing countries, it realized that a lot of money for larger projects was already available from other sources, and loans were also available for smaller enterprises, but there was a surprising gap in the middle that needed to be filled. We decided to concentrate on setting up and supporting small- to medium-sized enterprises, enabling them to become profitable, sustainable, and self-sufficient. By using the power of Shell's name and a close partnership with Grofin, a specialist developer and financier, the Foundation pioneered a new business model specifically designed to service this Growth Finance Sector. Grofin now manages well over $100 million of finance within some of Africa's larger countries. The Foundation also offers business training and ongoing support to the people involved. I found it both interesting and exciting to be involved in this pioneering work.

In the meantime, of course, other things were going on. In 2006 I was awarded the Japan Prize, the Japanese Nobel equivalent. Like the Nobel Prize won by the IPCC, I regard this as recognition of the importance of the science in which I've been privileged to be involved. The Japan Prize is awarded to two people every year. In 2006 the other prizewinner was a Japanese man called Akira Endo, who had discovered statins and their ability to reduce cholesterol. I'm very grateful to him actually, as I take statins myself.

Sheila and I were invited to a week-long ceremony and celebrations in Tokyo, which we thoroughly enjoyed sharing with Endo-San and his charming wife. At the award banquet, I sat next to the Japanese Empress, which was an enormous honour and absolutely fascinating. I found her to be delightful company: interested in everything and very well informed. With a BA degree in English Literature, the Empress speaks excellent English. Sheila sat between the Emperor and a lady who was the Leader of the Upper House, known to us only as "Her Excellency".

During the meal, Her Excellency asked Sheila through an interpreter whether I ever discussed my work with her. Sheila replied that, although she had no scientific background, she was interested in my work and that I often shared it with her. Sheila confessed to Her Excellency that she had been surprised by a discussion with Mrs Endo the previous day. Following her husband's lecture on statins, Mrs Endo had admitted to Sheila that most of the information in the lecture was new to her, because her husband never spoke about his work. Her Excellency explained that this was typical of Japanese marriages.

At the end of the meal, Her Excellency was the first to make a speech. All the speeches had been written in advance and published in a souvenir booklet for the banquet, but when Her Excellency approached the end of her speech she obviously strayed from the text because laughter rippled round the room. Of course, we couldn't understand the Japanese speech, but the Emperor kindly explained to Sheila that Her Excellency had used her comments to lecture the Japanese men that they should take a lesson from Western men and share their work with their wives. Sheila and I both thought this a very bold thing to say on such a formal occasion.

Once I had delivered my formal reply to Her Excellency, Mr Endo made his speech. Just as with Her Excellency's speech, he followed the typed speech until the end, when he departed from it. Again, there was laughter that Sheila and I didn't understand.

Whatever it was, the Emperor and Empress both appeared to enjoy his comment, while Her Excellency put her hands together and bowed in appreciation.

Once Sheila and I had formally processed out behind the Emperor and Empress, they fully explained the joke to Sheila. Mr Endo had commented that his subject is medicine, and he realized that he must take the medicine Her Excellency prescribed and start discussing his work with Mrs Endo. Sheila responded by saying that she had learned her lesson: that you have to be very careful what you say to a politician. Such good humour continued into a small evening reception. The Empress, a keen musician, talked fondly of her visit to Wales and, in particular, of a tune she had learned. Sheila had the privilege of joining with the Empress in singing together the tune of the well-known Welsh song "Ar Hyd yr Nos".

All in all it was a very happy occasion.

The Japan Prize itself was a very generous sum of money. Determined to use some of this money in a purposeful way, I decided to establish the John Houghton Fellowship at my old college, Jesus College in Oxford. I wanted the prize money to support scientific research into areas of sustainability. The Shell Foundation kindly accepted my invitation to join me in funding the research. The successful applicant was an excellent young chemist called Zheng Jiang, who pursued research into the science and technology of bio-waste-generated energy. Zheng completed his fellowship in 2012, having demonstrated the enormous potential of using biomass for energy generation. I hope it will not be long before his ideas have developed sufficiently to be put into practical application, especially in rural areas in the developing world.

The developing world should be of immense concern. As people try to lift themselves from poverty, their energy demands are increasing, and we need to help them find sustainable ways to meet this demand.

In 2006, as well as my trip to Japan, I also travelled to India to see the Shell Foundation in action. I went first to Gujarat, a state north of Bombay, which, having suffered three years of drought, was on the brink of agricultural catastrophe. Farming of their most profitable crop, cotton, was becoming unsustainable because of the combined difficulties of growing it efficiently, particularly in drier conditions, and selling it at a profit. Farmers were losing money. An NGO called Agrocel was already working with the farmers, trying to help them farm in technically and scientifically sensible ways, so the Foundation worked alongside them to make farming more viable. I visited a large and profitable farm, where the farmer thanked the Foundation for having turned things around for him. The funding and guidance he had received had enabled him to replace chemical-based pesticides with organic pest control, derived from the leaves of indigenous trees. He was also using organic waste from the farm as fertilizer, saving further expense, and was able to employ many members of his extended family. Another problem he had faced was the scarcity of water, his borehole often running dry. He was taught how to use water more efficiently on his crops. It was a joy to see his success, which was soon consolidated when the Foundation created a joint fair trade enterprise with Marks & Spencer to offer farmers like him guaranteed prices for their produce. This has enabled the development of thousands of profitable and sustainable farms that make sustainable use of local resources and employ local people.

From Gujarat I went to the state of Pune where the Foundation had been addressing problems arising from the "stoves" used in village homes. Traditionally, these were inefficient fires on the floor, which pumped out huge amounts of smoke, so much so that indoor air pollution was a very significant killer, particularly affecting children. Indeed I believe it is still the fourth biggest killer in the world. The object was simple: more efficient and less polluting stoves. Again, an NGO was already working on this, but they needed help. Shell worked with the NGO to design a better stove, which could be made locally in the villages, thus creating another small industry for the people. I was shown stoves being made in the village, and I met women whose work was arranging loans for families to buy these stoves. Although the sums involved were very small, they were valuable to the villagers. Still more people were employed in testing the stoves. These were good examples of villagers working within a newly flourishing local economy. Unfortunately, although the stoves on the whole showed much reduced pollution, they were not all a success, because some villagers found them difficult to use and maintain. Recognizing these problems, the Foundation has since developed improved stoves and distribution arrangements with the aim of providing millions of stoves in places where this is a major problem.

In Bangalore the Foundation had supported several enterprises, including cotton-spinning and the utilization of photovoltaic cells. I met a man who had a small business charging batteries during the day from solar cells on the roof of his house. He would take the fully charged batteries to the stalls in the night markets and take away their empty batteries to charge again the next day. The Foundation has continued to help such people scale up similar enterprises.

While in India I also visited Delhi where I met up with Dr Pachauri, the Chair of the IPCC who, through his position as director of The Energy and Resources Institute (TERI) of India, is providing scientific and technical support for the development of renewable energy in India. I also lectured in Delhi to a large audience on climate change and energy provision.

Through the Shell Foundation I also got involved in what was to be a very important public transport project in the developing world. About half of the world's population now live in cities, many of which are being brought close to a standstill by traffic congestion and smog. This disproportionately impacts the urban poor, who are affected by the pollution and separated from employment opportunities by inadequate public transport. Under a project called Embarq, the first city to be tackled by the Foundation in partnership with the World Resources Institute in the USA was Mexico City, which was in gridlock for much of the time. There it helped to develop "Metrobus", a 20-km-long bus corridor, serviced by 97 articulated buses that carry more than 300,000 people each day. Embarq has also been able to work with governments, business, civil society, and transport experts to deliver results in other congested cities especially in South America.

Shell can achieve these things because the powerful combination of their money and their big name opens the world's negotiating tables to them. It is great to see such wealth and influence being put to good use. Through my relationship with Shell I've had interesting and useful discussions with senior people within the company and the director of the Shell Foundation, updating them on climate change. I have always found them very supportive and willing to listen. Given the low probability that Shell will think of changing the very core of their oil business in the short term, it has nevertheless been great to witness, through the Shell Foundation, this major oil company using their money and might to a good end. It was a privilege to be part of that.

23

AMERICA THE POTENTIALLY GREAT

When people, businesses, and nations have been blessed with wealth and power, it is surely their responsibility to do great things for those less fortunate. This sense of responsibility may be rooted in faith or it may stem from instinct. Wherever it comes from, perhaps none of us do as much as we might, whether as individuals or as nations.

I would argue that the USA is the world's most influential country, and among the most politically powerful and wealthiest. It is also a predominantly Christian country with a large evangelical movement. Surely it should therefore be reasonable to expect Americans to take a strong line on climate change.

However, during the 1990s, while working on the first two IPCC reports, particularly the second, I gained my first understanding of the immensity of the obstacle to progress presented by the influence of the Right wing in American politics. As I have shown in earlier chapters, contrary to what I would hope to hear from America, the effect upon American energy policy of some of the voices and organizations influencing the more conservative voters and politicians has been and continues to be close to disastrous.

In terms of global statistics, China, rather unfairly, has gained notoriety as the world's biggest emitter of CO_2, producing more per year than the USA and Canada put together, with levels rapidly increasing. However, the statistics upon which this comparison is usually based don't present a very accurate picture. When it comes to per capita emissions, which are a fairer measure, Americans take some beating among the large economies, with emissions per head of population about four times that of China, at the moment anyway. We in the UK shouldn't feel too pleased with ourselves either, as we are still around tenth in terms of per capita contributions to atmospheric CO_2.

Although ranking high in total emissions, China and India rank low when we measure per capita. Another factor making it is unfair to single out China and India for blame is that when we in the developed world buy their products, as we so frequently do, the carbon load of the manufacture and the transport is borne by them. If the carbon load of these imports were to be added to the UK's figures, the statistics would look very different, with UK emissions over the last decade actually rising rather than falling.[1]

Not only that, but China in particular is actually doing something to deal with CO_2 emissions. Aware that their own people and economy will suffer from the effects of climate change, they issued in 2011 a five-year plan for energy and emissions in which they set some demanding targets for industry. Although, because of China's rapid growth, their targets may seem inadequate, it is actually quite a progressive plan.[2] Ambitious to become the world's prime manufacturer of renewable energy technologies, they are preparing for the future. They are sensibly keen to get on with it to gain advantage. Why aren't we in the West doing the same as China in positioning ourselves, our industries, and our economies for the future? Even if politicians can't see the importance of action, surely they can see the opportunities.

In general, per capita emissions tend to reflect GDP, supporting my belief that the moral imperative rests with the wealthy people and nations of the world. Emissions are not the only reason I believe this. Wealthier economies are better equipped to deal with the effects of climate change. We have more money, more knowledge, and better infrastructures. In addition to this, in a terrible example of injustice, it is the poorer people of the world, those with very low emissions indeed, who will suffer the worst effects of the changing climate, such as more frequent and intense heat waves, droughts, and floods. This returns us to the moral imperative and accountability argued in the previous chapter.

It's not about guilt or blame. There's no point in beating ourselves or indeed each other up about the state we've allowed the earth to fall into. For many decades, we had no idea of the potential impact of our actions. But now we know. Now that we realize and understand the disproportionate effects, there must surely be a tremendous moral imperative to act upon our knowledge. The current stand-off between the developed and the developing world, perhaps epitomized by that between the USA and China, is crazy. For the USA to rely upon China to take the first action, or to match their own action, is to occupy the moral low ground.

The USA still carries enormous political and cultural influence all around the world. George W. Bush's failure to ratify the Kyoto Protocol was a huge blow to progress on climate change, and the ongoing reluctance of the American Right to accept the scientific evidence of climate change has long been a major obstacle.

If we combine the Christian moral imperative with the American belief in their country as world-savers, we might expect Americans to be jumping up and down to do something about it. They could be shouting, "We will save the world!" Because they still can. They could rapidly transform the whole situation. I still hope they will. They just need to be convinced of the truth and integrity of the science, reinforced by the strong economic case for the benefits to the economy that will also come from positive action.

Since retiring from the IPCC, and running parallel to my work with the Shell Foundation, I have felt it important to try to put the science of climate change before Christian leaders in the United States, as I feel that therein lies an important key to international progress.

In 2000 I was at an environmental conference in St George's House in Windsor Castle. A distinguished ecologist from the University of Wisconsin, Cal de Witt, was there too. Cal was also the director of the Au Sable Institute of Environmental Studies, a Christian environmental association which does great work among students to promote Christian environmental stewardship. Between sessions, Cal and I took a walk in Windsor Great Park, a wonderful place to be on such a lovely afternoon. I remember saying to him, "If only American Christians would come on board, it would make an enormous difference. What can we do about it?"

After some discussion, Cal suggested that we organize a conference in Oxford. Americans, as I'd experienced before, love coming to Oxford. Cal offered to invite Christian leaders from the USA, especially some from the conservative side. Would they come? Could we persuade them of the reality of climate change and the imperative of tackling it? My role was simpler. I had to invite the very best IPCC scientists I could find to present the best, most recent scientific material. I also had to find prominent church leaders who would speak well on stewardship. With funding from a surprisingly enthusiastic UK Foreign Office, and organizational support from the recently established John Ray Initiative, the conference began to take shape.

The conference eventually took place two years later, in 2002. Unfortunately, we didn't get as many Americans as we would have liked because it was soon after the awful events of 9/11 and many Americans, understandably, were afraid to fly. Nevertheless, it was a very good meeting. Bob Watson, still at the time Chair of the IPCC, gave an excellent, compelling presentation of the science. The Rt Revd James Jones, the Bishop of Liverpool, talked authoritatively and passionately on theology and the environment. Others spoke about the scientific case and the economics. All in all, I felt that it was a powerful meeting, and I was not alone.

A key delegate was Richard Cizik, the vice president for Public Policy in the National Association for Evangelicals (NAE). Cizik is a charismatic man with lots of drive. The NAE has around 50,000 member churches and represents or at least has connections with about 25 per cent of the whole American population. If we could convince NAE leaders of the need to take climate change seriously, we would be making significant progress towards succeeding in the USA.

Cizik came to Oxford as a sceptic. As he himself has said, he was "dragged" there by a friend.[3] I am very grateful to that friend, because reluctant though Cizik may have been to attend, he was prepared to listen with an open mind, and what he heard made a great impression upon him. He has since spoken and written about the conference in glowing terms, saying he never realized scientists could be so humble. He was impressed by the reluctance of IPCC scientists to claim absolute certainty, and by the fact that we were so open about our degrees of uncertainty. More importantly, in the same interview, he said that what he heard made him realize that the responsibility to address climate change was not something he could "shirk, shrug, or rationalize". In short, he said, "It changed me." He has since described the conference as his "Damascus moment".[4] He returned to the USA determined to interest and influence American evangelicals in what he called "creation care" and climate change. Walking in through his own front door, he said to his wife, "Ginny, we're gonna have to change some things."

Unfortunately, Cizik faced an uphill battle. How could he convince fellow evangelicals that efforts to halt climate change should be high up on the political agenda, when everything they had previously been told had argued the contrary? After all, they'd been subjected to, and ideologically inclined to believe, the fossil fuel industry's misinformation campaign. In her 2012 book *Between God and Green*, Katharine K. Wilkinson suggests that although Cizik did succeed in moving climate change from the Left to the Centre of the American evangelical movement, he still has not won over those Right of centre, from whom he continues to face a lot of opposition.

Adding to Cizik's problems was the fact that, as he explained to me, scientists in the USA are perceived by many evangelicals to be Darwinian evolutionists. Many evangelicals reject evolution because it seems to them inconsistent with the biblical account of creation, and so distrust scientists in general. As a result they tend to reject what scientists say about climate change. Thus, climate change becomes a victim of the evolution debate (see Appendix 1). However, an optimist by nature, Cizik was convinced that evangelicals could change their minds because, as he said, if Christians don't care for God's earth, who will?

In June 2004, Cizik and others in the USA followed up the Oxford meeting with a two-day conference in Sandy Cove, Maryland, on the shores of Chesapeake Bay, to which were invited over 30 mostly sceptical evangelical leaders. The conference was daringly entitled "What to do about climate change". On the first evening, we heard an excellent speech by Howard Snyder, a professor of theology from Philadelphia. Snyder spoke about the doctrine of creation and its importance in the Bible. It was the perfect beginning because it made people very receptive to what was to come later. This made my job the following morning a little easier when I addressed the conference as a scientist, and spoke about the science of climate change.

At lunch time, bringing things to a more immediate and local level, we were shown a short film about what had happened on Tangier Island in Chesapeake Bay, where a 200-year-old fishing community had failed to keep to the official state guidelines about waste disposal and fishing quotas, thereby exhausting their fish stocks and polluting their own waters. The guidelines were there to protect the area's fragile ecological balance, so the community's very survival was now at risk. And yet, as a community, these people were largely Christian and churchgoing.

Susan Emmerich, a student of Cal de Witt, had recently worked on her doctoral thesis on the ecology of Tangier Island. During her stay there, she had felt a responsibility to point out to the community the errors of their ways, in terms of both their own survival as a fishing community and their environmental responsibility as Christians. She had planned to visit each of the churches in turn, but in the end, because of a big storm, they all gathered together in the largest church, where she addressed them en masse. As a result of her efforts, 20–30 per cent of Tangier Island's fishermen "covenanted" to keep to Maryland's rules. Within a short time, the island was cleaned up, the fish came back, and the community was saved. Problem solved.

Two fishermen from Tangier Island had come to Sandy Cove and talked to us over lunch about their covenant. They were accompanied by experts in the ecology of the bay. After that, inspired by their success story, we were treated to a trip around the bay on board a skipjack, an old type of oyster fishing boat. As well as being a welcome breath of fresh air, this was a wonderful opportunity to see for ourselves something of the ecological challenges of Chesapeake Bay.

Our job on the penultimate evening of the Sandy Cove meeting was to agree and sign a statement before midday the next day. Although it had already been drafted, it was very difficult to reach a consensus because people still felt insufficiently informed. Impressed as they might have been by what they had seen and heard throughout the conference, they quite rightly felt that there was much more to learn and more to consider. Although very happy with the theological part, they still felt that they knew too little about climate change to be able to promise any specific action. Someone suggested, "Let's agree a covenant rather than a statement, like the fishermen on Tangier Island." Thanks to our recent experience, we all knew what he meant. So, the Maryland meeting agreed to a covenant, in which all present committed to engage with, and learn from, the best climate scientists available. They promised to engage their own churches with the issue and write a more specific statement on climate change. Once the statement was ready, they would sign their names to it and seek other signatories among evangelical leaders.

Perhaps the most prominent figure among American evangelicals at the time, and possibly still today, was the Revd Rick Warren, one of the best known, highest profile Christian leaders in the world. He is pastor of Saddleback Church in California, a mega-church with a congregation of over 20,000. A remarkable man, Warren has written an excellent book called *The Purpose-Driven Life*. With sales of over 30 million copies, this has become one of the bestselling Christian books ever. In his book, Warren encourages Christians to tackle the world's biggest problems, which he identifies in a list of five, including dire poverty in the developing world. Unfortunately, he doesn't list climate change among them.

The team gathering signatories for the Sandy Cove Covenant rightly felt that Rick Warren's signature, if they could get it, would carry significant weight. Finding it remarkably difficult to get in touch with him, they asked me whether I might be able to help. I immediately contacted my old friend John Stott, and was astonished to discover that he was on the point of leaving for California, where he already had plans to meet with Rick Warren. Reporting back to the delighted team in the USA that John Stott would be happy to put the matter before Rick Warren, I helped them to prepare a letter and supporting materials. When John Stott presented the letter to Rick Warren on the Friday, he agreed to sign the covenant.[5]

The eventual statement and list of signatories proved to be an interesting and important step in influencing American opinion. Published prominently in the *The New York Times* and *The Washington Post*, the "Biblical Vision for Creation Care" recognized the problem of human-induced climate change and agreed that action needed to be taken. It had at the time 89 signatories, all prominent evangelical leaders. This number has continued to grow ever since. The delay between conception and publication was due to two reasons: one was simply the time-consuming nature of collecting signatories; the other was more political. Being predominantly of Republican leanings, nobody involved in the covenant wanted to hinder the re-election of George W. Bush to the White House by raising the issue of climate change. In spite of the delay, I've heard it said that the statement did actually have some impact within the White House. Since then, the issue has been recognized further within the evangelical movement, although against considerable opposition.

Throughout this period of preparing and publishing the "Biblical Vision for Creation Care", the rise and fall of climate change science within theological discussion continued to be a feature of the American evangelical movement. While Cizik's efforts met with some success, he faced formidable, powerful opposition. In 2007, there was an attempt to oust Cizik from the NAE because of his "relentless campaign" on global warming.[6] As expected, the pressure came from the political Right of the movement who claimed that Cizik's focus on climate change was shifting the emphasis "from the moral issues of our time", which they defined as abortion, homosexuality, and abstinence.[7] They also argued that market forces should be left to deal with any climate change problems. Thanks to significant support from the board of the NAE, Cizik survived on this occasion. However, a year later he was somewhat the author of his own downfall when he made the mistake of commenting that he was not 100 per cent convinced by NAE policy on a completely unrelated issue. Having publicly alluded to a possible flaw in NAE policy, he recognized that he had to bow to pressure and resign. Jacqueline L. Salmon's article in *The Washington Post* reported that "Cizik had increasingly earned enemies in the conservative evangelical movement for pushing to broaden the evangelical agenda, particularly into the area of 'creation care'".[8] Perhaps he had been a marked man. Perhaps he'll be free to have a greater influence outside the NAE. I hope so.

In spite of Cizik's difficulties, and in spite of all of the above, it is important to note that the NAE is officially onboard regarding climate change. Their president at the time, Rev Dr Leith Anderson, supported Cizik, and has also signed the Sandy Cove Covenant. For him to have done more would have jeopardized his position in the NAE and been counterproductive. Some people within the NAE admit to feeling powerless on climate change because of the oppressive weight of general disbelief. How can they shift a whole movement, when the voices against them are so established, so powerful and so determined?

In the USA there exists an influential Christian movement called the Cornwall Alliance for the Stewardship of Creation. In 2009, the Alliance issued a counter-document in answer to the "Biblical Vision for Creation Care". Carrying the signatures of 90 Christian leaders, their high-profile statement, *A Call to Truth, Justice and Protection of the Poor*, opens by asserting:

The world is in the grip of an idea: burning fossil fuels to provide affordable, abundant energy is causing global warming that will be so dangerous that we must stop it by reducing our use of fossil fuels, no matter the cost. Is that idea true? We believe not.[9]

They name this "idea" "global warming alarmism". Their website invites well-meaning visitors to endorse this view by signing their names to it, and many do.

The unintended irony in the title of their "Call to truth" is clear. Surely any "call to truth" should take into account, not ignore, scientific truth. Nevertheless, their document has earned the Cornwall Alliance both support and influence, which extends into powerful places. As they say on their website, they have become "one of the most prominent voices in America and internationally on issues of religion and environment". Often cited in American newspapers, on TV, and on the radio, they have provided testimony before both the US Senate and the Vatican.

At the heart of the Alliance's theology is an argument that creation can care for itself: after all, it was created by God and so were we, so what can go wrong? Ignoring the biblical principle of stewardship and accountability regarding the world and its resources, they encourage us instead to squander the earth's resources with no view to the future. The Alliance argues that we have been blessed with resources such as fossil fuels to improve life for everybody, and that using these, not questioning their use, should be our priority. They propose that the money spent on combating climate change ought instead to be spent on such things as wealth generation and international development. This view defies scientific evidence, and it defies economic research such as that of the IEA. Surely, any theology that argues on such grounds at the expense of addressing our immense responsibility to one another and to future generations isn't sensible at all.

I've no doubt that there are many good people among those we might call climate change sceptics. They believe that they are acting honourably. Of course they care about world poverty and suffering, but the standard Republican doctrine tends to say that we can only ease poverty abroad if the USA economy is strong; that is, if America remains wealthy. To say that our wealthy behaviour contributes to poverty overseas is contrary to their thinking. They distort the cost of action by focusing on the short-term up-front costs rather than the average costs over the next 20–30 years, which represent long-term savings. In this way, economic and political ideologies take the place of science in the debate. The result of all this pseudo-debate is that many good people genuinely believe that climate change is all nonsense, or is at least terribly exaggerated.

In January 2009, President Obama was signed in as President of the United States of America. Rick Warren was his controversial choice to read the inaugural prayer at the ceremony. I felt optimistic that the new president might help to lead the world forward in efforts to meet the challenge of climate change.

Later that year, I contacted Rick Warren myself and asked if I might call on him on my way home from the IPCC meeting in Honolulu. He very kindly invited both me and my colleague Michael Naylor to attend his church and to share Sunday lunch. At the heart of our conversation was Warren's belief that we have to solve with great urgency the world's problems of dire poverty and of water supply and sanitation. With these priorities, he asked, why should we prioritize the less concrete issue of climate change? My answer was that unless we do something about climate change, the poor will be poorer, and the consequences will be devastating for enormous groups of poor people. I explained that it was imperative that climate change should reach the top of any Christian agenda. At the end of our conversation, Rick Warren joked that he could perhaps make climate care the sixth on his list of the five most important issues for Christian action. I felt that our stop-off had been worthwhile.

Just prior to the November 2009 UN Climate Change Conference in Copenhagen, I attended an Institute of Politics conference on the US and Climate Change at the University of Aberystwyth, close to my home in Wales. Experts from around the world discussed the problems we are all facing, with a particular focus on the upcoming conference. On my short journey home, I thought, "What on earth can I do about Copenhagen at this late stage?" Arriving home, I went straight to my study and drafted "An Urgent Call to Prayer and Action". Once Bishop James Jones had agreed the document, I emailed it to Rick Warren. His reply was immediate. He said what great timing this was, as he was going to the White House for a meeting with President Obama the following week. He offered to share my Call to Prayer with the president.

The outcome of Copenhagen must have been a great frustration for Obama. It provided, I believe, evidence of the extent to which his hands were tightly tied by an uncooperative, conservative Congress. Sadly, the four years of Obama's first presidency saw little progress on climate change in America.

The Lausanne Movement's 2010 Cape Town Congress mentioned in Chapter 21 led to the setting up of a series of international workshops to address action on several key issues, one of which was Care for Creation and Care for the Poor. That workshop was to meet in Jamaica in October 2012, about the same time as Superstorm Sandy hit the east coast of America.

Prior to the Jamaica conference, I was aware that Calvin Beisner,[10] the national spokesperson for the Cornwall Alliance mentioned earlier, had been corresponding with the conference organizers, requesting some input into the meeting. As this was likely to be damaging, I felt it incumbent upon me to contact him. I wrote him a letter detailing the integrity of the IPCC and climate science, and mentioning some of the opposition we had faced, some by name. I really wanted to convince him of the reality of the climate change problem.

However, Beisner's impressively thorough reply was an absolute defence of his own position, and also that of his friends among whom he mentioned Seitz and Singer, both of whose stance on climate change has been discredited, as described in previous chapters. In his argument, Beisner ignored the scientific evidence of human-induced climate change, replacing it with his own politically driven agenda. Not only does Beisner fly in the face of scientific truth as represented by the IPCC, but he continues to assert that poverty in the developing world is being worsened by efforts to stop climate change. While I respect Beisner's genuinely strong feelings about such poverty, which he has experienced at first hand both as a child and as an adult, his argument is unfounded. In the longer term, climate change will make the problems of poverty very much worse. I had to respond with another letter, this time including a summary of present climate science. Much of this is included in the final chapter of this book.

It was a polite but heated exchange of letters between the two of us. Although the correspondence felt significant at the time, I'm not sure that I achieved anything. Sheila felt that I was wasting my time and energy; that someone like Beisner, approaching the issue from a predetermined viewpoint rather than in a quest for truth, is unlikely to consider the possibility that he might be mistaken or have been misled. Perhaps Sheila is right, but then again, we never know what influence our words and actions might have. I feel that I just have to keep telling the truth, as far as I know it.

For this reason I was particularly disappointed when, having been invited to speak at the Jamaica workshop, a severe throat infection prevented me from travelling. However, I was privileged to be able to speak to the meeting through a Skype link, and I am currently involved in helping to edit the book arising from the conference addressing the question, "What can Christians do?"

At about the same time as the Jamaica conference, and just before the 2012 American election, Superstorm Sandy hit the east coast of America. The devastation, particularly in New York, led the mayor of New York, Michael Bloomberg, to state:

Our climate is changing. And while the increase in extreme weather we have experienced in New York City and around the world may or may not be the result of it, the risk that it might be – given this week's devastation – should compel all elected leaders to take immediate action.

Bloomberg's words boosted Obama's re-election campaign.

Although opinion in America is still divided on whether or not climate change is attributable to human activity, I was greatly encouraged by President Obama's bold statement on climate change in his January 2013 inaugural address. Speaking with clarity and determination, he devoted more words to this policy than to any other:

We, the people, still believe that our obligations as Americans are not just to ourselves, but to all posterity. We will respond to the threat of climate change, knowing that the failure to do so would betray our children and future generations. Some may still deny the overwhelming judgement of science, but none can avoid the devastating impact of raging fires, and crippling drought, and more powerful storms. The path towards sustainable energy sources will be long and sometimes difficult. But America cannot resist this transition; we must lead it. We cannot cede to other nations the technology that will power new jobs and new industries – we must claim its promise. That is how we will maintain our economic vitality and our national treasure – our forests and waterways; our croplands and snowcapped peaks. That is how we will preserve our planet, commanded to our care by God.

The following day, the UN Secretary General Ban Ki-Moon stated that tackling climate change was one of his own priorities for 2013. Again, I found this encouraging, and I'm sure Obama must have felt the same. At the time of writing this book, I hope that in his second term, Obama will be able to find more freedom to act. I hope so, because I'm sure that this intelligent, well-informed man understands the immense significance of climate change. Whether or not he'll succeed in moving the USA to take the actions that are so necessary, we shall see. It's an exciting possibility.

Some US states such as California are already moving forward with targets, and encouraging positive action in industry and economies. Many US businesses have combined to create an Advisory Committee on Renewable Energy (ACORE), giving evidence that there is a will to move forward. That message needs to reach the politicians. Perhaps if the progressive states and businesses can demonstrate success, other states and the White House will follow. I have no doubt that if conservative American evangelicals could be convinced of the reality of climate change and of our Christian responsibility to tackle it, and of the immense benefits of doing so, the rules of the game could change dramatically for the better.

I am still involved with events which allow me to explain climate science to American Christian leaders. Over the last few years in the UK, Bishop James Jones has arranged a number of discussion meetings with pastors from churches in the United States, some of which have included a visit to Highgrove, the home of His Royal Highness Prince Charles. The prince is passionate about climate change and very well informed; his presence on these occasions contributed significantly to their success. Many American evangelical pastors are in fact convinced that climate change is an important issue, but they realize that they face a big challenge conveying this to their congregations.

At the time of writing, international negotiations are in stalemate: nobody can move. Because significant global action requires global agreement, we need somebody to catalyse international action. However, given the proven difficulties of making progress in world negotiations, it might be more effective for smaller groups of countries to come together to form binding agreements; for example if the USA and China could agree targets between them. After all, it would be in both of their political interests to reach an agreement. How great it would be if these two big powers and two big polluters could get together and say, "We're going to do this." The rest of the world would then follow. It is still not too late, but we're cutting it rather fine, and at the moment such agreement seems a very long way off.

Although I'm getting slower now and I have a little less energy for travel, I try to devote as much time and action, thought and prayer as possible to achieving this end.

24
TODAY

My very gradual move back to North Wales began back in the mid 1970s when Peter went to St David's in Llandudno. At about the same time, Margaret and I bought a holiday cottage in Abergnolwyn, within the Snowdonia National Park. Not only did this mean that we could at times be closer to Peter, but it was an area we loved, and we could all join Peter in learning to sail near Aberdovey. Peter, Janet, and I became keen sailors, spending many happy hours together on the water as the children grew up.

Just after my retirement, Sheila and I sold the holiday cottage, Sheila having found an old farmhouse on a North Wales hillside with a wonderful panoramic view of the Dovey estuary. As it had been unoccupied for 40 years and was without either water supply or an access road, we first had to make it habitable. Over the next few years we had an exciting time visiting and developing it to meet our needs before finally moving in in 1995. It has been home ever since. Before us we have the sea, and behind us the glories of Snowdonia. For years, I have been able to sail and walk in what to me is some of the world's most beautiful scenery.

I have climbed and sailed with a friend, Don Harris, most of my life. Don and I met at Oxford where he taught law at Balliol College. In the 1960s, we learned to ski together, and in 1995, shortly after Sheila and I moved into the farmhouse, Don and I bought a 26-foot sailing boat. Sailing from Aberdovey, we enjoyed adventures on the Irish Sea, sailing to the Isle of Man and several times to Ireland. Only recently did we feel that we were becoming less agile and less able to move safely around the boat or to deal with any incidents or mishaps that might occur. The time had come to give up sailing. Sad though the decision was, we were pleased to be able to give our boat to the Aberystwyth Sea Cadets.

Back on dry land, there are many fine mountains within easy reach of Aberdovey. At about 3,000 feet and less than 10 miles away, Cadair Idris is possibly my favourite. Snowdon, the highest mountain in Wales, is only about 50 miles away.

In spite of the idyllic and rather remote setting in which I now live, "retirement" seems hardly an appropriate word to describe my life. My time in recent years has been occupied by an interesting mix of continuing hard work, illustrious occasions, and precious, quieter moments with Sheila in our converted farmhouse. Occasionally we manage to make time to retreat to a favourite place of ours on Anglesey. I enjoy it all.

I have been blessed with seven grandchildren of whom I'm very proud. Janet and Paul have five children who at the time of writing range in age between 14 and 23 years. The eldest, Daniel, is in his final year of a traditional course at Oxford called "Greats", which includes classics and philosophy. Hannah has been studying Anglosaxon, Norse and Celtic at Cambridge and now Theology; Esther is working as a supervisor at Starbucks and pursuing Culinary Arts at City College, Norwich, before applying for university; Johnny is pursuing science subjects at school and has won top awards as a juggler; Jemima, the youngest, is keen on sport and wants to be a sports teacher. Peter and Kendra's two sons, Max and Sam, aged 17 and 11, live in the United States. Max is keen to attend a military service academy after graduating from high school, and Sam is starting middle school this year. They both enjoy school and sport, excelling particularly at lacrosse.

All my grandchildren, as all children, have different talents and interests. Like all young people, each one of them has so much potential to contribute to the world. I hope that I have always worked to the very best of my ability to leave them and their generation with hope for the future. I intend to continue to do so.

I am still occupied giving speeches, lectures, and presentations; sometimes about climate change and science, sometimes about faith and stewardship. Occasionally I am interviewed for radio, newspapers, and magazines, and twice I've spoken on a popular UK Sunday evening programme, *Songs of Praise*. It's all great fun and as I've said before, I have to take these opportunities because I never know who might be listening and what action they might take as a consequence.

The increasing awareness and understanding of the scale of the likely impacts of climate change continues to lead to the involvement of more scientists all around the world, including Wales. Three years ago, scientists in Welsh universities formed the Climate Change Consortium of Wales, inviting me to be its honorary scientific adviser. It has been most encouraging to be involved, and once again I find that when scientists from different but related areas get together, exciting progress can be made.

Sheila and I are both kept very busy by normal day-to-day life on our Welsh hillside. We're involved in the local church community, where I occasionally lead the services and through which we have developed valued friendships. Over 10 years ago Sheila bought a shop in a nearby town where, with others, she established a Christian bookshop and café providing fair trade food and gifts.[1] More recently, with a group of volunteers, Sheila took over the management and created a Christian fair trade café and gift shop that raised over £30,000 for a Christian charity in Uganda. The charity, WATSAN, supplies clean water and sanitation for some of the poorest Ugandan people, making a big difference to their health and to their lives. Sheila was saddened recently when she had to close the shop due to a shortage of available volunteers to help her to run it. However, she has since been able to set up a small Christian Fairtrade shop in our local village of Aberdovey.

Sometimes, as has happened throughout my life, events occur to lift us temporarily out of our day-to-day lives. In 2012 Sheila and I were honoured with an invitation to Queen Elizabeth's Diamond Jubilee in St Paul's Cathedral. It was a wonderful occasion, and we have often enjoyed reflecting upon it from back in the comfort of our home.

I frequently find myself, in quiet moments, reflecting too upon my career. Over the decades, I have learned a great deal about the world's climate, the effects of human influence, and the changes that lie ahead. These changes trouble me, and they should trouble us all. With such knowledge, how can I avoid my responsibility to do everything in my power to persuade the world to address the problem?

Perhaps we scientists haven't done this well enough. Perhaps I haven't been shouting loud enough, but I'm afraid that has never been my style. It doesn't come at all naturally to me to seek the limelight or to shout from the rooftops. However, my limitations have not all been those of my personality: during my IPCC years I simply could not be seen too much as an advocate for action. Although in recent years I've been free to talk about it more openly, I'm still more comfortable working away behind the scenes to try to make things happen.

This book is perhaps a means by which I can use my quiet, studious style to create something that might do a bit of the shouting on my behalf. There's a place for all kinds of action and we all need to do whatever we can.

25

GLIMPSES OF TRUTH

One of my most memorable experiences on Snowdon was about 25 years ago when Don Harris and I walked the Snowdon Horseshoe, a favourite climb of ours and one of the country's finest. Setting off from Pen y Pass, we left the Penygwryd track to begin the scramble up Crib Goch. We were soon in mist, an uncomfortable experience on Crib Goch's narrow, steep-sided ridge. The rocks were so wet and slippery that we needed handholds as well as footholds. By the time we reached Crib Goch's summit, any sight of the precipitous drop to each side was obscured by the mist.

From that first summit, the ridge widens, and a short descent leads to a comparatively flat, grassy area. Here we stopped to regain our breath and our nerve before the climb up to Snowdon's second peak, Carnedd Ugain. By now the cloud was beginning to lift. Areas of thinner mist swirled around us, affording us occasional brief glimpses of the features below before thickening again, obscuring them from sight. Beautiful vistas came momentarily into view, as did shadowy figures of walkers on other routes up the mountain.

As we stood enjoying the ever-changing scene, we also became aware of wider perspectives opening and closing before us. To our east, the unmistakable profile of Moel Siabod with its gentle green slopes appeared in sunshine for just a few seconds before the misty curtains closed again. Then the more jagged features of the Glydderau appeared, only to disappear just as rapidly. Fascinated by these snapshots of the sunlit peaks to the east, we turned to see the same gradual process of disclosure occurring to the west. The impressive rock faces on Lliwedd appeared, dark and threatening: the sun had not reached them yet. We could just discern the outline of Yr Wyddfa, Snowdon's summit, still veiled by fairly thick mist. To the north, parts of Anglesey beyond the Menai Strait began to appear. More windows were opening all around us. The cloud was fighting to stay, the mountains battling to come through to show their beauty, the sun pressing to declare its glory. Don and I stood transfixed for 20 or 30 minutes until finally the sunshine won.

This gradual unveiling provided one of my most enduring impressions of Snowdon's beauty and grandeur. Perhaps creation is best appreciated in small, even fleeting doses like these; I doubt that our minds are capable of perceiving at one moment the complexity of the whole. It is also very effective in whetting the appetite for further exploration and discovery.

I have spent most of my life exploring, through science and faith, the marvels and mysteries of creation. Like the clouds on Snowdon, the windows to truth tend to open slowly, revealing only tantalizingly small parts of the whole at a time. Our understanding and knowledge, like the sun, shine on some parts, leaving others in shadow. Occasionally, however, circumstances bring us closer to seeing and understanding the big picture, closer to seeing how all the small parts fit together to create one magnificent whole.

In contrast to those fleeting glimpses of Snowdon's scenery, astronauts in a spaceship can look back at the earth and see its immense beauty, complete with clouds and mist. They are rare and privileged viewers of one particular big picture, but still they cannot see everything. The big picture for which I have always been searching is different. Unlike a photo of the earth, it has to include the truth about everything. For me, it has to include the vastness of the universe and its complexity of systems; it has to include the smallest organisms; it has to include science and it has to include God.

Perhaps the most compelling aspect of my quest for truth is that it has led to more questions than it has produced answers. I cannot say that I have all the answers to life, the universe, and everything. As I said earlier, the more I've found out along the way, the more I've realized just how much more there is to know. It's a marvellous, endless, and constantly engaging quest in which the most important thing of all is to maintain a truthful mind, which I have tried to do. Only with a truthful mind can we be objective observers of creation, recording and reflecting upon the wonders we see. Affording us glimpses of truth and beauty, the world rewards our search, compelling us to continue. Don Harris reminded me once that as we stared at the scenes emerging from Snowdon's swirling mist, I turned to him and said, "I think heaven might be like that."

I am sure that God has a very much bigger picture of the whole of creation in terms of both time and space than we can ever hope to understand; all we might be privileged to gain are brief occasional glimpses. In spite of my necessarily imperfect understanding, I am committed to finding a way to live as God would want me to live, and to trying to find a way to work in partnership with him in everything I do, including my work.

Alan Brewer once said something to me that I have remembered ever since. Reflecting upon my career to date and upon the exciting direction in which things seemed to be going for me at the time, my former mentor observed, not unkindly, "You know, John, you have been able to do things I wouldn't have believed you capable of." His implication was that things had happened to me beyond my abilities. I understand and accept his meaning. Alan always was a very perceptive fellow. The relationship I feel I have with God reminds me of a song Sheila often sings, called "You Raise Me Up".[1] The chorus ends with the words, "You raise me up to more than I can be." It's as though I've been supported or developed beyond my own abilities by a force external to anything within me.[2]

I don't want it to seem as though I am special, because I'm not. That's the point. Nor do I wish to suggest that my faith has influenced my science in any improper way, because it hasn't. Both science and faith have a high concern for truth: to be concerned with either is to be concerned with a quest for truth, so there can be no conflict between the two.

As humans we have two eyes to view the world; their combined binocular vision brings depth not available to either eye on its own. Similarly, as I have sought to put my science and my faith alongside each other, the combination of my material eye and my spiritual eye has brought and continues to bring richness beyond my imagination. In my ongoing quest for truth I have been treated to true beauty. I feel immensely grateful for this.

26
WHERE ARE WE NOW?

It seems important to end with as clear a picture as possible of the most current information on climate science. With invaluable help from the UK Meteorological Office's Hadley Centre, I am currently updating my global warming textbook for the fifth edition, to be published by Cambridge University Press in 2014, work which is helping me keep abreast of much of the science.[1]

Climate change is an increasingly serious issue that we cannot ignore. It demands the urgent attention of everybody in the world. Most of us are part of the problem and we all need to accept the challenge of being part of the solution.

The latest situation

Current global average temperature is about 0.75 °C above pre-industrial levels. The most widely quoted current international "target" is to keep this figure below 2 °C. This was first proposed by the European Union Council in the 1990s, and is the adopted target of the United Nations Framework Committee on Climate Change. Although the target of 2 °C has been recognized internationally for well over a decade, there is as yet no international agreement about the emissions targets that need to be set to achieve it. It may in fact never be possible to set the necessary emissions targets on a wholly international scale. It is probably more realistic to hope for smaller groups of nations to agree targets. However, even some of those already with emissions targets, such as the UK, are not on track to meet them.

The figure of 2 °C has not just been randomly plucked from nowhere. It represents a realistic, challenging, and achievable target. Even a 2 °C rise will bring consequences to which it will be very difficult to adapt. However, staying below a 2 °C rise will go a long way towards limiting the extent of future problems.

I have described in earlier chapters how, over the past 25 years, through a series of IPCC reports, confidence has grown in the scientific evidence for human-induced climate change, although substantial uncertainties remain in some of the details of the likely changes and their impacts.[2] The main features of our current understanding are summarized in the following bullet points.[3]

- There is no doubt that over the last 200 years, the amount of carbon dioxide (CO_2) in the atmosphere has been increasing because of human activities, particularly the burning of coal, oil, and gas. That these are the source of most of the increase in atmospheric CO_2 has been chemically proven. Unless drastic action is taken, CO_2 levels are expected to double from their pre-industrial value before the end of this century. That's within the lifetime of our children and grandchildren.

- Carbon dioxide is one of several factors affecting the earth's climate. In recent years, through what are called "detection and attribution studies", climate scientists have thoroughly investigated possible climate changes and considered all known factors that play a part in such changes. Some of these, known as "feedbacks", occur within the climate system itself. Some influences have a positive (warming) effect, while others have a negative (cooling) effect (see Box 26.1).

Box 26.1 Some Factors and Feedbacks Influencing Climate Change

Along with CO_2, other factors influence the earth's climate, the extent of their impact constantly changing. When these factors are part of the complex climate system itself, they are called "feedbacks". Some feedbacks add to the warming (positive feedbacks) and some reduce the warming (negative feedbacks). Computer models include such factors and feedbacks in their formulations.

Some warming factors and feedbacks

• The greenhouse effect was explained and illustrated in Box 4.1 on p. 45. A straightforward calculation tells us that, if nothing else changes, doubled CO_2 would lead on average to an increase of surface temperature of about 1.2 °C.

• Because of warming, the oceans warm and more water vapour evaporates from the oceans' surface and enters the atmosphere. Water vapour being a powerful greenhouse gas, this is the largest positive feedback.

• As the earth warms, snow and ice melt. With a reduced area of the earth being covered in white, solar energy, instead of being reflected back into space by the ice, is absorbed by the earth's surface, making it warmer. This is another significant positive feedback.

Some cooling factors and feedbacks

• An important negative feedback occurs because increased CO_2 acts as a fertilizer for most vegetation, encouraging further growth, which in time has the effect of removing CO_2 from the atmosphere.

• Aerosols in the atmosphere (see Box 15.1 on p. 161) arising from human activities have grown substantially over the past century. These are an important influencing factor upon the climate. Sulphate aerosols from the burning of coal are acting to cool the atmosphere, masking some of the warming effect of greenhouse gases.

- The greenhouse effect, and the role played in this by CO_2, has been recognized as a solid piece of physics for over 200 years (see Box 4.1). IPCC work on detection and attribution has demonstrated that emissions of CO_2 due to human activities have been a major driver of the warming seen over the past century.

- The IPCC estimates that the result of doubled CO_2 levels would be an increase in global average temperature of 2–4.5 °C, an estimate that has remained about the same since the 1980s. This may not sound very much, but in terms of the global average it is very significant. The difference in global average temperature would be about the same as the difference between half an ice age and now. Such a rapid rate of climate change would be far greater than occurred on average during the ice ages. Both humans and ecosystems would find it very difficult to adapt.

- The average temperature rises over the past 50 years are already typically 0.5–1.5 °C over most of the earth's land surface with up to 2 °C over much of the Arctic. Because of their thermal capacity, the oceans take a long time to warm. The increases in surface temperature there are therefore smaller, typically in the range of 0.2–1 °C. As the oceans occupy over 70 per cent of the earth's surface, this helps to keep global average figures down. Observed global average temperature increases are in general consistent with what is expected and with what is simulated by climate models. Consistent small temperature rises in the deeper ocean have also been observed. Note especially that because of the substantial lag of several decades in ocean response, even if the increase of greenhouse gases were halted tomorrow, the average surface temperature would continue to rise for many decades into the future.

- So far we have only experienced a small part of the climate response to the greenhouse gas emissions that have already occurred. This is because some of the CO_2 can stay in the atmosphere and continue to affect climate for 100 years or more and also because, as with the oceans mentioned above, many of the systems on earth and within the atmosphere have a delayed or continuing response to climate changes already started. If greenhouse gas emissions were halted tomorrow, climate impacts much greater than we have so far experienced but to which we are already committed will be realized over the next 30 years and more into the future. Further emissions from now on just add to that commitment.

• An important result of rises in average temperature is the injection of more energy into the atmospheric circulation. This arises as follows. Increased surface temperature brings more evaporation of water from the ocean and the land surface. As well as increasing the greenhouse effect, this means more water vapour in the atmosphere and more rainfall on average. Observations are now showing this increase. It means too that more water vapour condenses into clouds, releasing extra latent heat into the atmosphere. This latent heat provides the largest single source of energy for the atmosphere's circulation and the hydrological cycle. Increased energy in the hydrological cycle means that rainfall in many areas will tend to fall with greater intensity. This all suggests a likelihood of greater frequency and intensity of climate extremes such as heat waves, intense rainfall, floods, and droughts, especially in vulnerable parts of the world.

• The expansion of seawater because of its increased temperature, together with some melting of glaciers and ice caps, could increase sea levels by around 1 metre by 2100, under the doubled CO_2 scenario. Many developing countries have large populations living in low-lying areas; for instance 10 million people in Bangladesh live below the 1-metre contour (see Figure 26.1 on the next page). Hundreds of millions of people around the world live close enough to the sea to be seriously affected by such a sea-level rise.

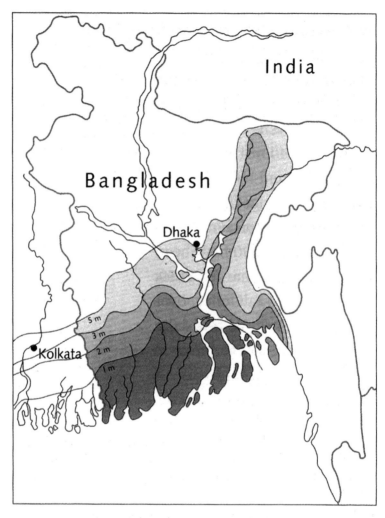

Figure 26.1 Map of Bangladesh showing the 1 m, 2 m, 3 m, and 5 m contours above sea level

- Observations over recent decades provide evidence for this increase in the frequency and severity of climate extremes, with some places being much more affected than others. Modelling studies (see Box 26.2) covering the rest of the twenty-first century demonstrate a very substantial continued increase in the number and severity of such events and the likely damage that will ensue. A careful report by the IPCC provides much more detail.[4] It is hard to imagine just how damaging the future would be if these estimates are anywhere near correct. In his award-winning and well-researched book *Six Degrees*,[5] Mark Lynas sets out to describe this future. It's a frightening picture.

- Due to the increasing CO_2 dissolved in the ocean, it is becoming more acidic, again at a rate to which many ecosystems, for instance coral reefs, are unlikely to be able to adapt.

- Melting land ice exposes the tundra below, allowing it to be warmed. This could lead to large emissions of methane, another greenhouse gas, which has been stored below the surface for millions of years. This process, which would be unstoppable, could have a large global warming effect. Although there is uncertainty about how big the change would be to trigger that release on a large scale, and although it is not likely this century, it is something on which scientists need to keep a vigilant eye.

- Melting ice, whether land or sea, means less reflective white on the earth's surface, meaning less reflection of the sun's heat, and an ever-faster rate of warming – another positive feedback.

- The likely impact of climate extremes and greater variability in weather and rainfall on the poorer parts of the world is extremely worrying. Aid agencies have stressed the urgent need for the world to address this problem. An excellent Tear Fund report, "Dried up, Drowned out", about the current dire situation in many parts of the world, can be read on their website.[6]

• Even if we do succeed in stabilizing global average temperature to within 2 °C above pre-industrial levels, the world will be a different place at the end of this century. Sea level will have risen; water availability will have changed in many places; the risk of floods and droughts will have increased substantially; and many ecosystems will have disappeared. Hundreds of millions of people who can't make a living where they are today will be displaced. It is beginning to happen already. Mass migration of whole populations and major disruption are likely to be widespread.

In spite of all this, and even though we will not be able to reverse much of the change already introduced into the system, it is not too late to act. We can still have a very positive impact on managing the extent, effects, and longevity of climate change. We can still take responsibility for the future, even if our potential to affect the present is limited. Clearly, we need, as a world, to take positive and urgent action to reduce carbon emissions to keep below the 2 °C target.[7] To fail in this would be very irresponsible. If we succeed, future generations will look back and thank us. This is an important moment.

Box 26.2 Computer Modelling of Climate

To ascertain the likely scale of future climate changes requires the use of computer-based climate models. Such numerical models provide the only means we have of integrating the relevant equations over time. Box 6.1 on pp. 72–73 gives a short description of computer models of the atmosphere that provide the basis for weather forecasting today.

Climate models have been developed from weather forecasting models. They also need to include the oceans and how they are coupled dynamically to the atmosphere, also the sea ice and ice sheets in the polar regions. Further, since climate models are run for years at a time, they also need to follow the relevant properties of the land surface and how they might change with time.

It was not until the late 1980s that computers became sufficiently powerful (~1 billion operations per second) to begin to couple the atmosphere and ocean circulations together. Today climate models are run on computers with a speed of many thousand billion operations per second, which is still nothing like enough to describe all the processes with the detail that is really required.

It is sometimes thought that climate models are like models in other complex areas – for instance models of the economy where predictions for the future are created from detailed statistical studies of the past. Such statistical models are bound to be severely limited in their predictive capability. Since the processes and equations that govern the behaviour of the climate system are mostly precisely known, the power of climate models is not limited in this way.

To test the accuracy of a model's simulations, the model is run from an initial state in the past defined by observations at that time. The evolution of the model's climate can then be tested by comparison with the climate observed at later times. By this means confidence can be generated regarding model predictions for the future.

Climate models can begin from a set of observations at a particular time. They need to include many more processes than weather forecasting models, so they can only be run with a relatively coarse spatial resolution.

The future emissions diagram (Box 26.3) illustrates how emissions from energy sources will have to be reduced between now and 2050 if there is to be a good chance of achieving the 2 °C target. In addition, deforestation will have to be much reduced.

Box 26.3 Necessary Future Emissions Targets

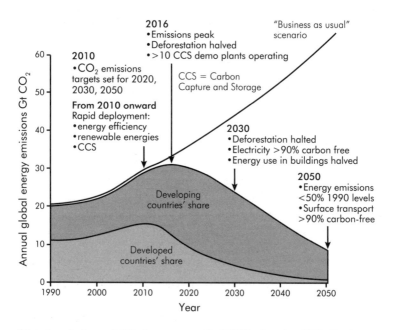

Global emissions of CO_2 from energy to 2050, showing IEA's Business-as-Usual Reference Scenario (top line) and a profile (lower lines) aimed at <2 °C temperature from pre-industrial levels. The division between developed and developing countries from today until 2050 is based on developing countries' share peaking earlier and reducing further.

What is the political situation?

Regrettably, voices arguing that climate change is not a result of human activities are still influential on public and political opinion, particularly in industrial countries in the Western world, for instance the USA and the UK. It seems ridiculous to me that they are frequently presenting objective science as a subjective issue that can be decided by conjecture, opinion, or popular vote.

The Kyoto Protocol, now drawing to the end of its validity, needs replacing. Negotiations began in Durban in 2011, with the aim of negotiating a new treaty on global emissions for agreement in 2015. What would help a great deal is agreement on emissions targets between the USA, India, and China: three of the biggest emitters, all of whom are exempt from the Kyoto Protocol. It can only be a good thing that President Obama will be at America's helm at this time.

What can we do?

I remember a particularly pertinent joke by the stand-up comedian Sean Lock, although I can't remember the actual programme. He told his audience that when he puts out his bottles and cans for recycling, he feels like a person turning up at the scene of a devastating earthquake with a dustpan and brush, saying, "It's OK everyone, I'll sort it out." Many people share that sense of powerlessness: our individual efforts seem completely ineffective in relation to the enormity of the problem we face.

Nevertheless, as Edmund Burke once famously said, "No one could make a greater mistake than he who did nothing because he could do only a little."[8] It is important that we do as much as we can to live as sustainably as possible, for instance by:

- switching to a green energy supplier;
- improving our home insulation and energy efficiency;
- recycling as much of our waste as possible;
- installing solar panels or even ground source heat pumps;
- limiting the miles we drive;
- driving electric or hybrid vehicles, or even none at all;
- limiting our flying;
- buying locally to reduce transportation costs.

If we all played our part, these would be valuable steps towards sustainable lifestyles, and small though they may seem, their effectiveness shouldn't be dismissed.

What we can also do as individuals is to lobby politicians and businesses to take action on a national and global scale, because that is what is really needed. There are several bodies very effective in this, collecting individual voices together to ensure that opinions are heard in the right places. None of us should be afraid to share information about climate change and about how we can tackle it. This is where people's power really lies.

To tackle climate change, the world needs to change its power source. This means reducing our dependence on fossil fuels. Current investment in further attempts to extract fossil fuel resources from the earth is alarming because it suggests business as usual without a thought to the impact upon the climate. If we cannot yet free ourselves from carbon, we must at least ensure that global legislation demands that any new coal- or gas-fired power stations have integrated carbon capture and storage.

However, we really need to invest in viable and safe alternatives to fossil fuels, such as wind power, biomass, solar, and tidal.[9] As no single clean and renewable technology will be able to meet our enormous demand for energy, we must develop a well-managed combination of renewables. In the UK, being windy islands surrounded by sea, we should develop tidal and wave energy. Other nations have similar resources, while others, with lots of sun and lots of space, could make excellent use of solar. The Sahara Desert has great potential, as do vast areas of America and Australia. Even in the UK, solar is a viable energy source. All countries should develop biomass energy; it has been estimated that at least 10 per cent of our total energy needs worldwide could easily come from biomass and waste.

In addition to the wave power of our stormy seas, the UK has some of the world's biggest tides. As tidal energy also offers great potential, I'm trying very hard to encourage the Welsh and British governments to invest in further research and development.

There are some excellent proposals concerning the coast of North Wales, and I'm a great supporter of the Severn barrage proposals. Put together, these schemes could provide enough electricity to meet the entire demand of Wales for the next century and beyond, at the same time boosting the economy. There are big companies willing to invest in both projects. They realize they won't make money for the first 30 years or so, but then they'll keep making more and more. What is needed is for the Welsh Assembly and the Westminster government to provide the framework and assurances required for these projects to proceed. Wales can serve as a microcosm of the world.

To enable technology to meet our demands, we need to work on reducing this demand in spite of increasing world population. It's another difficult challenge, but it's one we can and must meet. In countries like the USA and the UK there needs to be a more determined effort on the part of government, both national and local, to increase the energy efficiency of the housing stock. This would make a valuable difference. Other measures we can take include creating smarter electricity distribution grids in which waste is reduced.

Globally we also need to tackle the huge problem of deforestation. It is a shocking fact that, worldwide, CO_2 emissions from deforestation exceed those of transport, while deforestation removes our means of capturing that CO_2. We really need to reverse this. We in the West must take care to inform ourselves well and then make conscientious decisions about what we buy, paying particular attention to how our food is sourced.

Nuclear energy is in principle good because carbon emissions related to it are very low. Its disadvantages are its high cost and the possibility that, in the wrong hands, it might be used as a cover for making nuclear material for bombs. However, in the short term, it makes sense to buy time through prolonging the life of existing nuclear power stations and also to look into the possibility of making use of material in nuclear weapon stockpiles that under international agreements are redundant.

Developing all of these technologies globally would enable us to move successfully from a carbon economy and would greatly assist our efforts to stop at that crucial 2 °C. Most of the technology is ready to go. There are already companies able and desperate to do all of this and more, but governments need to provide the rubrics to encourage investment in the necessary research and development. In the UK, government-supported energy research and development is less now than it was in the 1980s, despite the great need. Government needs to work with industry to encourage rather than hinder investment in clean energy.

It is often assumed that the required action to control emissions will be costly and not appropriate at a time of world economic crisis, but this is not so. I refer again to the work of the International Energy Agency mentioned earlier. Their detailed blueprint for the world's future energy and the balance of costs is highly credible and sensible. The cost of taking action, they assert, is not large, especially when viewed in the long term. It will in fact bring net savings and many other benefits such as reduced pollution, better energy security, and the creation of new jobs. Nations taking action now will find substantial economic returns from their technological advantage so gained. The early bird will catch the worm.

In 1941 the British Prime Minister Winston Churchill went to see the USA's President Roosevelt. He desperately needed tanks, aircraft, and guns to help defend Europe against Nazi Germany. Although at the time America was still struggling out of the recession of the 1930s, Roosevelt asked US industry to provide these things. Within six months, he had created jobs and income in his own country, as well as providing invaluable help with the war. Western economies could benefit in the same way from tackling climate change at a time when the world economy needs a new way forward. There's nothing quite like a job that needs doing to stimulate purposeful action.

As this book was about to go to print, the IEA issued a report freely available on the Internet.[10] The report stresses the importance of meeting the 2 °C target. It also stresses the affordability of doing so, and shows how it can still be achieved. It is a challenging document providing both the urgency and clarity the world so desperately needs, particularly concerning the technical possibilities. However, there are major challenges to be faced in the areas of policy and economics where big changes are required. For instance, so powerful are fossil fuel lobbies that worldwide subsidies for fossil fuels are still many times greater than subsidies for renewable energy. The IEA has pointed out that carbon emissions will not reduce fast enough while this enormous disparity remains.

In his 2013 e-book, *Nuclear 2.0: Why a Green Future Needs Nuclear Power*, Mark Lynas presents a strong case for his title. Another recent book I would recommend is Dieter Helm's *The Carbon Crunch: How We're Getting Climate Change Wrong – and How to Fix It*, in which the author argues convincingly about the inadequacies of present policies and indeed about the inadequacies of all sides of the current debate.

There are numerous positive arguments for taking serious action now; I have not yet heard a convincing argument against. It is, as my grandchildren might say, a no-brainer. So why aren't we getting on with it? I strongly suspect that political delay is largely because of two factors: political short-termism and effective international lobbying by bodies with vested interests in the continued use of fossil fuels.

This chapter so far has concentrated on climate change mitigation: the need to reduce as rapidly as possible global emissions of greenhouse gases. However, it is equally essential and urgent that we find ways to adapt to the changes in climate that are already occurring; changes that will increase in their intensity and impact over the foreseeable future. Sea-level rise, changes in water availability, and the climate extremes of heat waves, floods, and droughts mentioned above are all challenges we will have to face.

During recent years, some parts of the world have experienced the most damaging climate extremes ever recorded. The impact of our changing climate upon worldwide agriculture and the management of water and food chains will be serious, and it has become increasingly clear that the world community needs to coordinate action in facing these great and immediate challenges. Acceptance that climate change is actually occurring and that its severity is increasing has galvanized scientists and concerned policymakers to work together on how human communities can best adapt to the expected changes, all under the title of climate services.[11]

Just as this book was being prepared for going to press in June 2013, the UK Meteorological Office hosted in London a day's event to consider the development of climate services both in the UK and around the world. The presentations were at once fascinating and encouraging. Speakers included senior climate scientists, and representatives from government, industry, research councils, and the World Meteorological Organization. They all demonstrated a high degree of awareness of the growing problems and of the cooperation and coordination required to address them.

I came away from the meeting excited about the scale on which climate services are being developed internationally. The impacts of climate change do not respect national or other boundaries. It is therefore encouraging to realize that by facing and tackling these challenges together, communities and nations could make a positive contribution to understanding, peace, and prosperity around the world.

The next IPCC report is due out in 2014. Although I'm no longer involved, I have little doubt that by the time the world has read and considered the report, people will be asking why we didn't act sooner. It will be a very valid question. I dedicated the fourth edition of *Global Warming: The Complete Briefing*[12] to my grandchildren and their generation. It is to their generation and to those that follow that I now dedicate, in retrospect and in prospect, all of my efforts past, present, and future.

Although the situation is increasingly serious; although political action is inadequate; and although the truths, as far as we know them, about climate change are still being unjustifiably questioned, despair is simply not an option. Despair in the face of the immense challenges posed by human-induced climate change can only hinder progress. Besides, I think the fiercest opposition is gradually dying away and once the world accepts the integrity of the scientific evidence of human-induced climate change, progress will be swift. It has to be.

I am optimistic for three main reasons. First, I have experienced the commitment of the world scientific community, including scientists from many different nations, backgrounds, and cultures, in painstakingly and honestly working together to understand the problems and assessing what needs to be done. Secondly, I believe the necessary technology is available for achieving satisfactory solutions, and there's still time to do so. My third reason is that I believe we have a God-given task of being good stewards of creation. As God gave us this task, he has given us the means of achieving it. But we really must get on with it.

By acting now we can save money, species, and lives. We will all be better off as a result. However far along the path of climate change we have so far come, we can still do something about it. People who say we can't afford it are wrong; people who say we'll be less happy are also wrong. There are those who say we should first solve the problems of gross poverty and hunger in the world, then tackle climate change. That too is wrong because failing to tackle climate change will lead to much greater poverty and hunger. There are also those who say we have first to tackle the world's economic problems. That is wrong too: as the history of tackling crises has constantly shown, taking the necessary actions to deal with climate change will create jobs and stimulate economies.

If we all work together to make human life on earth sustainable and equitable, it could be a much better, much happier, much more peaceful, and much safer place. I'm not naïve enough to think that such action will create heaven on earth, but it would be better than the alternative.

APPENDIX 1

CREATION, EVOLUTION, AND THE BIBLE

In 1859, Charles Darwin published his *On the Origin of Species* in which he proposed natural selection and survival of the fittest as the evolutionary processes through which life on earth developed from simple beginnings and eventually to *Homo sapiens*.

Some Christians were happy to accept evolution as a scientific description that in no way ruled out God as Creator. Others found conflict between Darwin's theory and their religious beliefs based upon the account of creation in the first chapter of Genesis in the Bible.

In the late nineteenth century some biologists began to extend the concept of evolution and argued that the development of life was just the product of chance forces. As this removed any need for God as Creator, those opposed to Darwin's theory became stronger and more vocal in their views.

How does evolution match up with the account of creation in Genesis in the Bible? Today, many Christians, especially in the USA, still insist on a literal interpretation of creation as described in the Bible. However, leading theologians in the early centuries of the Christian era and since have recognized that the Genesis account has many allegorical and poetic features that preclude a completely literal interpretation. For instance, there is reference to evening and morning on Day 1, while the sun was not created until Day 4.

I have always argued that science and faith can exist side by side and mutually support each other. I believe that this applies to discussion and debate about origins.[1]

APPENDIX 2

FROM THE CONCLUSION OF *CHRISTIAN HEALING*[1]

The ministry of healing is often thought of in a restricted sense, but it is important to understand that it includes the practice of medicine (addressing both physical and mental health) with caring and counselling, the call to repentance, the offer of forgiveness, and prayer. Forgiveness and restored relationships can be a powerful aid to healing of apparently physical disorders. We emphasize that all of these are God's work. Medicine makes use of what is available in the world God has created; healing through "medical" means is not to be thought of as inferior to healing through other "spiritual" means. God's will is that, in the Christian ministry of healing, all available resources should be brought to bear in a comprehensive and complementary manner. The work of God in the world is characterized by a combination of *nature* and *grace*. The pattern of healing is of *cooperation* between God and his creation, of divine initiative and creaturely *response*. That cooperation is evident in medical work, in prayer and in caring and spiritual ministry.

APPENDIX 3
PEER REVIEW AND THE IPCC

Peer review describes a process that is very important to the progress of science. Before a scientific paper can be published in a reputable journal, it has to be reviewed by expert scientists to confirm that it is describing scientific work that has been honestly carried out and that takes account of related scientific work carried out by other scientists.

The chapters for IPCC reports are prepared in accordance with firm rules and procedures. First, lead authors are agreed by the bureaux of the individual working groups. Draft chapters are then subject to two rounds of review, first by scientific experts, then by governments and international organizations as well as a wider range of individual scientists. All the review comments are considered by the lead authors. For the 2007 report over 30,000 written comments were received, and for that report independent review editors were appointed for each chapter to ensure that all substantive review comments received appropriate consideration.

APPENDIX 4

SUMMARY CHALLENGES

1. The world is facing environmental crises of unparalleled magnitude, including some on a global scale.

2. Looking after the earth is a God-given responsibility. Not to look after the earth is a sin.

3. Christians need to re-emphasize that the doctrines of creation, incarnation, and resurrection belong together. The spiritual is not to be seen as separate from the material. A thoroughgoing theology of the environment needs to be developed.

4. Our stewardship of the earth, as Christians, is to be pursued in dependence on and partnership with God.

5. The application of science and technology is an important component of stewardship. Humility is an essential ingredient in the pursuit and application of science and technology – and in the exercise of stewardship.

6. All of this provides an enormous opportunity for the church, which has too much ignored the earth and the environment and neglected the importance of creation and its place in the overall Christian message.

NOTES

"It has to be absolutely true"

1. An interview between Sir John Houghton and Dr Paul Merchant for the Oral History of British Science project. The project, undertaken by National Life Stories, based in the British Library, has been recording British scientists since 2009. The reference for Sir John's interview is C1379/45. More information is available at <www.bl.uk/historyofscience>.

1 Why Weren't We Warned?

1. A UK national tabloid newspaper with a circulation, at the time, of almost 4 million.

2 The Incubation of a Scientist

1. Alfred Powell Morgan, *The Boy Electrician* (Lothrop, Lee & Shepard Company, 1913).

2. Strict Baptists are distinguishable from General Baptists by their adherence to the theology of John Calvin, and by their closed communion.

3. The Plymouth Brethren began in Dublin in the 1820s. Originally they were informal interdenominational meetings of evangelicals. They rapidly became a distinct church.

4. A spectrometer is an instrument that splits light into its constituent wavelengths.

4 Return to the Spires

1. For clarification, the "ranks" at Oxford are, in ascending order, (1) lecturer; (2) Reader; (3) Professor.

2. Radiative transfer is an important means of transferring energy in the atmosphere by the emission and absorption of infrared radiation from atmospheric constituents such as water vapour, carbon dioxide, and ozone.

3. David Bourgeois, *Researches Sur L'Art de Voler* (Paris, 1784) cited in Richard Holmes, *The Age of Wonder* (Harper Press, 2008).

4. Leah Bendavid-Val (ed.), *Through the Lens: National Geographic Greatest Photographs* (National Geographic, 2009).

5 Breakthrough

1. For further information about the SCR, see J.T. Houghton and S.D. Smith, "Remote Sounding of Atmospheric Temperature from Satellites", *Proceedings of the Royal Society of London* A320 (1970): 23–33; and P.G. Abel et al., "The Selective Chopper Radiometer for Nimbus D", *Proceedings of the Royal Society of London* A320 (1970): 35–55.

2. J.T. Houghton and S.D. Smith, *Infra-Red Physics* (Oxford University Press, 1966).

7 Further Work with NASA

1. *Oxford University Gazette*, 29 June 1979.

2. For further information about the PMR, see P.D. Curtis, J.T. Houghton, G.D. Peskett, & C.D. Rodgers, "The Pressure Modulator Radiometer for Nimbus F", *Proceedings of the Royal Society of London* A337 (1974): 135–50.

3. More about our work within the Nimbus programme can be found in J.T. Houghton, F.W. Taylor, and C.D. Rodgers, *Remote Sounding of Atmospheres* (Cambridge University Press, 1984).

4. Mark Lynas, *The God Species: How Humans Really can Save the Planet* (Fourth Estate, 2011), p. 220.

8 *Nullius in Verba*: Take Nothing for Granted

1. John T. Houghton, *Does God Play Dice?* (Intervarsity Press, 1988).

2. Quoted in R. Hooykaas, *Religion and the Rise of Modern Science* (Scottish Academic Press, 1972), p. 52.

3. This is a very brief summary of Chapters 1 and 2 of my book *The Search for God. Can Science Help?* (Lion Publishing, 1995).

4. Roger Penrose, *The Emperor's New Mind: Concerning Computers, Minds, and the Laws of Physics* (Vintage, 1990), p. 445.

5. Edwin Abbott, *Flatland: A Romance in Two Dimensions* (1884).

6. Isaiah 57:15.

10 Learning on the Job

1. Geostationary orbit means that the speed of the satellite's orbit is the same as the rotation speed of the earth. The satellite therefore stays above one position on the earth.

11 The Weatherman

1. Malcolm Walker, *History of the Meteorological Office* (Cambridge University Press, 2011).

2. John Houghton, "The Predictability of Weather and Climate", *Philosophical Transactions of the Royal Society: Physical Sciences and Engineering* 337, no. 1648 (15 December 1991): 521–72.

3. For instance, cloud-radiation and ocean circulation feedbacks.

12 Loss and Optimism

1. Ernest Lucas (ed.), *Christian Healing: What Can We Believe?* (Lynx Communications, 1997).

13 The Formation of the IPCC

1. To find out more about the IPCC see <http://www.ipcc.ch>.

2. Scientific Committee on Problems of the Environment.

3. Report of the United Nations World Commission on Environment and Development: *Our Common Future* (1987) also known as the Brundtland Report. Available at <http://www.un-documents.net/our-common-future.pdf>.

4. Obasi held this position from 1984 until 2003.

5. Further information in Bert Bolin, *A History of the Science and Politics of Climate Change* (Cambridge University Press, 2007), p. 48.

6. Bolin, *History*, p. 49.

7. John Balzar, "Bush Vows Zero Tolerance of Environmental Polluters", *Los Angeles Times*, 1 September 1988.

8. <http://www.margaretthatcher.org/document/107346>.

9. The remit of this group changed slightly for later reports, with socio-economic considerations largely moving into Working Group 3.

10. Bolin, *History*, p. 50.

11. The cryosphere consists of places where water is in its solid form, frozen to ice or snow. Cryospheric studies, therefore, deals with such things as ice caps and glaciers.

14 The First IPCC Assessment Report 1990

1. Isotopes are atoms of the same element that have the same number of protons but a different number of neutrons.

2. This figure is now over 40 per cent.

3. Interview by David Lascelles, "A Scientist's Belief in God and the Earth", *Financial Times*, 18/19 March 1995.

4. Paraphrased from the speech available at <http://www.margaretthatcher.org/document/108102>.

15 The Second IPCC Report 1995

1. John Houghton, *Global Warming: The Complete Briefing*, first edition (Lion, 1994). It is now in its fourth edition (Cambridge University Press, 2009) with a fifth edition to be published by Cambridge University Press in 2014.

2. At this time, we still had to use artificial adjustments to keep climate models stable. These attracted some criticism. The need for these was gradually decreasing, to become completely unnecessary a few years later.

3. Latvia.

4. Ben Santer.

5. Canada.

6. India.

7. "Meetings That Changed the World: Madrid 1995: Diagnosing Climate Change", *Nature* 455, no. 7214 (9 October 2008), pp. 737–38.

16 Dirty Tactics

1. Naomi Oreskes and Erik M. Conway, *Merchants of Doubt: How a Handful of Scientists Obscured the Truth on Issues from Tobacco Smoke to Global Warming* (Bloomsbury Press, 2010), p. 1.

2. Frederick Seitz, "A Major Deception on Global Warming", *Wall Street Journal*, 12 June 1996.

3. Will Buchanan, "Merchants of Doubt: How 'Scientific' Misinformation Campaigns Sold Untruths to Consumers", *Christian Science Monitor*, 22 June 2010.

4. S. Fred Singer, "Disinformation on Global Warming?" *Washington Times*, 13 November 1996.

5. Dr Benjamin D. Santer, 12 June 1996.

6. William K. Stevens, "U.N. Climate Report Was Improperly Altered, Overplaying Human Role, Critics Say", *New York Times National*, Monday 17 June 1996.

7. Oreskes and Conway, *Merchants of Doubt*, p. 207.

8. *Bulletin of the American Meteorological Society*, 25 June 1996.

9. Bert Bolin, *A History of the Science and Politics of Climate Change* (Cambridge University Press, 2007).

18 The Third and Fourth IPCC Reports

1. "Clouds' Effect on Climate Change Is Last Bastion for Dissenters", *New York Times*, 30 April 2012.

2. IPCC Third Assessment Report (2001), *Working Group 1: The Scientific Basis*, Chapter 7.

3. IPCC Fourth Assessment Report. *Climate Change 2007: Synthesis Report*, Summary for Policymakers. Available at <http://www.ipcc.ch/pdf/assessment-report/ar4/syr/ar4_syr_spm.pdf>.

4. IPCC Fourth Assessment Report. *Climate Change 2007: Synthesis Report*, Summary for Policymakers, Section 5 "The long-term perspective", p. 19.

19 The Truth Will Out

1. Nigel Lawson, *An Appeal to Reason: A Cool Look at Global Warming* (Gerald Duckworth and Co. Ltd, 2009).

2. There's an interesting summary of the credentials of some of the GWPF's key people, and other people mentioned in this chapter, at <http://www.campaigncc.org/> hall of shame.

3. *The Telegraph*, 20 November 2009.

4. Christopher Booker, "Climate change: this is the worst scientific scandal of our generation", *The Telegraph*, 28 November 2009.

5. Christopher Booker, *The Real Global Warming Disaster: Is the Obsession with Climate Change Turning out to be the Most Costly Scientific Blunder in History?* (Continuum International, 2009).

6. Steve Connor, "Fabricated Quote Used to Discredit Climate Scientist", *The Independent*, 10 February 2010.

7. Sir John Houghton, *Global Warming: The Complete Briefing*, first edition (Lion Publishing, 1994).

8. BBC *Horizon*, "Science Under Attack", last broadcast on 19 February 2011.

9. "We Climate Scientists are not EcoFanatics", *The Times*, 15 March 2010.

10. Connor, "Fabricated Quote Used to Discredit Climate Scientist".

11. James Delingpole, "The Crazy Climate Change Obsession That's Made the Met Office a Menace", *Daily Mail*, 10 January 2013.

12. Julia Slingo, "Decadal Forecasting – What is it and what does it tell us?" The Met Office, January 2013. Available at <http://www.metoffice.gov.uk/research/news/decadal-forecasting>.

20 Towards a Sustainable World

1. Much of this analogy is borrowed from my Briefing no. 14, "Global Warming, Climate Change and Sustainability: Challenge to Scientists, Policymakers and Christians". Available at <http://www.jri.org.uk/brief/BriefingNo14_4thEdition_July.pdf>.

2. Speech to the Economic and Social Council of the UN, Geneva, Switzerland, 9 July 1965.

3. Buckminster Fuller, *Operating Manual for Spaceship Earth* (E.P. Dutton and Co., 1968).

4. In a publication in 1966, Professor Kenneth Boulding, a distinguished American economist, employed the image of Spaceship Earth. He contrasted an "open" or "cowboy" economy (as he called an unconstrained economy) with a "spaceship" economy in which sustainability is paramount.

5. The 1987 Report of the UN World Commission on Environment and Development: *Our Common Future* (often known as the Brundtland Report) provides a milestone review of sustainable development issues.

21 Progress and Obstacles

1. The report is edited by Sarah Hobson and Jane Lubchenco and published as *Revelation and the Environment: AD 95–1995* (World Scientific Publishing, 1997).

2. JRI briefing papers are available on the website <http://www.jri.org.uk>.

3. *Energy Technology Perspectives* (IEA, 2012).

22 Making Money Work

1. <http://www.shellfoundation.org>.

23 America the Potentially Great

1. Louise Bateman, "Act now to Tackle Imported Emissions, Head of Climate Watchdog tells Business", 24 April 2013, available at <http://www.greenwisebusiness.co.uk>, is helpful on this.

2. An interesting appraisal of the plan can be found at <http://climateactiontracker.org/countries/china>.

3. <http://www.thegreatwarming.com>.

4. There is a detailed account of the effects of the conference upon Richard Cizik, and his position in the NAE, in Katharine K. Wilkinson's *Between God and Green: How Evangelicals are Cultivating a Middle Ground on Climate Change* (Oxford University Press, 2012).

5. There is a detailed account of this in Wilkinson, *Between God and Green*, p. 44.

6. Sarah Pulliam, "Richard Cizik resigns from the National Association of Evangelicals", *Christianity Today*, 11 December 2008.

7. Wilkinson, *Between God and Green*, p. 68.

8. Jacqueline L. Salmon, "Richard Cizik's New Venture", *The Washington Post*, 19 April 2009.

9. *A Renewed Call to Truth, Prudence, and Protection of the Poor.* An Evangelical Examination of the Theology, Science, and Economics of Global Warming. First published in 2009.

10. Wilkinson in *Between God and Green* singles out Calvin Beisner as a leading voice against climate care: "If climate care can be said to have a primary opponent, Beisner is it" (p. 65).

24 Today

1. Fair trade is a very practical way to help people in the developing world to help themselves.

25 Glimpses of Truth

1. Words and music by Brendan Graham and Rolf Lovland; arranged by Roger Emerson; published by Hal Leonard Corporation, USA.

2. St Paul often describes his experience of an external force or influence, for example in Philippians 4:13 and Ephesians 3:16–21, as does King David in Psalm 23.

26 Where Are We Now?

1. Sir John Houghton, *Global Warming: The Complete Briefing*, fourth edition (Cambridge University Press, 2009).

2. The reports can be downloaded from <http://www.ipcc.ch>.

3. For more information, see <http://www.metoffice.gov.uk.climate-change>.

4. "Managing the Risks of Extreme Events and Disasters", IPCC SREX Report 2012, available at <http://www.ipcc.ch>.

5. Mark Lynas, *Six Degrees: Our Future on a Hotter Planet* (Harper Perennial, 2007).

6. <http://www.tearfund.org>.

7. See <http://www.avoid.uk.net>.

8. Edmund Burke (1729–97), Irish orator, philosopher, and politician.

9. See David Mackay, *Sustainable Energy – Without the Hot Air* (UIT Cambridge Ltd, 2009). Available at <http://www.inference.phy.cam.ac.uk/sustainable/book/tex/sewtha.pdf>.

10. See <http://www.worldenergyoutlook.org/energyclimatemap>.

11. See <http://www.wmo.int/pages/themes/climate/climate_services.php>.

12. Cambridge University Press, 2009.

Appendix 1 Creation, Evolution, and the Bible

1. For further information on this subject, see R.J. Berry, *God and Evolution* (Regent College Publishing USA, 2001).

Appendix 2 From the Conclusion of *Christian Healing*

1. Ernest Lucas (ed.), *Christian Healing: What Can We Believe?* (Lynx Communications, 1997), Appendix 1, p. 194.

INDEX

Abbott, Edwin   90
Abel, Peter   43, 62
Advisory Committee on Renewable
  Energy   255
aerosols   161, 181, 203, 267
Agrocel   238
aircraft, damage to ozone layer
  80–81
Al-Sabban, Mohammed   168, 170,
  172–76, 178–79
Allen, Geoffrey   96–97
Along Track Scanning Radiometer
  102
American Meteorological Society
  189–190
Anderson, Leith   250
Appleton Research Laboratories
  96–101
Arctic, loss of sea ice   198
atmosphere   28–29
  satellite measurement   36–38, 72
Au Sable Institute of Environmental
  Studies   244
aviation, effect on climate   195–96

balloon test   61–65
Ban Ki-Moon   255
Bangalore   239
Bangladesh   269–270
banks   232
Barker, Greg   155
Barnett, John   43
Bartholomew (Patriarch of
  Constantinople)   225
Becquerel, Henri   85

Beisner, Calvin   253–54
Benedict, Bill   54
Berry, Sam   227
Bible
  doctrine of creation   246, 282–83
  and evolution   24, 282–83
  and stewardship of the earth   223
  student discussion of   26
big bang theory   87
biomass energy   237, 276
Bloomberg, Michael   254
Bolin, Bert   127, 133, 187, 190
  breaks conference deadlock
    177–78
  death and tributes   207–208
Booker, Christopher   213–14, 215,
  216–17
Boyd, Robert   26
BP   227–28
Brewer, Alan   28, 30, 31, 41,
  51–52, 263
Browne, John   227–29
Bruce, Jim   129, 130, 133
Budyko, Mikhail   49–51, 144–45
Bush, George   132
Bush, George W.   131, 202, 204,
  243, 249
business   234–35

Callander, Bruce   135, 198
cancer   75–77, 121–22
carbon capture   276
carbon dioxide
  and developing countries   242
  drives climate change   127–28,
    150, 266–68
  emissions   92–93, 222
  natural/human origins
    distinguishable   140
  targets for reduced emissions
    130, 242, 256, 274
  use in measuring atmospheric
    temperature   38, 44, 54–55